Wild Enlightenment

Wild Enlightenment

The Borders of Human Identity in the Eighteenth Century

Richard Nash

University of Virginia Press

Charlottesville and London

University of Virginia Press
© 2003 by the Rector and Visitors of the University of Virginia
All rights reserved
Printed in the United States of America on acid-free paper
First published 2003

1 3 5 7 9 8 6 4 2

LIBRARY OF CONGRESS CATALOGING-IN-PUBLICATION DATA

Nash, Richard, 1955–
  Wild enlightenment : the borders of human identity in the eighteenth
century / Richard Nash.
      p.   cm.
"Winner of the Walker Cowen Memorial Prize."
Includes bibliographical references and index.
    ISBN 0-8139-2165-1 (cloth : alk. paper)
    1. English literature—18th century—History and criticism.   2. Wild
men in literature.   3. Great Britain—Civilization—18th century.   4.
Enlightenment—Great Britain.   5. Human beings in literature.   I. Title.
    PR448.W54 N37 2003
    820.9'352—dc21

                                                          2002151256

To
Nancy Rutkowski
and
Carolyn Nash

Contents

Illustrations

Wild Enlightenment

Acknowledgments

In a project that has spanned as many years as this one, it is impossible not to incur more debts than one is able to repay, and perhaps more than one is even able to recall. Of the many real pleasures encountered along the way, none has been greater than the very real gratitude I feel toward each of those who have assisted me. The research has introduced me not only to new texts and ideas in the archive; it has also introduced me to new friends along the way.

I am grateful to Indiana University for a one-semester sabbatical leave and to the Office of Research and University Graduate School of Indiana University for several summer research grants. I am very grateful to the library staffs at the Lilly Rare Book Library, Indiana University; William Andrews Clark Library, UCLA; New York Public Library; British Library; the Natural History Museum, London; and the Ehrenpreis Center for Swift Studies, Muenster. The photographs of the marginalia from *The Manifesto of Lord Peter,* including the woodcut of Peter attributed to Swift, appear courtesy Lilly Library, Indiana University, Bloomington, Indiana. The photographs of the panels of the King's Staircase in Kensington Palace are reproduced by permission of Historic Royal Palaces under licence from the Controller of Her Majesty's Stationery Office. An earlier version of part of chapter 1 appeared in my essay "Satyrs and Satire in Augustan England" in *Theorizing Satire: Essays in Literary Criticism,* edited by Brian A. Connery and Kirk Combe (New York: St. Martin's Press, 1995). A version of part of chapter 2 appears in my essay "Did Swift Write *It cannot Rain but it Pours?*," *Swift Studies* 17 (2002): 44–58. I am also grateful to the many colleagues who have commented on various aspects of this project at numerous conferences and professional meetings. Although these have been many, I am especially grateful to the intellectual support provided by five organizations in particular over the years: the Pithecanthropus Congress at Leyden, the Central Regional Johnson Society, the William Andrews Clark Library Workshop, the American

Society for Eighteenth-Century Studies, and especially the Society for Literature and Science. Here at Indiana University, I have been particularly blessed with a rich array of valuable colleagues, stimulating graduate students, and challenging conversations across disciplinary divides. I am particularly grateful to two local reading and discussion groups: the Science and Literature Affinity Group (SLAG) and the Bloomington Eighteenth Century Group.

I am deeply appreciative of the friendship and constructive criticism of Janet Sorensen, Oscar Kenshur, Dror Wahrman, H. James Jensen, and Michael Rosenblum. Pat Brantlinger and Steve Watt have been supportive colleagues, good friends, and helpful chairs. Among dozens of remarkably helpful and stimulating colleagues in the Society for Literature and Science, I am especially grateful to Ken Knoespel, Alan Rauch, Eve Keller, and Susan Squier. Among those who have read and discussed early drafts of several chapters of this manuscript, I am especially grateful to Chris Fox, Julia Douthwaite, Helen Deutsch, Linda Merrians, and Hermann Real. I continue to benefit from the teaching of Martin Battestin. I am especially grateful to my first teacher, and still one of my best friends in the field, Dennis Todd; his work and his integrity have been an inspiration to me. I cannot begin to say how much I have benefited from the criticism, friendship, and support of Lee Sterrenburg. Over the years, I have had the pleasure of working with many talented and perceptive graduate students. This book has benefited from their input in a number of ways; I am grateful to each of them and especially to Tobias Menely, Louise Economides, Jeffrey Galbraith, Scott Maisano, Martin Harris, Kathy Gehr, and Evan Davis. Cathie Brettschneider, the anonymous readers, and everyone associated with the University of Virginia Press have helped me in many ways to make this a better book than it would otherwise have been; I am grateful to each of them. In many ways, I could not have imagined writing this book without the example of my father's love of the wild. Always, my deepest gratitude is to my family. No one inspires me more than Carolyn, and no one has encouraged me more than Nancy. This book is dedicated to you both, with love beyond language.

Introduction

In 1712, the year Jean-Jacques Rousseau was born, little Samuel Johnson, age three, became one of the last children in England to participate in a superstitious ritual and receive the Royal Touch from Queen Anne, in an effort to cure his scrofula. The Tory ministry of Henry St. John, Viscount Bolingbroke, and Robert Harley, Earl of Oxford, began the secret negotiations that would culminate the following year with the treaty of Utrecht. Jonathan Swift, who had recently completed his stint as editor of the Tory newspaper *The Examiner,* continued writing on behalf of the ministry, but his most significant contribution to the party came when he detected and disarmed a mail bomb intended to assassinate Oxford. John Gay published *The Mohocks,* inspired by the purported savageries committed the previous year by a gang of youths who took their name from the "four Indian kings" visiting from America. Woodes Rogers, the privateer who had returned the previous year from a series of maritime adventures, published *A Cruising Voyage Round the World,* in the pages of which the world first became acquainted with the remarkable survival story of a solitary castaway, Alexander Selkirk. Selkirk told his story to Daniel Defoe, who was then editor of *The Review.* A young Alexander Pope, twenty-four, published the first version of *Rape of the Lock;* he had attracted considerable notice and acclaim the year before with the publication of *An Essay on Criticism,* much praised by Joseph Addison, who was widely acknowledged as England's chief man of letters in his role as "The Spectator." And about this time in the forests of Hanover, near the village of Zell, a poor peasant woman gave birth to a boy. Perhaps he was autistic, or perhaps he was mentally disadvantaged; perhaps not. Certainly, however, he was severely tongue-tied. Certainly, too, some time—though exactly when and where remain a mystery—he was abandoned in the forest by his parents.

In 1785, Thomas Love Peacock was born in Dorset. William Wordsworth, age fifteen, wrote the earliest of his poems that have survived. Samuel Johnson had died the previous December, and James Boswell rushed *A Journal of the Tour of the Hebrides* into print, as a sample of the mammoth biography he was composing. A few months before Johnson's death, Immanuel Kant had published "What Is Enlightenment?" the essay that gave the era its most enduring label. Benjamin Franklin returned to America from his post in France, retired from public life, and invented bifocals. Louis XVII was born, the last of that unhappy line, who, while still a child, was to perish in prison or disappear into the mists of legend as "the lost dauphin." Addison, Pope, Swift, Defoe, and all of that era were, of course, long dead. William Pitt introduced a bill calling for parliamentary reform; it was defeated, and he never authored another. And in Hertfordshire, that tongue-tied, possibly autistic son of an obscure Hanoverian peasant died quietly in retirement. His lifetime had spanned almost precisely the same years as Samuel Johnson's; during that lifetime, he had traveled—like his first sovereign—from Hanover to England. Commonly known as Peter, he had visited court and had been the topic of pamphlets, poems, and pointed discussions; he had fled from captivity and had been taken for the Pretender; he had retired to a quiet farming life, where he was periodically visited by the learned men of the day. The culture belongs to him, as well as to them.

A generation ago, Hayden White seemed to close the door on a familiar topic in eighteenth-century studies: "the theme of the Noble Savage may be one of the few historical topics about which there is nothing more to say" (183). White's own admirable discussion constituted an "archaeology of an idea," drawing as readily on Foucauldian theories of an archaeology of a knowledge as on the intellectual histories of Lovejoy and others. The fundamental argument of *Wild Enlightenment* is that much remains to be said on the subject, if we shift perspective slightly from the thematic approach of intellectual history to a more eclectic cultural criticism. Indeed, such a simple shift enables us to challenge a common presupposition shared by these discussions: that the "noble savage" is to be considered as other than (quite literally, "alien to") the Enlightenment. One recent study in this tradition concludes, "as we have seen, the monster is a concept that we need in order to tell ourselves what we are *not*" (Hanafi 218). Cultural criticism insists on our attending to the remarkable degree to which the figure of the wild man was located within, and thus, in part, constitutive of, the bourgeois public sphere.[1] Where this book most clearly parts company from those earlier discussions is in the ways those discussions begin with a premise that ideas may be examined independent of their material embodiments, as purely semiotic markers: "to be sure, expressions such as 'Wild Man' and 'Noble Savage' are metaphors; and insofar as they were once taken literally, they can be regarded simply as errors, mistakes, or fallacies" (184). I contend that while expressions such as "wild man" and "noble savage" operated as metaphors, they also always served as markers for real material beings; that, if anything, the trajectory was not one of a metaphor being "taken literally . . . [by] mistake," but rather that a preexisting mythological terminology actually shaped the preconceptions and hence perceptions by which real beings were observed and recognized by Europeans. In short, I want to return consideration of these material beings to the stage of this intellectual discussion. The phrase "noble savage," in particular, seems long ago to have lost its embodied moorings and to have taken up a ghostly, disembodied existence as merely a *topos* for discussion. Precisely because I insist on grounding in material conditions those abstract rational discussions that typify public sphere discourse, I want to distance myself from those earlier discussions of the "noble savage" that take for granted a continuity between their own intellectual discussions and those Enlightenment conversations that constitute their subject matter. Although such a distinction seems important to me, I also recognize how heavily indebted I am to that extensive critical heritage.

In brief, this book argues that the figure of the wild man constitutes a complex *alter ego* to the idealized abstraction of "the Citizen of Enlightenment," and that following his movements through the public sphere helps illuminate the process by which that idealized abstraction is reified into a particular construction of what constitutes "human nature." Jürgen Habermas's thesis that a fundamental social transformation in eighteenth-century Europe may be usefully charted in terms of the emergence of a bourgeois public sphere has enabled and

demanded critical discussion of the early modern period that explores the negotiations between discursive and material culture. Collectively, these discussions have enriched our understanding of the cultural process that produced
the Citizen of the Enlightenment. Habermas's contention—that the emergence
of a bourgeois society in seventeenth- and eighteenth-century Europe is
marked by a corresponding emergence of a "public sphere" as a discursive
space mediating state authority—has enabled a consideration of literary texts
and their relation to social organization more nuanced than that of traditional
social histories. Central to this contention is the notion that within a market
economy the relations of state authority and private citizen are mediated by the
construction of "public opinion," and that the historical conditions of that mediation constructed this discursive space around rational critical argument.
Both the operation of such a mechanism (how novels, periodicals, and other literary productions mediate the citizen's relation to the state)—and the construction of that mechanism (what conditions of inclusion and exclusion shape
what will count as "rational critical argument")—have become matters of critical debate within early modern cultural studies. With some justified trepidation, Habermas offered a schematic to describe the mediating role of the public sphere:

Private Realm		Sphere of Public Authority
Civil Society (realm of commodity exchange and social labor)	Public sphere in the politi-cal realm Public sphere in the world of letters (clubs, press)	State (realm of the "police")
Conjugal family's internal space (bourgeois intellectuals)	(market of culture prod-ucts) "Town"	Court (courtly-noble society)

Habermas's exposition of this schematic, suggesting as it does considerable
overlap in the categories and a dynamic fluctuation of their relative positions at
different historical moments, may be helpful:

> The line between state and society, fundamental in our context, divided the public
> sphere from the private realm. The public sphere was coextensive with public au-
> thority, and we consider the court part of it. Included in the private realm was the
> authentic "public sphere," for it was a public sphere constituted by private people.

> Within the realm that was the preserve of private people we therefore distinguish
> again between private and public spheres. The private sphere comprised civil soci-
> ety in the narrower sense, that is to say, the realm of commodity exchange and of
> social labor; embedded in it was the family with its interior domain. The public
> sphere in the political realm evolved from the public sphere in the world of letters;
> through the vehicle of public opinion it put the state in touch with the needs of so-
> ciety. (30–31)

If Habermas's configuration of the public sphere constitutes a discursive space
in which the private citizen and state authority negotiate their relations, we
should recall that "discursive space is never completely independent of social
place and the formation of new kinds of speech can be traced through the emergence of new public sites of discourse and the transformation of old ones"
(Stallybrass and White 80). In the discussions that follow, I want to always keep
one eye on the material location and embodied agents of those discursive spaces
that play such a critical role in the formation of early modern culture. At the
same time, however, I also want to attend to the semiotic role of those material
agents that contributed directly to an emerging construction of human identity.
Here it is helpful to follow the lead of those in science studies whose work insists on paying attention to science as a discourse about the world, rather than
as a transparent rendering of the world itself. In characterizing the wild man as
a complex alter ego to the idealized abstraction of the Citizen of the Enlightenment, I am thinking of a relational grid of contrasting and complementary attributes that swirled around the contested term *human*. Particularly helpful to
me in thinking through the arrangement of these attributes beyond simple binary opposition has been the particularly inelegant version of Greimas's semiotic square deployed by Donna Haraway in "The Promises of Monsters":

> "Promises of Monsters" will rely on an artificial device that generates meanings
> very noisily: A. J. Greimas's infamous semiotic square. The regions mapped by this
> clackety, structuralist meaning-making machine could never be mistaken for the
> transcendental realms of Nature or Society. . . . I like my analytical technologies,
> which are unruly partners in discursive construction, delegates who have gotten
> into doing things on their own, to make a lot of noise, so that I don't forget all the
> circuits of competences, inherited conversations, and coalitions of human and
> unhuman actors that go into any semiotic excursions. The semiotic square, so
> subtle in the hands of a Frederic Jameson, will be rather more rigid and literal here
> (Greimas, 1966; Jameson, 1972). I only want it to keep four spaces in differential,

relational separation while I explore how certain local/global struggles for mean-ings and embodiments of nature are occurring within them. (304–5)

Like Haraway, I am less interested in the efficient generative potential of Greimas's structural machine, but more interested in keeping four conceptual spaces "in differential, relational separation." Ultimately, I share Timothy Len-oir's skepticism about the commitment to a realistic ontology that underwrites Greimas's semiotic square; but while such a skepticism must necessarily prompt a degree of caution when approaching the so-called semiotic turn in science studies, I think that turn (if it isn't taken at excessive speed) can facilitate a more complex and nuanced articulation of the complexities of how scientific de-scription operates within a larger cultural frame.

The eighteenth century has long been accepted as a foundational period for the establishment of anthropology and "the human sciences."[2] Alan Bewell touches on some of the same concerns that animate this study, though we some-times approach similar subjects from rather different perspectives. "The pur-pose of this book," Bewell writes, "is to show how many of Wordsworth's shorter narratives and lyrics contributed to this anthropological history. . . . I have treated [Wordsworth's poems] as anthropological narratives, indebted to, yet simultaneously at odds with, Enlightenment anthropology . . . my hope is that the reader's patience will be rewarded by the recognition of the specific ways in which Wordsworth, as he reflected on human origins, consistently drew upon and transformed the anthropological methods he inherited from the En-lightenment" (44–45). My reservation about Bewell's approach is that he some-times seems to have been too apt a pupil of the poet he studies, and that his "En-lightenment anthropology" comes filtered through a Wordsworthian lens. That discourse, in his study, seems to me often flattened and arid without the turbu-lences and anomalies that this study hopes to more fully acknowledge. Bewell, of course, is not alone; the eighteenth century often seems to be envisioned as an endless procession of tea-table talk and salon seminars. If I wish to empha-size features of "Enlightenment anthropology" that were less significant to Be-well's project, it should not minimize the degree to which this book continues his larger project of reading literary works within a specific context of emergent anthropology as a form of cultural criticism.

While this book was in press, Julia Douthwaite published *The Wild Girl, Natural Man, and the Monster: Dangerous Experiments in the Age of Enlighten-ment,* in which she describes a change in literary attitudes toward scientific ideas about "perfectibility": "At the beginning of the eighteenth century, literary discourse was largely optimistic about science's ability to discover the truth about human nature. . . . For many writers, such schemes took on increasingly sinister overtones in the postrevolutionary years . . . the representation of human experiments in literature became increasingly fraught with anxieties about the regulatory public eye and the dangers of meddling with nature" (1, 10). *Wild Enlightenment* takes a slightly different approach to literature and science in the eighteenth century: while Douthwaite seeks "to track how literature reacted to developments in science" (2), *Wild Enlightenment* examines how literary and scientific discourses interact with one another as part of the process by which culture constructs a particular notion of what counts as "human." Within the broad sweep of the changing attitudes charted by Douthwaite (from "largely optimistic" to "fraught with anxieties"), this book seeks to ground itself in detailed discussions of the tensions and instabilities that characterize considerations of human identity throughout the period.

Certainly, the question of "man's place in nature" constitutes a central theme in the richly varied philosophical tradition identified with the Enlightenment. The relationship of man and beast was more than a simple binary, of course, and enjoyed a complex and varied history prior to the eighteenth century; nonetheless, certain strands of that discussion enjoyed widespread general acceptance. Texts frequently deploy the binary of man/beast in tandem with its cognate binaries, reason/passion and social/solitary. Georges Louis LeClerc, comte de Buffon, spoke for many when he wrote: "The animals have only one mode for acquiring pleasure, the exercise of their sensations to gratify their desires. We also possess this faculty: but we are endowed with another source of pleasure, the exercise of the mind, the appetite of which is the desire of knowledge. . . . Uninterrupted passion is madness; and madness is the death of the soul" (1:295). This is a familiar articulation, one that is frequently identified as being turned upside down in Gulliver's fourth voyage, where the Houyhnhnm beasts exemplify reason, and the anthropoid Yahoos seem motivated by passion. Just as important to the particular construction of human nature that emerges at this time is what is identified as a "natural" tendency to friendship and sociability. Buffon continues: "Friendship is the offspring of reason. . . . Thus friendship belongs only to man; . . . Man commands the universe solely because he has learned to govern himself, and to submit to the laws of society" (1:303, 306). A central concern of this book is an exploration of those cultural mechanisms by which a particular construction of citizenship, associated with

Habermas's characterization of an emergent bourgeois public sphere, is reified as constituting a definition of the "human" within the natural world. We may deploy a version of Greimas's semiotic square to help us map the shifting semiotic binaries that shaped the naturalizing of this particular construction of the human, as follows:

Social/Passionate	*Social/Rational*
(passionate sounds, domesticated brutes, herds)	(express ideas, teachable, public societies)
	Citizen of the Enlightenment
Orang-outangs, Yahoos, travelers' reports of native peoples	

Solitary/Passionate	*Solitary/Rational*
(inarticulate cries, anarchic solitude)	(contemplative, withdrawn exercise of liberty and reflection)
Feral children	
	Castaways, exiles, and solitaires

If the discursive manipulations of the emergent bourgeois public sphere sought to naturalize a particular definition of the "human" as that which found its fullest expression in rational societies in which private individuals came together to discuss and consolidate public opinion as the basis for collective action, then the "other" to that figure might appear in any of the three guises described in the remaining quadrants. Against the normative description of the citizen as human, one found quasi-human sociability in descriptions of Swift's Yahoos, travelers' accounts of the Khoi-San and other native peoples, and those nonhuman primates collectively identified as "orang-outang," meaning, literally, "wild man of the woods." These figures all possessed no written language but verbal utterances that defied European efforts at translation. At the same time, they manifested forms of social behavior that corresponded to behavior that seemed the prerogative of the human. But one also found those quasi-humans who, without abandoning reason entirely, withdrew (either voluntarily or by circumstance) from human society. Castaways such as Peter Serrano and Alexander Selkirk, as well as Defoe's fictional Robinson Crusoe, entered, as did hermits and recluses, a liminal status of border identity, frequently characterized by what was termed "degeneration theory"—a notion that, outside of society, humans underwent a degeneration both physical and moral, frequently characterized by becoming more hirsute, less bipedal, stronger, faster, and less articulate. Even more extreme in their liminal condition were those feral children (roughly a dozen cases) reported in varying degrees of detail through the late seventeenth and eighteenth centuries. These children were doubly separated, trapped in the passionate interiority of a solipsistic subjectivity, apparently raised in total isolation from their own species and beyond the reach of language and communication. Each of these three identities (each of which is, in turn, complexly figured) marks a separate facet of the complex figure of the wild man, for that label operated generically to include them all in a quasi-human identity that constituted an "other" to the implicit normative human identity of the Citizen of the Enlightenment.[3]

This book belongs to the genre of "adventures and strange encounters," for it seeks to chart the travels of the figure of the wild man, in each of his guises, through the mythical realm of the bourgeois public sphere. We follow him not only through the discursive networks of novels, broadsheets, pamphlets, and advertisements, but also through their material locations and topographical sites of the fair booths, Royal Society, court, and Parliament. This is not primarily a story of the English gentleman abroad in the realm of the wild man (though from time to time it will have that flavor); instead, it focuses more on the figure of the wild man abroad in the realm of the English gentleman. Although the discussion focuses on particular individuals, my emphasis is not on Peter alone, or on Robinson Crusoe, or Madame Chimpanzee, but always on their shared identity as momentary articulations and embodiments of the material/semiotic actor, of the figure of the wild man. The notion of a "material/semiotic actor" I borrow from those contributions to science studies (notably those of Donna Haraway and Bruno Latour) that seek a productive analysis of nature/culture that does not originate with an a priori separation of the human and the world.[4]

I want to retain from Latour his particular mode of double vision, in which the world is simultaneously viewed as consisting of nature and culture, humans and nonhumans, and also necessarily as populated by hybrid nature/culture networks of humans and nonhuman affiliations. From Haraway I wish to retain that especially crude noisy version of the semiotic square, in which four conceptual spaces are held in "relational separation" to enable a meaningful exploration of how certain struggles for meaning take place within them. From Habermas, I wish to retain the notion that in the eighteenth century a discursive space emerged that enabled private subjects to forge, through rational discourse, a public opinion that mediated between the individual and the state authority. Now the idealized actor hero of Habermas's public sphere is the Citizen of the Enlightenment, a reasonable, property-owning, bourgeois, English gentleman. Such an identity points to no one in particular but pointedly excludes a great many (such as women, laborers, people of color).[5] Nonetheless, his anonymity makes him no less real; as a matter of historical fact, we know that a great many such citizens once lived and died. To avoid particularizing the abstraction, however, it is important that the label *Citizen of the Enlightenment* not be attached to any one person circumscribed by a particular set of contingent beliefs. Such a figure may usefully be thought of as a "material-semiotic actor"—at once, a fully embodied, real material being and a representative sign; he is, at once, doubly meaningful, and the trajectories of his significances are sometimes complementary, sometimes contradictory.[6] Though few studies have made use of this terminology, a great many works concerned with the "public sphere" in early modern culture have dealt with the doubled significance of this particular figure (though a great many more have considered the "citizen" as a purely semiotic figure, while according purely material status only to those human figures denied access to the public sphere).

In a supple and subtle discussion of "the Tory critique of the public sphere" (543), Christian Thorne acutely observes one of the alienating features of Habermas's argument: "One often has the feeling—and this is the strange quality of his book—that Habermas is giving the history of an institution that never existed in the first place and then came, over time, to exist even less" (542). Such a characterization neatly echoes Bruno Latour's argument about "modernity" in *We Have Never Been Modern*. For readers who too quickly identify Latour with postmodernity ("Postmodernism is a symptom, not a fresh solution"), the conjunction of Latour and Habermas may at first appear incompatible. Latour's active resistance to the illusion of modernity—a stance he identifies as "nonmodern"—offers us an opportunity to engage Habermas's public sphere in terms of the very complexity Thorne notes. The work Latour challenges us to do is to return to the arena in which the modern delusion was framed, re-view it, and reconceive it in terms that consciously resist the temptations of the modern. Having first articulated that challenge in *We Have Never Been Modern,* he has subsequently elaborated that challenge in *Pandora's Hope:* "there is a fight in the social sciences and the humanities between two opposite models, one that can loosely be called postmodern and the other that I have called nonmodern.

Everything the first takes to be justification for more absence, more debunking, more negation, more deconstruction, the second takes as proof of presence, deployment, affirmation, and construction" (21). One way (not the only way) to superimpose Latour's nonmodern double perspective over Habermas's public sphere is to see the structural transformation of the bourgeois public sphere that Habermas describes as enacting a kind of purification of discourse, which thereby engenders the very hybrids whose representation it denies. In Latour's formulation, purification separates culture from nature, humans from nonhumans; the Citizen of the Enlightenment is imagined by modernity to be the reasonable human representative of culture, distinct from those passionate nonhuman brutes who populate the natural world. If such a separation "above the line" is required to imagine the Citizen of the Enlightenment, then it will, Latour says, engender "below the line" hybrid quasi-humans on the nature/culture boundary. Here we find the figure of the wild man, the material-semiotic actor who functions within the culture of the Enlightenment as the alter ego of the Citizen of the Enlightenment; his existence is as requisite as its repression, and a nonmodern view of Habermas's public sphere challenges us to trace the traffic and exchange between these two figures.

Habermas's articulation of the transformation of the Bourgeois public sphere has a special significance for those of us interested not only in literary history but also in the relations between that history and larger cultural history.[7] His contention is, in part, fundamentally about the social and political agency of those discursive networks that operate under the broad sense of the literary. For Habermas, literary expression is not merely a by-product of the liberatory politics of the Enlightenment, but it also plays a constitutive role in bringing about the political change that we retrospectively identify with the Enlightenment. In this sense, it seems to me, radical critiques of Habermas often do a disservice to this aspect of his argument. The claim that the bourgeois liberalism of the Enlightenment was for some elements of the population oppressive may well be true but hardly undermines Habermas's argument. As Craig Calhoun rightly observes, "it was the society that was bourgeois, and bourgeois society produced a certain kind of public sphere." In a convenient old-fashioned literary history of the novel, in which literary history followed in attendance on political history, England first gave rise to republican politics, and a happy byproduct of that political change was a liberated literary expression that gave birth to the novel. The Habermasian framework for reconciling literary, social, and political histories identifies the work of literary texts as in part bringing about the political transformations that in turn enable new literary contributions to the public sphere discourse that continues to shape the changing relations of the individual subject and state authority. Such a notion of mutual reinforcement between public sphere discourse and society does indeed problematize Calhoun's observation by revealing its own circularity. This book attempts to come to terms with that circularity by recognizing up front two fundamental turbulences within the smooth flow of most public-sphere arguments. The imagined public sphere of a continuous circulation of salons and coffeehouses is doubly disrupted: first by those voices that can be heard from without, raising cries in the streets that penetrate into the clubs and salons; and again by those troublesome voices of those who have been allowed in but who prefer to speak out against the very organization that is assimilating them. One may think of the first as the various excluded voices (women, laboring classes, nonwhites, etc.), and one may think of the second as those satires within the public sphere that seek to attack the very conventions that construct their readership; one staple of Scriblerian satire was the "newsmonger" who played an integral role in constructing an audience for the satirist.[8] In this book, I try to keep alive not so much a tension, but an active exchange between those elements of public sphere discourse from the eighteenth century that effectively "passed muster" as contributing to bourgeois letters and those related contributions that were subsequently "drummed out" of such a social cannon.

Thus, my opening chapter moves back and forth between Tyson's Royal Society–sponsored seminal contribution to comparative anatomy and the history of science (an eminently bourgeois text) and several more ephemeral Scriblerian satires related to it that have long since slipped from the literary canon. Chapter 3 similarly moves back and forth between the novel that is perhaps most closely identified with the literary rise of the bourgeoisie in England, *Robinson Crusoe*, and Defoe's contribution to a more vulgar plebian literature prompted by the arrival in England of Peter, the wild youth. Chapter 5 follows those two representative English gentlemen, Samuel Johnson and James Boswell, on their bourgeois tour of Scotland; but in doing so, it pays serious attention to the voluble eccentric, James Burnett, Lord Monboddo, who Johnson more or less wrote out of the canon of eighteenth-century letters. My final chapter similarly poses two texts in discussion with one another: Mary Shelley's *Frankenstein*—well established by now as a central text of Romantic fiction— with Thomas Love Peacock's *Melincourt,* a novel written at the same time as

Frankenstein by a member of the same circle but seldom reprinted since the mid-nineteenth century. Two exceptions to this general pattern of double-voiced chapters occur in chapters 2 and 4, and perhaps these chapters should be read as in some ways speaking with and against one another. The former concerns itself almost exclusively with a plebian literature focused on Peter, the wild youth, that has long ago been dropped from the eighteenth-century canon; the latter focuses almost exclusively on perhaps the most famous fiction of the early eighteenth century, Jonathan Swift's *Gulliver's Travels.* Since the literature surrounding Peter was all published during the summer while Swift was in England arranging for the publication of *Gulliver,* it makes a good deal of sense to see the arguments of these two chapters as engaging one another. Cumulatively, the aim of this organization is to reconsider the puzzling circularity that Calhoun voices in his articulation of the bourgeois identity of Habermas's "bourgeois public sphere." The eighteenth-century public sphere was a much richer and more turbulent cacophony than a retrospective review of the complete *Tatler* and *Spectator* might suggest.

Habermas's thesis that a fundamental social transformation in eighteenth-century Europe may be usefully charted in terms of the emergence of a bourgeois public sphere has enabled and demanded critical discussion of the early modern period that explores the negotiations between discursive and material culture. Collectively, these discussions have enriched our understanding of the cultural process that produced the citizen of the Enlightenment. At roughly the same time, the so-called semiotic turn within cultural studies of science has challenged practitioners to attend equally to the material and the semiotic dimensions of knowledge construction. These discussions frequently borrow from semiotics the heuristic of the "semiotic square" as a means of positioning conceptual terms in a more complex juxtaposition than that of simple binary opposition. Borrowing from these studies the notion of a material/semiotic actor as an agent distinct from the presuppositions of Enlightenment narratives of heroic individualism, this study identifies the figure of the wild man as such a candidate: he moves between the realms of daily life and narrative representations, oscillating between real living creatures, fictional characters, and a variety of mediating figures who are each distinct from, but affiliated with, one another. The resulting narrative of the wild man in the Enlightenment helps to clarify the process by which a particular "social" democratic ideal of the citizen of the Enlightenment collapses into a "scientific" discourse of natural philosophy's description of what it means to be "human." In doing so, it also sheds light on the ways in which this traffic contributes to an emerging British imperial identity.

Throughout the journey that this book traverses, the chapter headings playfully remind us not only of the narrative conventions of eighteenth-century travel narratives and novels but also of the peculiarly shape-shifting propensity of the material-semiotic figure of the wild man, as he traverses the globe, sometimes in fiction, sometimes in reality, sometimes as human, sometimes as nonhuman. The protagonist of this narrative is a "trickster" figure, a shape-shifter who resists and disrupts classificatory schemata. The overlapping episodes that constitute his narrative do not lend themselves readily to linear outline, but they do dissolve into one another in nonrandom ways. The subheadings accompanying each chapter borrow a convention of eighteenth-century narrative in order to provide a signposting that can help the reader as he or she attempts to navigate the nonmodern argument of this narrative.

1

a *Pygmy* in London

*in which an orang-outang
appears before the Royal Society,
a monster enters the coffeehouse,
and an infant makes a sometime curator of Bedlam famous
as a father while he remains
celebrated for celibacy*

We tend to think of it as a "matter of fact" that we are primates and, similarly, that it is also a "matter of fact" that there exist other, nonhuman primates.[1] In one very real sense, both of these notions are true. Those statements speak directly to our material identities, yet they need to be checked by the recognition that these ideas are ultimately historically contingent semiotic markers. Whatever material identity people enjoy (or endure), they were not "primates" before 1758, and only in that year were they distinguished from another set of fellow primates designated as "nonhumans." The relationship of man and beast, and its attendant anxieties of kinship and dominion, are at least as old as literate culture and probably older, but between the dawn of an age of global navigation and Darwin's publication of *The Origin of Species,* defining that relationship in the light of the proliferating evidence of other humans and humanoids brought back to Europe by travelers and discoverers became an increasingly challenging activity. John Ray's *Synopsis methodica animalium quadrapedum et serpentini generis* (1693) continued a longstanding practice of simply omitting humans from its description of the brute creation. Carl Linnaeus, a generation later, felt that man's animal nature and the obligations of his grand undertaking required our inclusion. In early editions, he listed men among the *anthropoids*, the first subheading under *quadrupeds*. That taxonomy was assailed on both fronts: it was circular to include men among other "man-like" beasts, and it undermined the dignity of bipedal humans to group them with quadruped brutes. Only in the tenth edition (1758) did Linnaeus, to appease these critics, introduce the categories of "mammals" and "primates."[2] However much our primate identities may appear today to be "a matter of fact," the uneven discourse of what may be thought of as "pre-primate primatology" in the early decades of the eighteenth century contributed much to the shaping of that identity.

In the summer of 1699, there appeared in London, among several other related essays, "A Philological Essay Concerning the Satyrs of the Ancients."[3] In spite of the title, the essay is concerned not with the "satyrs" of Horace, Juvenal, and Persius, but rather with those characters in Pliny and Diodorus Siculus, who "are always represented as Jocose and Sportful, but Scurrilous and Lascivious; and wonderful Things they relate of their Revellings by Night, their Dancing, Musick, and their wanton Frolicks" (46). That is, the subjects of the essay in question are "satyrs," and not "satires." At the same time, although the essay announces itself as philological in method, it is not commonly thought of as a contribution to literary criticism but to medical science. The title of the complete work in which it appears is *Orang-Outang, sive Homo Sylvestris: or, The Anatomy of a Pygmie Compared with that of a Monkey, an Ape, and a Man. To which is added, A Philological Essay Concerning the Pygmies, the Cynocephali, the Satyrs, and Sphinges of the Ancients.*

Considering Edward Tyson's "satyr" in relation to those of his literary contemporaries allows us to explore new ways of considering literary satire of the eighteenth century and as a consequence entertain more general ideas about our understanding of the nature of satire. For such a project, Tyson's book commands a special interest, for it is itself what we would term retrospectively a work of "literature and science"—its first half is detailed comparative anatomy; its second half is philological criticism. In this way, it belongs to those distinctly "modern" contributions to learning that attempted to bring a solid, material basis to the practice of philological criticism, and this parallels those antiquarian projects so well characterized by Joseph Levine in *Dr. Woodward's Shield.* Such an odd, hybridized quality defies easy generic classification in a way that is itself related to the practice of satire. Tyson's work is an anatomy, both in that word's principal sense of a dissection of the body, and in the secondary (and more literary) sense of a logical dissection or analysis of a body of knowledge. In this latter sense, it belongs to a tradition, popularized in the seventeenth century by Burton's *Anatomy of Melancholy,* that is frequently identified with Menippean satire. We should note that the difficulty in classifying Tyson's book reflects the difficulty in classifying the subject of that book and also is reflected by the persistent problem of classifying satire within the realm of literature.

Together, the various claims of Tyson's titles reveal his project as consisting of three interrelated activities: a comparative anatomy, a taxonomy, and a philological essay on the myth and literature of the wild man. The comparative anatomy is "hard science," the philological essay is literary criticism, and the taxonomy is the hybridized act of naming the world that underwrites not only this, but so much of eighteenth-century natural history. However much Tyson attempts to position literary criticism ("philology") as a supplement to the preexisting scientific discourse of "comparative anatomy," the two enterprises are in his narrative mutually reinforcing, drawing upon one another for support and subordinating both to the unidentified privileged discourse of taxonomy. Tyson's title provides us with six nouns, names that are to be compared with one another, not as words but as bodies: "Orang-Outang," "Homo Sylvestris," "Pygmie," "Monkey," "Ape," and "Man." The first term, from which the modern-day "orangutan" is derived, is a Malayan word meaning, literally, "wild man of the woods." It was first employed in Europe by the Dutch physician Nicolaas Tulp (the central subject of Rembrandt's *The Anatomy Lesson*) and was used generically to refer not only to creatures found in Borneo but to what are now referred to as "anthropoid apes." On one hand, it is important to recognize that Tyson uses the term in this generic sense; he is not confusing the creature he anatomizes with an orangutan. At the same time, we must also recognize that the very concept of "generic" in the Linnaean sense that we now use the term is anachronistic when applied to Tyson. While taxonomies existed before Linnaeus, nothing approaching the rigorous system he developed was familiar to Tyson. When he uses "Orang-Outang," he refers not to "anthropoid apes," but to all creatures commonly referred to as some kind of "wild man of the woods." Thus, his first title, "sive Homo Sylvestris," provides the proper scholarly Latin alternative name, "or man of the woods." If, for Tyson, "Orang-Outang" and "Homo Sylvestris" are synonymous terms, so too are "monkey" and "ape," as they will continue to be for Samuel Johnson fifty-six years later. Our current practice of using "ape" to refer primarily to the five so-called great apes—man, chimpanzee, gorilla, gibbon, and orangutan—and using "monkey" to refer to the lesser primates had not emerged. Of the two remaining terms, Tyson consistently uses "man" in one of the widely accepted usages of the day, "as distinct from beast"; "Pygmie" is used in the sense provided by Johnson, "one of a nation fabled to be only three spans high, and after long wars to have been destroyed by cranes." "Man," in this usage, is a term of science, locating a creature in the scale of beings, while "Pygmie" is opposed to it as a fabulous term of mythology. What Tyson is about to do is relocate the figure of myth in the discourse of science, position that figure between man and ape as a liminal figure of science, and then, denying the possibility of liminal status, demote it to the status of ape.

Late in 1697, or early in 1698, a ship arrived in London carrying among other things a young chimpanzee, captured in Angola. During the voyage, this little traveler fell against a cannon, knocking out a tooth and precipitating an infection that hastened his death in April 1698. Edward Tyson, arguably England's foremost anatomist, conducted a thorough anatomy, the results of which did much to establish both the method of comparative anatomy and the field of primatology. For one interested in studying culture, more remarkable than an evaluation of Tyson's successes and failures is a recognition of how interrelated and inextricably linked they are. On the one hand, Tyson's anatomy details— carefully and with admirable precision—the physical attributes of a young male chimpanzee. At the same time, Tyson nowhere uses the term "chimpanzee" (a word he did not know), and indeed his entire discussion participates in a confusion of terminology and taxonomy.[4] Thus, even as Tyson establishes a distinctly "scientific" method of constructing knowledge about the body, that knowledge is constructed within a context of confusion, marginality, and liminality that characterizes "pre-primate primatology."[5] Before Linnaeus's tenth edition established an order of primates that included apes and man in a ranked order, the discussion of their relation to one another was not only vexed, it was defined in fundamentally different ways. Certainly, Tyson's "Orang-Outang, sive Homo Sylvestris" was an important contribution to that discussion, but so too—in fundamentally different terms—were a range of popular (and, particularly, satirical) works, less obviously concerned with the same sets of questions.

At the time Tyson wrote, very little was known in Europe of anthropoid apes, and not surprisingly what was known was embroiled in confusion. Writing in 1602, Konrad Gesner assembled what has accurately been described as "an admirable account of the knowledge of the ancients, a vivid picture of the credulity, superstition, and fancifulness of the Middle Ages, and a determined effort to distinguish the true from the false" (Yerkes and Yerkes 8). Andrew Battell, an English privateer taken prisoner by the Portuguese in 1559, had spent several years in Africa, and in 1613 his narrative was published in *Purchas his Pilgrimes.* This account reported secondhand testimony of "two kinds of Monsters, which are common in these Woods, and very dangerous." These "monsters," known today as the gorilla and the chimpanzee, were referred to by Battell as Pongo and Engecko, respectively, though in such a way as made it unclear to Samuel Purchas that they were in fact two distinct creatures. Battell's account also included a brief discussion of "Pigmey Pongo-killers," presumably members of the Pygmy tribe today known as the Twa, though Purchas concludes that these must be the monsters labeled Engecko. Prior to Tyson, the most important contribution to European knowledge of other primate species was Nicolaas Tulp's description of what he termed the "Indian Satyr." Tulp assigned the term *Homo Sylvestris,* orang-outang, to what was probably a chimpanzee. This primate, like Tyson's, had been brought from Angola, and the phrase "the Indian Satyr" alludes to a description in Pliny: "there is an animal, a quadruped, in the tropical mountains of India, a most pernicious one; with a human figure, but with feet of a goat; and with a body hairy all over. Having none of the human customs; rejoicing in the shadows of the wood; and fleeing from intercourse with men . . . [other poets] call their Satyrs lascivious, shameless, two-formed, two-horned, and with the wanton inclinations of the woods. Which epithets of the ancients, if you explore with the level of truth, you will see themselves not far wrong" (Tulp 277). Within a few years of Tulp's description, Jacob Bontius offered a description of what we would now identify as a Bornean Orangutan, employing Tulp's terminology of *Homo Sylvestris,* orangoutang. Compounding the confusion, Bontius illustrated his text with an engraving of a pilose woman. Bontius's illustration returns us to Battell's phrasing in underlining what historians of science have often been happy to overlook: the discourse of pre-primate primatology was a discourse of monstrosity, monsters, and alterity. The subject Tyson anatomized and preserved for permanent display (now in the British Museum of Natural History) was already on display in Bartholomew Fair. The elite culture of science was appropriating the popular culture displays of marginal humans.

Tyson is something of an anomalous figure in the history of science. Long acknowledged, but generally ignored, for his contributions to the work of Huxley and Darwin, he found an enthusiastic champion in Ashley Montagu about fifty years ago. Montagu's biography begins: "This book is the outcome of a personal enthusiasm for Edward Tyson, its principal subject," and continues, unabated, in that vein for 418 pages (excluding appendixes), concluding, "It may be that I have overestimated Tyson's place in the history of our culture, for I have not been able to judge his work altogether dispassionately, my enthusiasm for the man and his work has been too great for that. In any event I do not like dispassionate biographies. If, as a scientist, Tyson had any faults I am not aware of them" (418). Between such effusions, it will not be surprising to learn that Montagu ranks the orang-outang along with Copernicus's *De Revolutionibus,* Vesalius's *Fabrica,* and Newton's *Principia,* as the four most important contributions to science before the eighteenth century. Indeed, such is Montagu's enthusiasm, and so engaging is his undisguised admiration, that one is almost obligated to overlook the aside on page 311 where Montagu acknowledges indirectly that Tyson was almost entirely in error in all of his conclusions.

Regarding Tyson's conclusion that the Pygmies of the Ancients were not humans but animals such as his orang-outang, Montagu writes:

> Tyson did his work so well that the notion of the existence of a pygmy race of man, in spite of several brilliant attempts to bolster it up, fell thoroughly into disrepute, so that when, in 1867, Paul Du Chaillu published an account of the pygmy tribe which he had discovered in Equatorial Africa, his story was received by scientific men with frank incredulity. The truth was but slowly accepted, and then only after the independent corroboration of Du Chaillu's report by several different investigators. The skepticism which so grudgingly gave way to a conviction of Du Chaillu's good faith, has since also given way to the substantiation, in almost every detail, of the truth of the accounts given of the pygmies by the many ancient authorities whom Tyson quoted. (311)

I suspect that with more "dispassionate" historians than Montagu, this latter fact accounts for the relative obscurity to which Tyson has returned. Today, this sometime curator of Bedlam and anatomist who discovered the preputial and coronal glands of the glans penis, is primarily acknowledged (and then ignored) as introducing comparative anatomy and is thus often given the title "the father of primatology." According to Montagu, "No man has ever been more truly the founder and the father of his subject than Tyson has been of Primatology" (399).

I wish to return our attention to Tyson, not in the vein of enthusiasm adopted by Montagu, but in a more ironic vein. If today Tyson is renowned as "the father of primatology," he was in his own lifetime no less renowned for his celibacy, inspiring Elkanah Settle to rhapsodize in a threnody on the occasion of his death: 'Nor Wonder ne'er by Beauty Captive led, / No Bridal Partner ever shared his bed. / No, to the blinder God no Knee e'er paid, / To great MINERVA his whole Court he made." An anonymous account of his life, published in *A Compleat History of Europe . . . For the Year 1708,* comments on both his celibacy and the sudden nature of his death: "This learned Physician having never been married, but I may say, devoted himself to Caelibacy"; "[death] overtook him suddenly, and in an Instant, deprived him of Life, on Sunday the first of August, about five in the Evening, as he was pleasantly Conversing with a Gentlewoman his Patient in her Apartment" (405–6). In an age notorious for innuendo, when "to converse" held connotations of sexual intimacy that no longer obtain ("To have commerce with a different sex" in Johnson's *Dictionary*), it is tempting to read reports of Tyson's celibacy as compromised by the circumstances of his sudden demise. But both for his anonymous biographer and for Elkanah Settle, Tyson's celibacy was in fact important as testimony to his devotion to science. Donna Haraway notes a similar dynamic at work in Carl Akeley's construction of his devotion to science: "The pace he was setting himself was grueling, dangerous for a man ominously weakened by tropical fevers. But science is a jealous mistress and takes little account of a man's feelings" (*Primate* 33). Constructing Tyson as a paragon of science requires him to sacrifice human bodily pleasures for the more refined and solitary pleasures of the mind. Settle's verse paragraph opens with the defining synecdoche for science ("Such the lost HEAD we mourn") and concludes with the consequent rejection of domestic happiness: Tyson hears only the Apollonian music of learning, "Musick so much beyond the poorer Cries / of unharmonious Cradle Nurseries." In reconsidering the work of this celibate father of a discourse whose subject was constructed thirty years after his death, we may tease open its ironic conjunctions and explore the underlying assumptions of colonial science. Ultimately, for all the excesses of enthusiasm Montagu may be guilty of, I believe he is right in his judgment that Tyson was an outstanding scientist, and in that light his erroneous conclusions become all the more interesting and revealing.

The simple facts of his biographical notice and funeral threnody indicate Tyson's relatively distinguished social status. His scientific eminence is inseparable from his social eminence, and the most important work of his life — the anatomy of a "pygmie"—is a social, as well as a scientific, achievement. Tyson rendered appropriate as a subject of science a figure who already enjoyed enormous popular appeal as a spectacle. Broadsheets and newspaper advertisements frequently announced new exhibitions at Bartholomew and other fairs and coffeehouses. Staples of this entertainment included giants, dwarfs, apes, and those who blurred the boundaries of the human: "A little Black Hairy Pigmy, bred in the Desarts of Arabia, a natural Ruff of hair about his face, two foot high, walks upright, drinks a glass of Ale or Wine, and does several other things to admiration" (Ashton 203; cf. Todd passim). These were popular entertainments, but they were also the subjects of scientific curiosity; Pepys and other fellows of the Royal Society were often in attendance at such exhibitions (Benedict 42).[6] Tyson's introduction of the disciplined procedure of comparative anatomy fundamentally alters the nature of the exhibition while claiming the subject for the realm of science. Dennis Todd has nicely articulated the disturbing economy of these monstrous exhibitions. Noting the troubling play of similarity and difference that is fundamental to our fascination with monsters, he shows how that tension is defused and recontained through public display: "Placed on a stage, shown during holidays, exhibited precisely because of their anomalousness, the monsters were, in the end, not us at all but just freaks in a fair booth. The intuition of identity that attracted the audience in the first place, instead of ripening into conscious self-awareness, was diverted into the mindless pleasure of spectacle. And so the economy of monster exhibitions answers perfectly to the dance of attraction and avoidance. What begins as titillation ends as mere entertainment, to the infinite satisfaction of an audience who 'purely come to hear, and stare'" (259).

If, on the one hand, Tyson's enterprise is antithetical to commercial exploitation of the managers of the fair, his anatomy is similarly dedicated to a comforting recontainment of the initially troubling resemblance of the "pygmie." The comforting conclusion of his anatomy is a list of thirty-four specific points wherein "the Orang-Outang or Pygmie differ'd from a Man, and resembled more the Ape and Monkey-kind" (94–95). That conclusion was foreshadowed in the book's opening declaration: "That the Pygmies of the Antients were a sort of Apes, and not of Humane Race, I shall endeavour to prove in the following Essay" (1). While Tyson, no less than the fair managers, recontains the potentially threatening monster as a diminished and abject imitation of the human form, his method is almost diametrically opposed to theirs. If, at the fair, troubling possibilities are "diverted into the mindless pleasure of spectacle," in

Tyson's anatomy they become the disembodied object of mental speculation. Such a difference is in no small part a function of class difference and social standing. Just after the death of "Tyson's pygmie," a handbill was published, as Todd notes, promoting a "tantalizingly unspecified monster shown at Moncress's Coffee House in June 1698, 'being Humane upwards, but Bruit downwards, wonderful to behold'" (246). The pleasures of spectacle depend upon the tantalizing lack of specificity with which the "monster" (in the handbill, this word appears in capital letters) is announced. But the "wonder" such a monster provokes is intellectual as well as visual. Tyson's dedication, "to the Right Honourable John, Lord Sommers, Baron of Evesham, Lord High Chancellor of England, one of the Lords of His Majesties Most Honourable Privy Council, and President of the Royal Society," locates his anatomy at once in the privileged space of aristocratic gentility, political privilege, and scientific eminence. Tyson's "pygmie" has been removed from the staring throng of the democratic mob, and that removal is directly related to the reaffirmation of a consoling hierarchical rank order. Just as Tyson himself will be memorialized as sacrificing bodily pleasure in his constant devotion to the "jealous mistress," science, so here he employs a similar conceit in his appeal to Sommers: "To serve your Country, you have defrauded your self both of Meat, and Rest; which, my Lord, is the only Act of Injustice, that was ever charged upon you. Your immoderate Labours make daily Encroachments upon your Health; or at least 'tis the fear of every good Man, that they should. And yet your Lordship, notwithstanding all Disswasions, perseveres inflexible; as if, animated by the Noble Spirit of an Old Roman, you were resolved to Sacrifice your Life, for the Good of your Country" (ii).

Here are paired conceits that have long since become clichés: the scientist placing knowledge above the pleasures of the body; the statesman neglecting to nourish his own body so that he may better serve the body politic. These mutually supporting roles reinforce one another in constructing the social space of science. Sommers "has lately condescended, to Preside over the Royal Society." This is the paradoxical rhetoric of modest self-assertion, the elliptical dance where deference enables self-promotion.[6] The underlying concern of both Tyson's anatomy and the exhibits at the fair is one of troubling taxonomies. The nine terms offered in Tyson's complete title all jostle with one another, contesting for privilege in a rank order. The most pressing commitment of Tyson's anatomy is to locate his pygmy outside of—but adjacent to—the human species. Doing so, his dedication indicates, serves a social as well as a scientific purpose: "The Animal of which I have given the Anatomy, coming nearest to Mankind; seems the Nexus of the Animal and Rational, as your Lordship, and those of your High Rank and Order for Knowledge and Wisdom, approaching nearest to that kind of Beings which is next above us; Connect the Visible, and Invisible World" (iii).

Tyson mobilized his description to construct the bonobo beneath his knife as nonhuman and non-ape. Tyson concluded that his creature was a pygmy, but in a confession of his own, he announces that he framed that conclusion not as the result of his scientific discoveries but as the precondition to their existence: "I must confess, I could never before entertain any other Opinion about [pygmies], but that the whole was a Fiction, and as the first Account we have of them, was from a Poet, so that they were only a Creature of the Brain, produced by a warm and wanton Imagination, and that they never had any Existence or Habitation elsewhere"("Philological Essay" 1). Tyson's anatomy of "a pygmie" allows him to "discover" the "real," nonhuman basis for the fabulous tales of poets. His anatomy was so convincing that well after human pygmies in central and southern Africa had been encountered by Westerners, their existence continued to be discredited.

The "creature[s] of the Brain, produced by a warm and wanton Imagination" that Tyson will reveal to be monstrous representations of a quasi-human hybrid sound very much like contemporary descriptions not of the fanciful productions of poets but of the monstrous reproductions of teratogeny. By Tyson's time the doctrine of the prenatal influence of the imagination had entrenched itself as the compelling explanation for monstrous birth, and the excited maternal imagination was the established reproductive technology for the generation of monsters.[7]

Cultural anxieties about teratogeny and the doctrine of the imagination's predominant role focused on the Mary Toft case of 1726, in which a woman was said to have given birth to seventeen rabbits. Explanations of how such an event could occur had recourse to the doctrine of the influence of an excited imagination; Mary Toft's rabbits could be rationalized, along with a long tradition of teratogenous reproduction, as belonging with Tyson's pygmy among the "creatures of the brain." That Toft's extraordinary delivery could be reconciled with an established doctrine did not, of course, make her story credible, and in a little more than a month the episode was revealed as a hoax. Some had doubted Toft from the beginning, some had been genuinely taken in, and most had been of a divided opinion, alternating between the poles of belief and disbelief. From the outset, one of this larger group had been James Douglas, a reputable man midwife who had doubted Mary Toft's story, even while retaining a belief in the doctrine of maternal imagination that rationalized that story. Dennis Todd's discussion of Douglas's position underlines the importance of species in considerations of reproductive potential:

> Douglas's ultimate rejection of Mary Toft's claim should not be taken as evidence that he doubted the doctrine of the influence of the imagination. He chooses his words with great care: "I begin by declaring it to have been always my firm Opinion, that this Report was false; in the First Place, because I could never conceive the Generation of a perfect Rabbit in the Uterus of a Woman to be possible, it being contradictory to all that is hitherto known, both from Reason and Experience, concerning the ordinary, as well as extraordinary Procedure of Nature, in the Formation of a Foetus" (Advertisement, 3). The important word here is "perfect," and Douglas's point is that a human cannot give birth to "an intirely different Species" (38). (Todd 284 n. 29)

The pygmies Tyson encountered in Pliny and other classical authors are identified as monstrous, unnatural impossibilities that, like the monstrous productions in nature, are to be accounted for as the offspring of a wanton imagination, "a creature of the brain." Correcting the errors of the poets and the excesses of imagination leads Tyson to identify the "real" pygmy of nature in the bonobo brought back to England. The painstaking anatomy that follows this creature's death is mobilized on behalf of fixing his identity as a natural pygmy—neither human, from whose anatomy he differs in thirty-four ways (94–95), nor ape, from whose anatomy he differs in forty-eight ways (92–94). The liminal status of Tyson's pygmy between human and ape at once naturalizes the monstrous pygmy created by the wanton imagination of poets and stabilizes that figure in a natural order that insists on species purity. For like Douglas, who will maintain "that a human cannot give birth to 'an intirely different Species,'" Tyson also insists that his pygmy is to be accorded its own species: "Now notwithstanding our Pygmie does so much resemble a Man in many of its Parts, more than any of the Ape-kind, or any other Animal in the world that I know of: Yet by no means do I look upon it as the Product of a mixt Generation; 'tis a Brute-Animal *sui generis,* and a particular Species of Ape" (Tyson 2).

As an anatomist, Tyson found the ape most closely approaching the human on an imagined "chain of being," or *scala natura* (Dougherty 66). Tyson's principle criteria were functionalist, and his comparative anatomy presented a strong case that the material form of his "pygmie" more closely approximated the functional requirements of the human form than any other species in the natural world. Naturalists tended to differ from anatomists in minimizing the importance of the ape's material approximation of the human form, in favor of a ranking of animal nature that emphasized the perceived uniqueness of human mental activity. In this version, the ape mimicked man, but without reason, whereas other animals approached man much more closely in their rational capacity. For neither naturalist nor anatomist did such proximity translate into anything approaching evolutionist logic. While the chain of nature needed to be complete, each link was imagined to be utterly distinct and independent; species was fixed.

Thus, despite the appearance of disagreement between naturalists and anatomists, their shared assumption of species fixity meant that where sexual activity crossed species lines it would be marked by the inability to reproduce.[8] Against the vulgar superstition that apes were the result of a "mixt generation" between man and beast, Tyson insisted on the species integrity of his pygmie. Yet even while Tyson presented his anatomy to the Royal Society as material evidence of that animal that "coming nearest to Mankind; seems the Nexus of the Animal and Rational," such a body (quite possibly, this very one) was on display in Moncress's coffeehouse for a shilling a view as "a MONSTER, wonderful to behold, being human upward and bruit downward," in the tradition of "mixt generation." The exemplary cases of "hybridous" mixt generation for enlightenment taxonomy were the mule and the hinny, the offspring of a jackass and a mare, and a stallion and a female ass, respectively. While such "hybridous" breeding was in some instances possible, the offspring was marked by an inability to reproduce. Thus, species identity was preserved by an inheritable capacity to reproduce.

Throughout the eighteenth century, as Europeans sought to identify their relation to those creatures we now identify as "nonhuman primates," narratives of such hybrid couplings signal anxiety over the limits of species identity in the absence of an evolutionary model. Since Darwin, the dominant metaphor for primate relations is one of kinship, and the anxieties surrounding debate over evolution almost invariably reveal themselves in the rhetoric of family, blood, resemblance, and so on. As Piet de Rooy has pointed out, this led in the case of Herman M. Bernelot Moens "to the conclusion that 'humans and anthropomorphic apes are literally blood relatives.' This in turn suggested that—just as in the case of related animals like horses and donkeys, or hares and rabbits— hybrids between these apes and man must be possible" (Rooy 195). For Moens,

a follower of Haeckel, the goal was to realize such a potential and prove empirically the possibility of "a missing link." For the eighteenth century, however,
such hybrid fantasies offered evidence not of evolutionary continuity but of either confirmation or refutation of a putative species distinction between man
and ape.

In the Enlightenment, the two tracks of a divided response to what we now
label "nonhuman primates" corresponded to a fundamental divergence over
questions of species and taxonomy that separated anatomists such as Tyson
from naturalists such as Buffon (Dougherty 67; Wokler 45). In spite of what
seems both general similarity and specific difference at a level of anatomical
function, specific behaviors—such as domesticating, or parenting, a kitten—
seem at times to reproduce "human nature." In some cases, such as the elephant, the consolation of significant anatomical difference could license narratives of dramatic similarity in nature; Buffon includes several stories of elephant
behavior that seem remarkably human.[9] Where anatomical resemblance threatens with a monstrous similarity, however, those narratives become more dangerous, particularly when the human nature being approximated is already
dangerously carnal. Among the ways that Tyson's pygmy resembled men more
than apes, or apes more than men, Tyson notes pertaining to reproduction only
that "the Orang-Outang or Pygmie differ'd from a Man, and resembled more
the Ape and Monkey-kind . . . in having no pendulous Scrotum" (94).

This observation was almost immediately challenged on the basis that Tyson's subject was by his own account an infant, but within Tyson's narrative it is
easy to discern a logic for inclusion: "whether the Testes being thus closely
pursed up to the Body, might contribute to that great salaciousness this Species
of Animals are noted for, I will not determine: Tho' 'tis said, that these Animals,
that have their Testicles contained within the Body, are more inclined to it, than
others. That the whole Ape-kind is extremely given to Venery, appears by
infinite stories related of them" (42). Without relating all of them (he has previously cited some), Tyson proceeds to an account from Licetus "of a Woman
who had two Children by an Ape" (42). Tyson's discussion, though it is careful in language ("I will not determine") unites anatomical findings with traditional lore regarding sexual appetite. According to this tradition, women were
more salacious than men because their organs of generation were folded inward, and consequently were warmer. Thus, the celibate anatomist can find in
the body of an infant bonobo a material justification for a species distinction
that naturalizes human behavior as modest and ape behavior as salacious, while
linking that species distinction to a gender distinction that identifies women

with apes. He then illustrates that finding with a classical narrative uniting woman and ape in salacious coupling, even though the reproductive success promised by the narrative contradicts the very species distinction he is seeking to affirm. Laura Brown has also commented on this passage, noting astutely the double game whereby Tyson simultaneously disowns and insists upon a species link: the narrative creates "a sense of the inevitability or even the anatomical necessity of this [cross-species] connection, so that the anecdote represents a leap of affinity, in which a posited alterity is reversed by a surprising connection. This leap is the hallmark of the fable of the nonhuman being" (*Fables* 239). Such a double game will become the signature of an emergent racist ideology of alterity and difference. Notoriously, it is to such narratives of natural history that Thomas Jefferson turns in the fourteenth query of his *Notes on the State of Virginia,* when he comments on the "superior beauty" of whites: "Add to these, flowing hair, a more elegant symmetry of form, their own judgment in favour of the whites, declared by their preference of them, as uniformly as is the preference of the Oran-ootan for the black women over those of his own species." This recourse to what Jefferson purports to describe as "the real distinctions which nature has made," testifies to the process by which a construction of alterity in natural history is enlisted in the service of a racist ideology. The problematic identity of the wild man calls into question the limit points of an unstable human identity. As the culture moves at the end of the eighteenth century to establish consensus about a normative definition of the human in terms that reify the Citizen of the Enlightenment as a natural (rather than a political) identity, it simultaneously grounds that identity in terminology that relocates previous uncertainty over species identity onto the problematic ground of racial identity, thereby enabling the tiresome racist ideologies propounded by Edward Long and others (Jordan 28–32, 457–61).

It would be easy to read some aspects of Tyson's anatomy ironically, and, in fact, I think we should. If there is to be a progressive component to Enlightenment science and the knowledge of the natural world that it enables, then surely the past three hundred years, building on the solid material foundation supplied by Tyson, has gone a long way to dispelling those myths and presuppositions that Tyson was willing to countenance as surely as the fables of "pygmies" that he set out to discredit. Such a reading enables us to locate Tyson's contribution to our knowledge of primate identities and reproductive technologies as both empirically sanctioned and socially constructed.

Swift's Pygmies and Yahoos, Pope's Monsters of Dulness, all occupy the liminal space defined by Restoration and early-eighteenth-century science as monstrous: at once failing to reproduce the same, they are too dangerously similar to be safely classified as "other" (Turner) They reproduce the stories contemporary science told of the "wild man" or satyr: on the one hand—weak, degraded, diminished, and abject; simultaneously dangerous, threatening, and too free, especially sexually. The monsters of satire, like the constructions of the wild man, are impotent in that word's dual construction—weak and ineffectual, yet given to unrestrained sexual excess and satyriasis. Swift's amorous Yahoo repeats (with reversed genders) the common stories of orangutans as satyrs, marauding the boundaries of forest and society in search of sexual prey. In *Tale of a Tub,* the Moderns are seen to realize the type of those priapic pygmies with enlarged genitalia recorded by Ctesias ("Digression in praise of Digressions"); the "monster breeding" dunces of Pope's *Dunciad* "get a jumbled race." The anxiety underwriting Tyson's anatomy is not dissimilar to a fundamental anxiety at the heart of satire—a concern over the limits and boundaries of what counts as human.

At the same time that early modern science sets about discovering in nature the physical embodiment of the legendary satyr—half-man, half-beast, English literary history marks itself as "an age of satire." The wild men, feral children, satyrs, orangs, and apes of eighteenth-century natural history represent a dangerous and degraded vision of ourselves against whom we define the category "human." The satirist, metaphorically reenacting the liminal predations of these creatures, subverts this reassuring boundary formation by revealing the bestial within the human. Thus both satirist and satiric victim wind up balancing on the boundary between "human" and "other" and threatening the security promised by such definitions.

Tyson's work, in short, is a study of "human" that proceeds by focusing attention on instances of monstrous alterity. It is, quite literally, a cataloguing of identity and difference that aims to fix and establish the boundaries of what constitutes the human. In this respect it mediates between the mythic role of its subject—the satyr—and the literary role of the satire. For the legendary figure of the satyr, half-man and half-beast, is a figure of (especially sexual) predation lurking in the shadows of the forest who polices the boundary between civilization and the wild, threatening to carry off those women and children who do not participate in their own domestication. Satire, too, performs a kind of border work and does so repeatedly by invoking an antithesis between the social and the animal. It is one of the important paradoxes of satire that the figure of

the satyr describes both the satirist and the object of satire. The satirist, often
characterized as a figure of rage and violence, serves through his attacks the social function of establishing the limits of social behavior. At the same time, his
attacks repeatedly take the form of stripping away the civilized veneer of social
respectability to reveal a bestial nature at the core. In the various descriptions of
"primate" behavior between Tyson and Linnaeus, and in the contemporary
satiric contributions of Pope, Swift, and Arbuthnot, one can find a similar impulse: a constructive projection of self-loathing onto those who threaten by resembling too closely.

In what follows I want to pay particular attention to an intercourse, a boundary crossing, that was clearly at work in the early eighteenth century and that is
frequently obscured for late-twentieth-century readers. Today we are likely to
treat as separate and isolated episodes narratives of gorillas, chimpanzees, pygmies, wild men, and the like, but as Tyson's account and other works of natural
history make clear, there was an extensive traffic in representations of these
creatures. All such creatures belonged to the class of orang-outang, a figure differing in degree but not in kind from man. Beeckman's voyage to Borneo (published in 1718) articulates the relationship of man and orang-outang in some
detail:

> The monkeys, apes, and baboons are of many different sorts and shapes; but the
> most remarkable are those they call Oran-ootans, which in their language signifies
> men of the woods: these grow up to be six feet high; they walk upright, have longer
> arms than men, tolerable good faces (handsomer I am sure than some Hottentots
> that I have seen), large teeth, no tails, nor hair but on those parts where it grows on
> human bodies; they are very nimble-footed, and mighty strong; they throw great
> stones, sticks, and billets, at those persons that offend them. The natives do really
> believe that these were formerly men, but metamorphosed into beasts for their
> blasphemy. They told me many strange stories of them, too tedious to be inserted
> here. (108–9)

This troubling and problematic kinship provides the central anxiety as well as
the crucial joke in *An Essay of the Learned Martinus Scriblerus, Concerning the
Origin of the Sciences.*

Pope described the design of this satire to Spence as being "to ridicule
such as build general assertions upon two or three loose quotations from the
ancients" (126), and that has usually suggested to critics that it is principally
directed toward a chief antagonist of the Scriblerians, Dr. Woodward, whose

Remarks upon the Ancient and Present State of London, Occasioned by some Roman Urns, Coins, and Other Antiquities lately discovered (1713) would nicely model such practice. If so, it would suggest that the essay was composed about 1714, which is not unlikely although it was not published until 1732. While such a target may well have been in Pope's mind, there is no specific mention of Woodward, and the essay does explicitly allude to Tyson's anatomy. I am less interested in substituting Tyson for Woodward as the focus of satire and more interested in exploring the work's relation to his anatomy—a relation that has tended to be obscured by reading the essay as an attack on Woodward.

Pope's characterization of the general design of the satire is born out by the title and opening line of the essay: "Among all the inquiries which have been pursued by the curious and inquisitive, there is none more worthy the search of a learned head than the source from whence we derive those arts and sciences which raise us so far above the vulgar, the countries in which they rose, and the channels by which they have been conveyed" (360). As one can see readily enough in Pope's other writings (notably, his preface to Homer), this view represents a fundamental perversion of what he considers an appropriate respect for "the Ancients." Those whose interest in the Ancients was nothing more than a diligent search for the most ancient missed entirely the aesthetic point that one should value the works of the Ancients because of their merit, not their age. This conceit leads Scriblerus to seek the ultimate origin of arts and sciences: "It is universally agreed that arts and sciences were derived to us from the Egyptians and Indians; but from whom they first received them is yet a secret" (360).

That secret is soon revealed through the mediation of Tyson's "Philological Essay Concerning the Pygmies, the Cynocephali, the Satyrs, and Sphinges of the Ancients." In arguing that these fabulous creatures had no real existence but were the distorted representations of such subhuman creatures as the one he had anatomized, he sought to bring the light of materialist science to the semiotic shadows of myth and legend. At the outset of his preface, he explicitly identifies his project with eclipsing the explanatory power of mythic narrative with that of scientific discourse: "I have made it my Business more, to find out the Truth, than to enlarge the Mythology; to inform the Judgment, than to please the Phancy." By proclaiming his essay "philological," he aligns himself with Richard Bentley and those other "verbal critics" who, by seeking to establish the study of literature on a material basis, challenged the aesthetic criterion of taste and judgment long accorded to the poets. His philological essays consist almost entirely of "loose quotations from the ancients" strung together in support of the view that whatever the creatures may have been to which the ancients referred, they were not men.

Like Tyson, Scriblerus begins his essay with references to accounts of "Pygmaeans . . . in Homer, Aristotle, and others" (361), and like Tyson, he quickly takes up Diodorus's description of the Satyrs encountered in Ethiopia. Where the entire force of Tyson's anatomy and philological argument had been directed to distinguishing man from these liminal figures, however, Scriblerus's use of Tyson's materials is to solidify the bond between humans and the monstrous other. Thus, Scriblerus takes from Diodorus precisely the same passage that Tyson extracted and ties the description even more tightly to Tyson: "He met . . . a sort of little Satyrs, who were hairy one half of their body, and whose leader Pan accompanied him in his expedition for the civilizing of mankind. Now of this great personage Pan we have a very particular description in the ancient writers; who unanimously agree to represent him shaggy-bearded, hairy all over, half a man and half a beast, and walking erect with a staff, (the posture in which his race do to this day appear among us)" (361). Tyson had reasoned that the creature's natural posture was erect, but that his illness had left him too weak to stand unsupported for long; as a result, he had provided the creature with a staff in the accompanying illustration: "Being weak, the better to support him, I have given him a stick in his Right-hand" (16). Subsequent illustrators perpetuated the trope of the walking staff in eighteenth-century illustrations.[10]

In opposition to Tyson's attempt to distinguish his creature from civilized humanity, Scriblerus finds this creature the very source of human civilization by pairing this quotation from Diodorus with another selected from Homer: "And, since the chief thing to which he [Pan] applied himself was the civilizing of mankind, it should seem that the first principles of science must be received from that nation, to which the Gods were by Homer said to resort twelve days every year for the conversation of its wise and just inhabitants" (361). In the pages that follow, Scriblerus traces the lineage connecting Tyson's fabulous references to subhumans to the flourishing of Classical Greece. Socrates, for example, is known to have had "an uncommon birth from the rest of men," to have demonstrated his lineage in his physiognomy, "being bald, flat-nosed, with prominent eyes, and a downward look," and to have shown a penchant for the writings of Aesop "probably out of respect to the beasts in general, and love to his family in particular" (363). This discussion continues through the ages and for several pages, culminating as it must in Tyson's own anatomy: "Nor let me quit this head without mentioning, with all due respect, Oran Outang the

1. Tyson's orang-outang (1699). The distinctive curvature of the hands of knuckle-walking primates confused Tyson, and he gave the creature a walking stick, "the better to support him." One result is that the figure conforms to what Richard Bernheimer identified as a defining trope of the wild man: "frequently the creature is shown wielding a heavy club or mace or the trunk of a tree" (1).

2. The four nonhuman primates illustrated by Hoppius (1760) perform a visual summary of nonhuman primate representation in the period, underlining the iconic significance of the staff and emphasizing the troubling human/nonhuman border identity posed by these actors.

great, the last of this line; whose unhappy chance it was to fall into the hands of Europeans. Oran Outang, whose value was not known to us, for he was a mute philosopher: Oran Outang, by whose dissection the learned Dr. Tyson has added a confirmation to this system, from the resemblance between the homo sylvestris and our human body, in those organs by which the rational soul is exerted" (366).

Now, the first thing to keep in mind here is that Scriblerus makes use of Tyson's findings in a way that is precisely opposed to Tyson's intent. I belabor that point because Montagu, Tyson's twentieth-century champion, has taken this passage as a tribute from Arbuthnot: "Arbuthnot makes serious reference to Tyson's work" (404). The reversal here (keeping in mind it is Scriblerus, and not Arbuthnot or anyone else speaking) is accomplished so blandly that it may escape notice. Tyson—maintaining proper scientific objectivity—considered only the material body, but his concern in being able to distinguish human from other must have been in no small part motivated by concerns about "the rational soul," especially in one who was renowned as "a strict Adherer to the Doctrine and Discipline of the Church of England." Nonetheless, in his summary list of attributes wherein "the Orang-Outang or Pygmie more resembled a Man, than Apes and Monkeys do," number 25 reads: "The Brain was abundantly larger than in Apes; and all its parts formed like the Humane Brain" (92). Scriblerus thus turns Tyson's observations to his advantage, blurring the very boundary Tyson intends to establish.

This reversal highlights the problematic role of impersonation on which so much satire depends.[11] Scriblerus, a "solemn fool" modeled on Don Quixote, embodies those aspects of false learning—particularly prevalent in the new science—that the Scriblerians set out to ridicule. He is, in this manifestation, a parodic alter ego to Tyson, the grave, studious scientist whose attention to the body is subordinated to the pleasures of the mind. Not least significant here is the rhetorical affinity between Martin and the proponents of the "New Science." In an acute critical discussion of this work, Lester Beattie calls attention to the persistent use of modest self-effacement: "This tentative idiom of the overconfident scholar is employed in all its known forms: 'I cannot but persuade myself'; 'if I should conjecture . . . it ought not to seem more incredible than . . . '; 'nothing is more natural to imagine'; 'it should seem that the first principles of science must be received from that nation'; 'I am much inclined to believe'; 'India may be credibly supposed'; 'I make no question that there are remains'" (228).

Historians of science have begun identifying the crucial role this "literary technology" of modest reporting played in the establishment of modern science. In describing the various means by which Robert Boyle lobbied for the belief of his readers, Steven Shapin and Simon Schaffer identify the form of the essay itself as calculated to emphasize the credibility earned by modesty: "The essay . . . was explicitly contrasted to the natural philosophical system. Those who wrote entire systems were identified as 'confident' individuals, whose ambition extended beyond what was proper or possible. By contrast, those who wrote experimental essays were 'sober and modest men,' 'diligent and judicious' philosophers, who did not 'assert more than they can prove'" (65). Moreover, within these essays, Boyle consciously adopted the rhetoric of modesty parodied by Martin, informing his son: "in almost every one of the following essays I . . . speak so doubtingly, and use so often perhaps, it seems, it is not improbable, and such other expressions, as argue a diffidence of the truth of the opinions I incline to, and that I should be so shy of laying down principles, and sometimes of so much as venturing at explications" (qtd. in Shapin and Schaffer 67).

The satire in Martin's essay will be effective precisely to the degree to which the parodic characterization transgresses the boundary that separates it from the original. To the extent that such an impersonation is successful, Scriblerus's argument—like Tyson's—will appear learned, leading to an equation between modern proponents of science and their pygmy originals. It was Tyson, after all, who after diligent examination was unable to distinguish his own brain from the pygmy's. Finally, such a successful impersonation also licenses a displacement, for it is ultimately not Tyson, but his pygmy, who is revealed as "the great . . . philosopher." If Tyson's triumph was, by introducing scientific method to popular spectacle, to establish an inviolable barrier between man and beast, the satirist, by challenging those barriers, subverts the very logic of domination on which they depend. Here, then, is a particularly compelling convergence of the two senses of "satyr," for both figures, dwelling on the boundaries of society, are committed to challenging our constructions of what it means to be human.

Tyson's appropriation of monstrous man from the liminal space of the fair to the domesticated space of the Royal Society was at once an act of containment and revaluation. Under the guise of science, the pygmy had become a subject of knowledge rather than display and, as a result, was now subject to a separate standard of valuation. At the fair, a pygmy might be valued at a shilling per viewing, but under scientific appropriation he became a different type of commodity, valued now not as spectacle but as a curiosity. The difference has to do with mentation and class: spectacles are vulgar, stimulating pleasure without thought; curiosities, offering philosophical pleasures, are the recreation of the nobility. The role of institutions such as the Royal Society in such cultural commodification has been noted by Barbara Benedict as contributing to the transformation of a bourgeois public sphere (Benedict 9–10, 18; cf. Mackie 98–99). When Scriblerus intones, "Oran Outang, whose value was not known to us, for he was a mute philosopher," he alludes to the pygmy's previous devalued condition as spectacle. Read straight, this praise elevates the pygmy at the expense of Tyson; read bathetically, Tyson's contribution is revealed to be nothing more than the detailed dissection of a monstrous spectacle; either way, Tyson is bit.

There is, however, a great deal more to Scriblerus's relation to Tyson and to the monstrosities of the fair. The satire on Scriblerus as arid pedant collapses into a satire on the vulgar credulity on which the fair depends. Such a movement not only reprises Swift's theme in *Tale of a Tub* regarding the Hobson's choice between curiosity and credulity, knavery and folly, but it also points to the artificiality of class boundaries: the genteel space of the Royal Society polices, domesticates, and makes orderly the chaotic, libidinous, and liminal space of the public fair. This theme comes to the foreground in "The Double Mistress Episode" of *The Memoirs of Martinus Scriblerus*.

The Memoirs are generally regarded as being principally by Dr. Arbuthnot, with some assistance from other members of the club; they were published by Pope in 1741, six years after the death of Arbuthnot. In the nineteenth century the Double Mistress episode was deleted (presumably on "moral" grounds), a practice followed by subsequent editors until the authoritative Kerby-Miller edition appeared in 1950 with the episode restored. Martin, wandering one day by Whitehall, finds himself at a fair, enters, and discovers numerous "Wonders," not the least of which is (are?) "the two Bohemian Sisters, whose common parts of Generation, had so closely allied them, that Nature seem'd here to have conspir'd with Fortune, that their lives should run in an eternal Parallel" (146). In brief, Martin falls in love with Lindamira, while her sister Indamora falls in love with Martin. After some complications the three elope and are married, but the Master of the Show, concerned for the future of his show, intrigues with the Black Prince (a pygmy) to marry Indamora while Martin sleeps, then brings suit against Martin for bigamy, incest, and unlawful cohabitation. After hearing all arguments and appeals, the final judgment is a general annulment of all marriages.

Confronted with such a bizarre fantasy, the reader may be assisted by sorting out the impressive number of topical allusions. Lindamira and Indamora are clearly modeled on twin sisters, Helena and Judith, who were exhibited in London in 1708. On June 10, Swift wrote to Dean Stearne: "Here is the sight of two girls joined together at the back, which, in the newsmongers phrase, causes a great many speculations; and raises abundance of questions in divinity, law, and physic."[12] Handbills from shows in 1711 indicate that most of what is on display with the two sisters—Libyan leopard, lion, jackal, cat-a-mountain, porcupine, peccary, and "of two Cubits high, the black Prince of Monomotapa"—were in fact displayed in London that year. The fragment of the Double Mistress episode that exists in the British Library shows that it was written by Arbuthnot and heavily edited by Pope. The master of the show, "Mr. Randal," likely refers to the proprietor of "Randall's Coffeehouse against the General Post Office in Lombard Street," who displayed exotic animals, including in 1738–39 "Madame Chimpanzee," the first chimp, so-called, displayed in England. In February 1739, an anonymous prose satire titled *An Essay towards the Character of the late Chimpanzee Who died Feb. 23, 1738–39* was published by Gilliver and Clarke. The essay parodied Alured Clarke's similarly titled panegyric to the late Queen Caroline.[13] Pope was preparing *Memoirs* for publication during 1739 and is likely to have borrowed Randall's name.[14]

This opposition satire of 1739 highlights not only the persistent influence of Tyson's *Anatomy* but also the considerable degree to which considerations of liminal border identity have entered the discourse of the public sphere in a form that blurs and destabilizes class identity, while at the same time weaving together the discourses of species and nation. Among those who visited Madame Chimpanzee during her stay at Randall's Coffeehouse was Sir Hans Sloane, president of the Royal Society. Echoing the findings of Tyson a generation earlier, Sloane "pronounced himself 'extremely well pleas'd' . . . and 'allow[ed] it to come the nearest to the Human Species of any Creature" (200). Moreover, again echoing Tyson's anatomical finding on the capacity for speech, he is reported to have said that "she has all the parts of speech in her, which is as much to say she is made to speak, which, whenever it happens, may, I suppose, be followed by school instruction; and who knows but she may become as famous a wit and writer as Madame Dacier" (201). But where Tyson drew a line, however fine, between human and nonhuman, the autopsy conducted by Sir Hans Sloane "formally pronounced her . . . 'perfectly of a human Specie'" (203). Madame Chimpanzee, in the satirist's representation, has not only the capacity for speech, but for literacy as well; and like the late queen, she spends her time in conversation with freethinkers, reading Deist tracts, and anonymously authoring political flackery on behalf of the Walpole administration. Of this Madame Chimpanzee, "it may . . . be said with Assurance, that from her appearance and Carriage, she must have been of a Gentleman's family; probably a younger Child: and being no great Favourite, and her father not being able to give her any great Fortune, and the Estate settled on the eldest son, she might be turn'd out into the wide World to shift for Herself" (9). This initial fiction of bourgeois romance rapidly climbs the social ladder, as Madame becomes ever more closely connected first to the "Quality" who "flock" to see her and take tea with her and ultimately to the queen herself, whom she "apes" in life as surely as in death. This time around, the dissolving of boundaries is at once more highly politicized than the earlier satire on Tyson, and at the same time it introduces into that more overtly political satire a more explicit linking of the discourses of nation and species: "Some imagine, from her Make, she must be *Dutch;* others judge her to be *French,* from her Complexion. Some, again, from her Inclination to sit still, suppose her *German;* and others, from her Gravity, think her *Spanish,* tho' it was never observ'd she was giv'n to *insult*"(9–10).

These particular manifestations of political division and nationalist tensions arise from a tension within the emergent public sphere a generation earlier. Swift's jesting letter of 1711, regarding the twin sisters, underlines the traffic between popular and elite culture that these exhibits encouraged. Those who would advertise such "monstrosities" to the general public (Swift's "newsmongers") repeatedly invoked the rhetoric of scientific curiosity: "[the display] raises abundance of questions in divinity, law, and physick." Martin's trial, exploiting these possibilities, hinges on questions of individual identity and the materiality or immateriality of the soul. The *Memoirs,* like other Scriblerian satires, seeks to collapse the class barrier separating the disciplined space of the Royal Society from the more chaotic, liminal world of the fair. The arid mock-pedantry of Martin's curriculum vitae comes to a ribald and vulgar climax in this episode, but as it does so, it continues to pursue the very same abstract speculations that had motivated the early chapters. As was the case in Swift's *Tale of a Tub,* the satire here unites attacks on the curiosity of the learned and the credulity of the vulgar. As far removed as Martin's conjugal relations with conjoint twins may appear from Dr. Tyson's celebrated celibacy, the *Memoirs*—like Tyson's anatomy—offers a knowledge construction about human identity as an unacknowledged by-product of a social space.

From the dizzying array of terms to be defined in the title of Tyson's anatomy

CHIMP-ANZEE

Scotin sculp. A.D. 1738

3. A print of Madame Chimpanzee by Gerard Scotin from 1738. In contrast to Tyson's male and his walking stick, Madame Chimpanzee signals her domestic status by prominently displaying the teacup with which she took tea in the company of London's nobility.

to the sexually transgressive fantasy of the Double Mistress episode, this chapter has been concerned with a kaleidoscopic depiction of the social location of species anxiety in early modern England. One might well seek at this point a moment of clarity, an intervention in which the actors assembled onstage are once again clearly identified with their respective performers. It is precisely that moment of clarity that I now wish to resist. For the presumption underlying such clarification is what Bruno Latour would characterize as the "modern" impulse toward "purification"; that trick of mental bookkeeping that arises with the immensely powerful Enlightenment construction of the autonomous individuated self that seeks to define the world by the interactions of discrete actors. Here I want instead to employ something akin to Latour's concept of a "nonmodern" perspective, in which our observation of knowledge construction focuses on the hybrid networks of material-semiotic actors that cross social and disciplinary divides to participate in what Karen Barad has termed "intra-actions." Re-orienting our perspective in this way challenges our often-unarticulated assumptions about actors and agency. For Ashley Montagu's purposes, the "actor" under consideration was Edward Tyson, and the orang-outang was merely the subject of his anatomy. Latour and Barad urge us to reconsider that relationship; as we do so, the boundaries continue blurring, for the material body Tyson dissects is inextricably linked with the one he displays before the Royal Society and the one put on display in coffeehouses and fair booths; moreover, that physical orang-outang is equally embroiled with the other quasi-human identities of pygmies and satyrs of his philological essay. Indeed, this proliferating network of intra-active identities is precisely what the Scriblerians in their collaboratively authored "satyr" point to when they insist on the indistinguishable features that Tyson shares with his pygmy. And just as Tyson and his "mute philosopher" find themselves confused, the problematics of identity that Tyson's study pretends to answer bubble up in the transgressive fantasy of the *Memoirs of Martinus Scriblerus,* as they do again in the political satire of *Madame Chimpanzee.* The modern era has from its inception been marked by the difficulties of primate identity; in the generation before Linnaeus invented the term, those difficulties—and their attendant anxieties—were (quite literally) on display.

Ultimately, Tyson's anatomy needs to be seen as an answer to a challenge. Confronted by a monster—one who distorted our self-perception while resembling us too closely—Tyson set about to police the boundaries of the human. Rescuing this monster from the arena of public spectacle and subjecting him to public scrutiny, Tyson laid bare the physical grounds for distinguishing the essential human. Returning the pedant to the fair, and marrying him to such a monster, the Scriblerians renew the challenge as to what constitutes the knowable boundary of humanity. Such an inversion—troubling and transgressive— is the characteristic of both the literary and the mythological form of the satyr. What happens when a wild man is brought to town and put on display, neither in the fair booth nor the Royal Society, but in the royal court, we shall see in our next chapter.

2

The Feral Child

at Court

*in which a wild child
from the forests of Germany
appears at the Royal Court
of his countryman, advertises
a remedy for venereal disease,
seeks a wife, and retires to
the country*

In the spring of 1726, a wild youth found running naked through the forests of Hanover was presented at the court of George I. It seems almost impossible not to seize on such a moment as defining the culture wars of that era, and yet with the exception of a trenchant discussion by Maximillian Novak, little has been said on the subject.[1] This chapter returns to consider the uses to which this "wild youth" was put in the interests of both science and satire and to reflect on the competing knowledge constructions articulated by commerce, court, and opposition within the public sphere. In doing so, we examine in some detail the literature pertaining to this feral child, present the case for some specific attributions, and situate those works in larger literary and cultural contexts.

Novak surveyed the literature generated by "Lord Peter" (as the wild youth was dubbed) and remarked that "his arrival produced a number of pamphlets, a sermon, a book-length satire by Daniel Defoe, and at least one poem" (185). The poem, entitled "The Savage," which appeared in a 1726 miscellany edited by David Lewis, is reprinted in Novak's article. The sermon, alluded to in the book attributed to Defoe, is no longer available (if it even was published).[2] Of the "number of pamphlets," Novak identifies four: one serious, *An Enquiry How the Wild Youth, Lately taken in the Woods near Hanover, (and now brought over to England) could be there left, and by what Creature he could be suckled, nursed, and brought up;* and three satiric, *The Manifesto of Lord Peter, The Most Wonderful Wonder,* and *It cannot Rain but it Pours,* "a work sometimes attributed to Swift and sometimes to Arbuthnot" (193). This latter work, as discussed later in the book, comprises in fact not one pamphlet but two, and the list might also be expanded to include two more pamphlets of the following year, *The Devil to Pay at St. James* and *A Little More of that Same,* both of which allude briefly to Peter.

Peter was found wandering in the forests of Germany, near Hameln, on Friday, July 27, 1724. The next year he was sent to the hospital at Zell, next to the House of Correction, and from there he was sent to the Court of King George in Hanover. In February 1726 Mr. Rautenberg brought him to London. He was the chief entertainment of the court that spring and was entrusted to the care of Dr. Arbuthnot. When Swift arrived in London in March to oversee publication of *Gulliver's Travels,* he lodged near Arbuthnot and spent much time with the doctor and "his merry pupil": "This night I saw the wild Boy, whose arrivall here hath been the subject of half our Talk this fortnight He is in the Keeping of Dr Arthbuthnot, but the King and Court were so entertained with him that the Princess could not get him till now. I can hardly think him wild in the Sense they report him" (Swift to Thomas Tickell, April 16, 1726).

It is extraordinarily difficult to uncover at this late date any reliable account of Peter's condition. Johann Blumenbach, who undertook to establish his history at the end of the eighteenth century, wrote: "the history of this idiot is always remarkable, as a striking example of the uncertainty of human testimony and historical credibility. For it is surprising how divergent and partly contradictory are even the first contemporary accounts of the circumstances of his appearance in Hameln" (334).[3] Blumenbach is able to produce a variety of conflicting and unreliable accounts, but his own research is shaped by a considerable bias—an insistence that Peter was an abandoned idiot and not the instance of "natural man" that James Burnett, Lord Monboddo had claimed. Any attempt to reconstruct the history of Peter must sort through a variety of incredible, contradictory, and unsystematic accounts that simply do not lend themselves to a uniform, coherent narrative. A history of the representations of Peter, on the other hand, demonstrates a remarkable degree of uniformity.

He was apparently an early adolescent, variously described as from about eleven to about fifteen, when discovered. He was naked, with dark skin, or covered with hair, or wearing the small fragment of a torn shirt still fastened with string about his neck, or having very white thighs, indicating that he had until shortly before his discovery worn breeches. He was found by Jurgen Meyer (a townsman of Hameln) or by King George while hunting, or it was necessary to cut down a tree in which he had taken refuge in the topmost branches. He walked erect, or on all fours, or at first walked on all fours and very quickly learned to walk erect. He jumped about trees like a squirrel and made a nest in a hollow tree trunk, or he had no known dwelling place. He ate grass and nuts and berries and vegetables, seemed to have an acute sense of smell (being wonderfully adept at finding truffles), but was unresponsive to noxious odors (including his own excrement); King George experimented with him, attempting to bring him "by degrees to human Diet." He laughed frequently or not at all. He was mute, made only inarticulate sounds, was unable to learn any words, or learned some words almost immediately, or learned to mimic words only, without comprehension. He was carried to England in an iron cage or in his own cabin. Thus, while specific descriptions of Peter vary considerably, a remarkable uniformity characterizes the various efforts to represent him through narrative. Repeatedly, Peter is constructed as identifiable with respect to five categories: diet, locomotion, nakedness, passion, and speech.

An Enquiry—which notes that Peter "is straight and upright, & not Hairy, except a bushy Head of dark brown Hair"—begins by finding in him the fulfillment of a prophecy of the noted (or notorious?) astrologer William Lilly:

> When Rome shall wend [go] to Benevento,
> And Spaniards break the Assiento;
> When Spread Eagle flies to China,
> And Christian Folks adore Faustina:
> Then shall the Woods be Brought to Bed,
> Of Creature neither taught nor fed,
> Great Feats shall he atchieve——
>   WILD   YOUTH

Associating Peter with Romulus and Remus and with Orson, the writer suggests "it is not impossible, that some She-Bear, somehow or other deprived of her Cubs, finding this Infant, and being full of a suckling, nursing, tender Temper, finding it a Living-thing, laid her self down to it, and suckl'd it and brought it up 'til it could shift for it self" (3). Many of us, considerably more suspicious of the universality of maternal instinct, would (I suspect) contend that this is

4. A crude triptych of Peter, the Wild Youth, from the frontispiece of a pamphlet advertising a quack anti-venereal remedy, Given Gratis . . . at the Sign of the . . . Anodyne Necklace (1726). The central woodcut clearly copies a painting in Kensington Palace; see figure 10 (page 127).

indeed "impossible" or, at the very least, implausible. This is tabloid science, the eighteenth century's version of the journalism for sale at our supermarket checkout line.

An Enquiry's representation of Peter brings together mythic and mystical elements: not only is he the realization of the types of Romulus and Remus and of Orson; Peter is also presented here quite literally as the fulfillment of the prophets. But the prophecy, in this case, is not biblical, but astrological. Peter is a sign, a token testifying to the power of "the famous Astrologer, Mr. William Lilly." The tripartite illustration on the title page represents Peter in three poses. In the left panel, we glimpse his past, suckled by a bear; in the right panel, we see his present wild condition as it was described on his discovery, scrambling on all fours up a tree; in the most prominent centerpiece, we are promised a future vision of what he shall become, a refined young gentleman, slender, elegantly attired and gracefully presenting a handful of acorns.[4] *An Enquiry* thus represents Peter as simultaneously fulfilling one prophecy (by his discovery) and projecting another ("great feats shall he achieve"). Those "great feats" are distinctly class oriented, for the illustration promises that Peter (under the sponsorship of his royal protector) shall rise from the class of animals to the class of gentleman.

An Enquiry, then, trades in the familiar currency of astrologers' almanacs prevalent during this period, offering (not unlike our own New Age almanacs) entrepreneurial success for a popular audience. In this respect, it is worth examining the details of Lilly's prophecy. The other predictions cited in the prophecy all come from the daily newspapers: the Pope (i.e., "Rome") in spite of ill health was insisting on traveling to Benevento; Spain was abrogating a treaty and threatening the peace; the Austrian empire had opened trade with China; and London was currently excited by the long-awaited arrival of Faustina Bordoni, reputed to be the greatest diva in the world. The context, then, for Lilly's prediction is the newsmongers' popular commodification of elite culture (national politics and opera) as vulgar entertainment. On these terms, then, *An Enquiry* seeks to participate in the public sphere Habermas describes as emerging from the "traffic in news" (16). Although the pamphlet is precisely of the sort derided in salons and in the pages of the *Spectator,* its hybrid status blurring the bounds of high and low culture is important to Habermas's term: "I think that a public sphere, in the sense in which I've tried to define it, only arose with the transformation of the split between high culture and popular culture that has been characteristic of premodern societies" (Calhoun 464–65).[5]

Indeed, *An Enquiry*'s very existence is as a form of popular culture advertisement. The treatise announces itself as "Given Gratis (for the Satisfaction of the Curious) Up One Pair of Stairs at the *Anodyne Necklace,* etc." The four-page description of Peter is immediately followed by four pages advertising other works "Given Gratis," including one on the Anodyne Necklace, one on the Gout, one on Shorthand, "A Short Way at once with the Cure of the *Secret Disease,*" "The Venereal Dispensatory," "The Gleet Dispensatory," and "Eronania," as well as the remedies advertised within these pamphlets. The author of *An Enquiry* is advertised as "the Author of *The Practical Scheme of the Secret Disease,*" which like these other treatises was given away at the Anodyne Necklace and other locations.[6] All of these treatises were printed by Henry Parker or another member of the Parker family, which may have also included George Parker, a well-known astrologer and purveyor of quack remedies. The Anodyne Necklace was the foundation for this patent medicine concern and was essentially a teething necklace. It promised relief from the torment of teething pain, but it was justified on rather fanciful grounds. One of the concern's treatises explained the necklace's curative powers by dressing up the claims of "sympathetic remedies" in the rhetoric of the New science, particularly the "Newtonian" principle of "action at a distance" (see "short Philosophical ESSAY"). Moreover, the "Anodyne Necklace" was the sign under which various venereal remedies were sold, and pamphlets on "The Anodyne Necklace" and "The Practical Scheme for the Secret Disease" advertised for one another. Thus, the innocent teething ring served as a screen for treatments for more scandalous disease. In the fifth plate of Hogarth's *The Harlot's Progress,* Moll Hackabout, wrapped in blankets and

5. William Hogarth's *The Harlot's Progress,* plate 5 (1732). In the final stages of her venereal infection, Moll Hackabout is treated by quacks.

6. A detail from Hogarth's *The Harlot's Progress* reveals the anti-venereal pamphlet from the Anodyne Necklace.

near death, is being sweated by the fire while two quacks quarrel with one another over which remedy to try. A table upended in the center of the engraving
has dumped on the floor the pamphlet labeled "Practical Scheme . . . Anodyne
Necklace."[7] In reading *An Enquiry's* representation of Peter, it is important
to keep in mind the commercial purposes of the pamphlet and the degree to
which the pamphlet seeks to exploit curiosity surrounding the New Science in
the familiar method of quacks and mountebanks.

In brief, the pamphlet begins by invoking Aristotle to the effect that won-
drous phenomena merit greater consideration the more marvelous they are. It
then rehearses briefly the few established matters of fact regarding Peter and
slides quickly into offering what the author speculates is "the most probable
Origin of this Youth's wildness" (2). This speculation on origins soon gives way
to a description of his behavior as currently on display at court, this description
frequently mixing in speculation both as to the origin of such behavior and as
to future alterations.

Of the four remaining pamphlets published in 1726, all have been thought to
be Scriblerian productions, but the various degrees of involvement on the part
of Swift, Pope, Arbuthnot, and Gay has been unclear. The pamphlet that has received the most bibliographic attention has been *It cannot Rain but it Pours:
or, London strow'd with Rarities,* which was included in the 1727 edition of the
Pope-Swift *Miscellanies.* Throughout the eighteenth century, this pamphlet was
commonly understood to have been written by Swift.[8] There are, however, good
reasons to question that attribution, and since publication of Temple Scott's
edition of *The Prose Works of Jonathan Swift,* the work has effectively disappeared from the Swift canon. The two most compelling reasons for this are that
in Swift's own annotated copy of the 1732 *Miscellanies,* the work is not marked;
and in the 1742 edition (generally thought to have been edited or at least over-
seen by Pope), the work is attributed to Arbuthnot.

Sorting out attributions among Scriblerian productions is a difficult task
and demands caution and circumspection.[9] Indeed, although the attribution to
Arbuthnot has been sufficient to remove the pamphlet from the Swift canon,
it has not quite carried enough weight to move it into the Arbuthnot canon.
Aitken listed both *It cannot Rain but it Pours* and *The Most Wonderful Wonder
that Ever Appeared* (another satire occasioned by Peter's arrival) as "Doubtful
Works" in his *Life and Works of John Arbuthnot* (1892): The former of these "is
probably Swift's, though it is sometimes attributed to Arbuthnot" (107). The
latter work, he thought, "may also be Swift's" (107), but Lester Beattie has cast

doubt on the attribution to Arbuthnot and, to a lesser degree, the attribution to Swift.[10] After observing the attribution to Arbuthnot in the 1742 edition of the *Miscellanies,* Beattie notes that one phrase in particular virtually disqualifies Arbuthnot as the author. At one point, the writer describes Peter as "ignorant of languages, 'that care being left to the ingenious physician, who is entrusted with his education."[11] It would be highly unlikely that Arbuthnot would refer to himself in these terms, and Beattie, who finds the pamphlet "makes a somewhat poor showing" in the collection, suggests that it may have been begun by Arbuthnot and finished by another hand.

I would quarrel with Beattie's assessment of the pamphlet, and in the discussion that follows I make a case for the considerable cultural interest that these pamphlets hold collectively, regardless of questions of authorship. Certainly, the pamphlets were generally understood to be by Swift and the Scriblerians, and I argue that they play a minor but significant role in the emergence of a political opposition during the summer of 1726. As such, they may be considered a species of "Gulliveriana," as Jeanne K. Welcher and George Bush contend.[12] Before entering into the details of that interpretive argument, I want to offer some mild resistance to the arguments against Swift's authorship. The various identifying marks in Swift's annotated copy of the *Miscellanies* (some are marked with an "S" and others with a pointing finger) are subject to interpretation but have generally been accepted as indicating Swift's acknowledgment of authorship. Several other works that we know to be Swift's, however, are also unmarked; the most relevant of these in terms of topical similarity and jesting tone may be "The Accomplishment of the First of Mr. Bickerstaff's Predictions." Whatever Swift may have meant by the marks he may have made, it would be unwise to lean too heavily on the absence of such marks in determining authorship. Of greater weight, but still not definitive, is the attribution to Arbuthnot in the 1742 edition, particularly if Pope was, indeed, behind the attribution. That latter assertion, however, remains for now conjectural and may be outweighed by other evidence, to which I now turn.

In the Lilly Library at Indiana University there exist copies of *It cannot Rain but it Pours: Or, The First Part of London strow'd with Rarities; It cannot Rain but it Pours: or, London strow'd with Rarities;* and *The Manifesto of Lord Peter.* These three pamphlets have been bound together in a leather binding bearing the bookplate of Maurice Johnson, antiquarian, book collector, and founder of the Gentlemen's Society of Spalding; they contain significant marginalia in his handwriting.[13] Before recording the details of those comments, it makes sense to clarify the confusing dual identity of *It cannot Rain but it Pours*. Both pamphlets were printed for J. Roberts; the first part (so named in the subtitle) carries a note to readers on the title page: "N.B. The Second Part of this Book by Mistake of the Printer was published first."[14] In Johnson's bound volume the first part appears first and consists of a paragraph concerning Faustina being taken hoarse, another concerning the wounding of Mr U****k, and eight pages devoted to "the Arrival of the two Marvellous Black *Arabian* Ambassadors, who are of the same Country with the wonderful Horse lately shewn in *King-Street*." The entirety of the second part of *It cannot Rain* is devoted to "a Description of *Peter* the Savage."

On the title page of "The First Part," Johnson has identified "U****k" as "Urrik, his Majesties Page," and has written at the bottom of the page: "this and the 2 following humorous Pamphlets were given me by Mr. John Gay and were written by him & Comp^n. Dr. Swift, Dr. Arbuthnot, Mr. Pope & al." The second and third pamphlets have had their pages cropped, so that it is sometimes difficult to make out all the marginalia. The complete title page of the second pamphlet reads: *It cannot Rain but it Pours: or, London strow'd with Rarities: Being an Account of the Arrival of a White Bear, at the House of Mr. Ratcliff in Bishopsgate-Street: As also of the Faustina, the celebrated Italian Singing Woman; And of the Copper-Farthing Dean from Ireland. And Lastly, of the wonderful Wild Man that was nursed in the Woods of Germany by a Wild Beast, hunted and taken in Toyls; how he behaveth himself like a dumb Creature, and is a Christian like one of us, being call'd Peter; and how he was brought to Court all in Green, to the great Astonishment of the Quality and Gentry.* Johnson has added marginal comments next to "Copper-Farthing Dean"[15] that are only partly legible: " [Author?] . . . of this and a pa[per? . . .] published at Dublin ag^t Woods patent for coining half . . . [pence] he would cheated [?] ye Nation of £10000 but his Maj[esty?]." At the end of the title page, Johnson has written, "he was glad in Green Wastcoat when I see him in May 1726." Below this he has written: "By the R̶e̶v̶ᵈ̶ & no less Witty than Revd Jonathan Swift DD Dean of S[t. Patricks?] . . . in Dublin then but lately come over to London wth Ld Carteret [Ld. Lt.?] . . . of Ireland." The third and final pamphlet, *The Manifesto of Lord Peter*, having the most blank space on the title page, contains the most detailed marginalia, though again the lines have been cropped at the edge. The comments read: "the Wild [Youth?] taken in the Forrest of Emlyn [Hameln] & presented to his Maje[sty] King George the First when over in his German Dominions. In May 1726 I went with 2 other Gentlemen out of Curio[sity] to see this Boy and Wee did see him

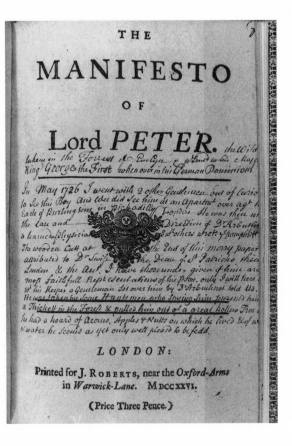

7. The title page of *The Manifesto of Lord Peter* (1726) with detailed manuscript notation in the handwriting of Maurice Johnson and including the attribution of a drawing of Peter to "Dr. Swift, the Dean of St. Patrick's." (Courtesy Lilly Library, Indiana University, Bloomington, Indiana.)

8. The woodcut at the end of the pamphlet, taken from Swift's sketch of Peter. (Courtesy Lilly Library, Indiana University, Bloomington, Indiana.)

at an Apartment over agt [the] Earle of Burlingtons in Pickadilly London. He was then u[nder] the care and Direction of Dr Arbuth[not] a learned Physician w° wth others wrote y^s pamphlitt. The wooden Cutt at the End of this merry paper attributed to Dr Swift the Dean of St Patricks then [in] London. the Acct I have hereunder given of him are most fathfull Representations of his Pson only I will here [add?] w^t his Keeper a Gentleman set over him by Dr Arbuthnot told Us. He was taken by some Huntsmen who Spying him pursued him . . . a Thickett in the Forest & pulled him out of a great Hollow Tree . . . he had a hoard of Acorns, Apples & Nutts on which he lived & of w[hich] & water he seemd as yet only well pleased to be fedd." On the final page of the pamphlet, beneath the woodcut, Johnson has written: "This Cutt presents a near Resemblance of Peter the Wild Bo[y] his Hair Bushy, coleblack, & harsh, Flat Faced, his Compl[exion] very pale yellow & swarthy, his Eyes little but sprightly. He seemd about 12 or 13, pronounced some few english words."

Taken together, these comments make a case for attributing the pamphlets to Gay, Swift, Arbuthnot, and Pope. *It cannot Rain but it Pours: or, London strow'd with Rarities* Johnson explicitly and unequivocally assigns to Swift, and *The Manifesto of Lord Peter* he attributes to Arbuthnot "wth others." The attribution on the title page of the first part of *It cannot Rain* clearly identifies the three pamphlets as a collaborative Scriblerian undertaking, whether each pamphlet was written separately or collaboratively. *The Manifesto of Lord Peter* is written in two distinct parts—the first in the voice of the "First Minister to a Minor Prince"; the second in the voice of the prince himself. This rhetorical fiction seems to me well suited to the pairing of Arbuthnot (to whose care Peter had been entrusted) and Pope. Johnson's comments are of excellent authority and can be dated with some confidence. We know that Johnson and Gay were friends as early as 1713, but there is little evidence of any correspondence between the two between 1713 and 1727. Johnson marked his pamphlets as dating from May of 1726 when he visited the wild boy and spoke with the boy's caretaker. While he may have made some notations at that time, the reference to "King George the First" clearly indicates that some annotations date from after the accession of George II in July of 1727.[16] The only record we have of a meeting between Gay and Johnson is in 1728. In that year, Gay went to Bath in May and remained there throughout the summer and fall, attending the Duchess of Marlborough, and was joined at one time or another by Pope, Arbuthnot, and Bolingbroke (as well as the young Lord Oxford). Letters indicate that Swift planned to winter in London that year and was intending to travel through Bath, until ill health prompted him to change his plans. In September, Pope joined Gay and remained with him for six weeks;[17] Maurice Johnson (whom Gay had introduced to the Duchess of Marlborough much earlier) joined the two at some point during this visit. At the October 21 meeting of the Gentlemen's Society of Spalding, Johnson records that both Gay and Pope were admitted as new members of the society. The most probable conjecture consistent with all the evidence available is that Gay presented Johnson with the pamphlets (as Johnson records in his marginal notes) on that occasion. Johnson was an antiquarian who took some pride in exact learning; moreover, the Spalding Society was, to a great degree, a literary and bibliographic society, presenting poems (including, among others, one addressed from the Earl of Orrery to Swift in February 1732) and discussing literary matters (Johnson prided himself on his possession of *Wynken de Worde* and one of Caxton's original books). The information recorded by Johnson on the title pages and in the margins (including a gloss on an obscure reference to Lord Wharton, former Lord Lieutenant to Ireland, that points to Swift's involvement) is of precisely the type that would have been of interest to the society. If that conjecture is followed, the testimony of Johnson's marginal comments, plausibly derived from Gay and Pope just two years after publication, seem of greater weight than the attribution made anonymously fourteen years later and presumptively assigned to Pope. Not least intriguing among the marginal comments is Johnson's confidence in assigning the drawing of Peter to Swift. Not only does this make Swift responsible for one of the only remaining realistic drawings of Peter at the time of his capture; to the best of my knowledge, it also makes Peter responsible for the only drawing executed by Swift preserved to the present day.

The first part of *It cannot Rain* promises on the title page "a full and true account of a Fierce and Wild Indian Deer that beat the breath out of Mr. U[rri]k's Body"; how Faustina (the celebrated diva) was taken hoarse; and "a true Relation of the Arrival of the two Marvellous Black Arabian Ambassadors, who are of the same Country with the wonderful Horse lately shewn in King-Street." The author makes short work of the first two topics in order to devote his attention to the ambassadors. Not least interesting in this arrangement is the economy of exoticism that such a title page establishes. The pamphlet brings together in interchangeable mélange court and servant, beast and human, *haute monde* and spectacle, in a circulation of tropes that begins with a "fierce and wild Indian deer" and ends with the one of the imported Arabian stallions that helped establish the thoroughbred racehorse. Bracketed between these animals are the Royal Page, a famous opera star, and a pair of Moroccan ambassadors, who in this satire stand in as the liminal "wild men" disrupting class order, offering alternative spectacles to fashionable opera, and destabilizing cultural norms of humanity.

Passing quickly over Faustina's illness, the author mocks at once superstitious enthusiasm and aristocratic taste for opera: "now whether this was a Judgement from Heaven to prevent the Quality and Gentry from going to the Opera, or whether it was only caused by a Natural Cold we'll leave to the Physicians and the aforesaid Reverend Divine [alluding to William Law, who had lately published on the unlawfulness of the stage] to determine" (3). In doing so, he articulates the two chief axes—class and religion—on which his satire will turn, and the vehicle for that satire, the "two marvellous black Arabian Ambassadors," will stand in as surrogates for Peter in the role of wild men.

The visit of these two ambassadors is a small part of a complex diplomatic history between England and Morocco. In 1726, Morocco was in the final year of the fifty-five-year reign of its powerful ruler, Muley Ismail. During that reign, five English monarchs had found Anglo-Moroccan negotiations both difficult and expensive. Formal diplomatic negotiations between the two countries had begun in Elizabeth's reign. Early in Muley Ismail's reign, he sent Mohammed bin Hadou to England for a six-month visit that was elaborately staged and widely described, including accounts of his visits to Oxford, Cambridge, and the Royal Society, as well as many other public appearances; Evelyn records the visit as "the fashion of the season" (Matar 38–39; see also Blunt 190–96). Over the next four decades, shifting alliances with respect to European conflicts, merchant trading, Barbary Coast piracy, and England's outpost at Gibraltar involved the two countries in a series of complex and difficult negotiations, frequently involving the exchange of captives. The most significant of these negotiations was that undertaken by John Windus and Commodore Stewart in 1720–21. When Stewart returned, he had signed England's first diplomatic treaty with Morocco; more spectacularly, he returned at the head of a procession of 296 English slaves, released by the settlement. Windus's account of their journey, published in 1725, was an immensely popular book. In 1727, John Russel would have to renegotiate this treaty with Muley Ismail's successor; perhaps the visit of the ambassadors in 1726 anticipated this necessity (by this time Muley Ismail was very old and in very poor health), or perhaps their visit was merely the next in a seemingly interminable series of difficult negotiations. In any case, the satiric treatment in *The First Part of London Strow'd* is not concerned with the subtleties of these diplomatic maneuvers.

Instead the ambassadors—Mahomet and Bo-ally—become the vehicle for an exchange of anxieties as the satire simultaneously works out a xenophobic indictment of an imagined Moroccan primitivism and a suppressed but equally present castigation of British corruption. This defining ambivalence is articulated through the marker of racial difference: "these two Gentlemen are Black of Complection, but of a clear Conscience" (5). They are marked as savages— "somewhat like the *Wild Irish*"—by their dress (which they can "use either for Sheets or Tablecloths, according as they are inclined for Sleep or Dinner"), their habitation (living in tents rather than houses), and their diet (a vegetarian practice rendered as "they eat Milk as well as grass"). In anticipation of notions of the "noble savage" usually identified with the latter half of the century, however, their innate innocence contrasts markedly with the corruptions of British society: they are "remarkable for their modesty," "learned in the Eastern literature," devout in the practice of their religion, unshakable on points of honor, temperate in their amusements, and courageous in adversity.

These virtues are particularly contrasted with the moral failings of British culture: the foppishness of English beaux; the erotic overtures and illicit desires of English ladies; the atheism of courtiers; the fraud and flattery of lawyers; the vices of gambling and intoxication indulged in by ladies and gentlemen, respectively; and the dishonesty of merchants. Throughout this catalogue of satiric contrasts, however, the pamphlet also registers more obliquely its anxiety about those social spaces in which rigidly drawn class barriers are subverted. That is, the satire deploys the figure of the wild man in a dual role: at times, his uncorrupted virtue contrasts with British behavior; at other times, his barbarism matches the socially sanctioned savagery of his English counterpart. In either role, the target of satire would seem to be those British beneficiaries of a rigid class system where social privilege and moral virtue are unrelated. Yet, repeatedly, this satire against English privilege identifies as problematic precisely those sites where the boundaries of a rigid class system are called into question.

When the ambassadors are presented at court, the details of their reception ("how they kiss'd the King's Hand," etc.) dissolve into the mysteries of political intrigue ("and how ——") as equally beyond the scope of the satirist's license: "These being Secrets of State, we must refer you to the News Papers." More than the emptiness of court ritual, what suffers in this attack is the empty pretension of the News Papers in recording superficial ritual as though it were matter of great importance.[18] Implicit in the satirist's restraint is the legitimation of the private conduct of public policy that is being compromised by the vulgar publication of News Papers. In a similar vein, the ambassadors provide the opportunity for swipes at the current vogue for "our Herald's Art of making *Lucky* and *Rich Men* descend from forefathers who never begat them"; at the Board of Trade, at such leveling meetings as those of deists and Dr. Cheyne's vegetarians: "they seem to be a Sect of those Vegetable Gentry the Herb Eaters" (7). Although the ostensible target of each allusion is to ridicule a species of British folly, all of them locate the arena of folly as defined by an erosion of so-cial boundaries: "These two Black Quality, as I was telling you, were introduced to His Majesty King *George* at St. *James's*, as you'll read in the News Papers. The Gentry and Quality Flock't round them, taking them for Masqueraders, and 'Squire *Heidegger* came Sweating from *Whites* in a great Fright, least his Ball should be brought from the Opera House without his Knowledge, and any body should presume to make Monkeys of Mankind besides himself" (6).

In the topsy-turvy world surrounding Mahomet and Bo-Ally, it is undecid-able whether "His Majesty" or Squire Heidegger enjoys greater presumption; whether the Masquerade Ball at the Opera House or the Court at St. James is the more privileged social venue; or, indeed, whether "the Two Black Quality" or England's "Gentry and Quality" represent the "Monkeys" made of "Man-kind." When the wild man is brought to England, it is not so much that his presence destabilizes the rank order that organizes a disciplined classed society; rather, his appearance underlines the fact that those apparent orderings are already subverted. As the allusion to "Masqueraders" indicates, this space of chaos and disrupted boundaries is an eroticized space of sexual license where disruption is marked along the axes of race and gender; the ensuing paragraph pursues this aspect of the allusion explicitly:

> But the Ladies soon found that their Faces were Flesh and Blood; and Boally's Eyes set Ms. [sic] ***'s Mouth a Watering for a Kiss, and Mrs. ***** was so fond of him, that her Spouse according to Custom presently invited 'em to Dinner. The Old Dutchess of S—— wanted him for her Page, and some body else wish'd she had deferr'd her Marriage fourteen Days longer. But, by their Ladyship's good leave, they were mightly out in their Judgments: For the Modest and Chaste *Arabians* were as little affected with them as a Man would be at the sight of a fine Mare, look-ing upon them as Strange, tho' beautiful Creatures. (6–7)

While the ostensible purpose of the satire at this point is the sharp contrast be-tween the moral virtue of the "noble savages" and the inflamed passions and luxurious vices of a debauched European aristocracy, wild black ambassadors and aristocratic white women are coupled here in an erotic fantasy of fetishized primitivism. In the erotic economy of the paragraph, first the bodies of the Moroccan ambassadors and then the imaginations of the English women are offered to the gaze of the reader, only to puncture that fantasy with a view of the bodies of those white women, which bestializes woman. In what has become the most clichéd trope in eroticizing racial difference, viewing the black male body inflames the white female imagination, and both views are simultaneously brought before a single white male gaze that without being implicated in the satire is invited to equate English ladies and Moroccan ambassadors as equally inhuman: "looking upon them [both] as Strange, tho' beautiful Creatures."

The gender politics of the wild man emerge centrally in *The Manifesto of Lord Peter*. This pamphlet is presented in two voices: the first (perhaps Arbuthnot's contribution) speaking "as first Minister to a *Minor* Prince" (4); the second speaking directly as "We Lord Peter" (5). The containing voice of the first minister frames Lord Peter's Manifesto in terms that explicitly evoke the Christian types of Adam and Christ. Identifying Peter as the son of a "great Philosopher," he locates Peter as having been sent, Christlike, to redeem mankind from its fallen, civilized state: "This Great Man, from a deep Sense of the Miseries brought upon Mankind by being civiliz'd, condescended to dedicate his only Son to an Experiment, by which he did not doubt but he should convince the World, how much a nobler Creature a Wild Man was than a Tame one" (3). This redemptive myth is layered over the Adamic myth of a lost innocence: "from the Height of Tenderness to the Child, as well as Love to Mankind, he turned out his Son into a desert Forest. Fortune has so far favored his Design, that the Boy is preserv'd, but the Girl, who was turned out with him at the same time, is missing" (4).

In one respect, this is a familiar *topos* in treatments, both satiric and straightforward, of the wild child: his natural, unsullied innocence offers redemptive possibilities. The minister's voice in the *Manifesto* is unusual only in locating those possibilities squarely within the context of Christian myth. The consequence of such a location, however, is to turn the course of the ensuing satire into an explicitly anti-feminist channel. When the story of Peter is presented as a retelling of *Genesis* after the fall, it becomes an elaborate personals ad—Single White (Innocent) Male desperately seeking Eve. The idiom is that of a royal proclamation, but the message clearly anticipates mail-order marriage markets: "To all Mistresses of Boarding-Schools, Governants, Waiting-Women, Poor Cousins, Matchmakers, and all other Couplers, howsoever denominated or distinguish'd, Greeting" (5).

The criteria enumerated—eighteen in all—as requisite in the bride-to-be are introduced by another convergence of the codes of race and gender. Peter has come to consider the possibility of an English bride only after being convinced that English women are capable of the necessary "wildness": "Whereas we were once resolv'd to send for a Consort to the Deserts of *Arabia,* amongst the Inhabitants of the *Cape of Good Hope,* or the wild *Americans,* that we might not degrade the Dignity of our Race by marrying any Tame Woman; yet being inform'd that the Country where we now sojourn, abounds with Females of those noble Qualities, which render them proper for our Royal Turf, we have suspended our said Resolution" (5). The same ambivalent logic of the "noble savage" that identified the Moroccan ambassadors as at once pure and degraded matches English women with the "Dignity of [a wild] Race." In the catalogue of qualifications that ensues, English women are doubly assaulted: for the affectation of "Tame Women" and for the savagery of those who resist normative gender coding. Several of the qualifications encode women as beasts, either identifying them with animal attributes or evaluating them in terms typically reserved for evaluating animals. Thus, Peter's wife must have "strong and sound Teeth"; "a Loud and Shrill Voice"; she must "be active, sound, and strong in her limbs"; and she must have made just use of "her natural Weapons, Teeth, Nails, and Fingers, by biting, scratching, and pinching"; finally, she must be one who delights in "Beasts and Birds, as Cats, Dogs, Monkeys, &c. And we require it as an indispensible Condition, that she has some time or other kept a great Dog, a squawling Parrot, or a Black Boy" (7–8). As the final unsettling term in that list reminds us, it is primarily "whiteness," and the license to possess that that racial marker guarantees, that distinguishes English women from beasts.

In pursuit of wildness, Peter courts those women who violate socially sanctioned gender codes; in doing so, he sometimes mocks social convention and sometimes reinforces the very assumptions on which those codes are based. Thus, while Peter's wife must have a loud and shrill voice, "if she speaks it must be insignificantly, so as to open her Mouth and say nothing. She must read indistinctly, spell false, and scraul Pothooks rather than write Letters" (9). These qualifications form the main part of Peter's preference for the least educated wife possible, as he wishes not to "have corrupted the Simplicity of Nature" (9). She should have been spoiled in her upbringing to encourage an untamed willfulness; she should resist makeup and even cleanliness; she should refuse to do needlepoint and "any sort of Manufacture of Tame-Women"; she should have contempt for fashion and indeed show a preference for nudity; she should refuse the restrained movements of a Dancing-Master, and be "one who rather frisks like a Satyr, than dances like a Tame Gentlwoman" (8); her contempt for money should lead her to throw it away for her diversion on all occasions; if she has been previously married, she should have abhorred staying at home and preferably have eloped from her husband; she must never be punctual; nor must she claim to be "vastly stupid" nor complain of the spleen; as Peter often goes on hands and feet together, his wife must not choose to stand on one foot only ("unless they can prove to us they learnt it at Scotch-Hop, and only do it to shew their Dexterity at that agreeable Diversion"); finally, Peter will be indulgent to a "female" aversion to light in the eyes and will allow his future bride a green leaf to shield herself from the sun rather than the affectation of a fan, a hood, or a bit of paper.

The satire here is inconsistent, at once faulting women for a cultivated affectation and for a violation of social decorum. Moreover, the satirist's attitude toward Peter's criteria seems to participate in the same inconsistency, sometimes validating and sometimes undermining them. In part, this inconsistency may indicate multiple authorship of the list, but it also speaks to the inherent instability of antifeminist satire that seeks to portray women as defined by inconsistency. Tellingly, I believe, the inconsistencies in Peter's criteria are clarified in a single moment where the satire shifts momentarily to the social space of the court.

In a long list of refusals, resistances, and aversions, item 14 stands apart: "We *allow* her to have a strong Inclination for Courts, where Men commonly lose, but Women acquire Liberty" (9, emphasis added). Within the pamphlet's running joke of the authoritarian voice of the royal "we," the allowance enacts the paternalist liberty it voices. In an antifeminist satire where the boundaries of race, gender, and species are all brought into play, however, the item calls attention to the gender anxiety located at court where women's acquisition of liberty coincides with male loss. The obvious joke of the passage is the traffic between male politico-economic liberty and female socio-sexual liberty. At court, men compromise their freedom as political subjects in economic self-interest, where women are granted a freedom and sexual license denied to them in the larger social world. Peter's understanding of this "inclination" is voiced in his anarchic predilection for liberty, the defining trait of British nationalism; yet that predilection is ironically at odds with the political reality of the current Hanoverian court. The wild child from Germany voices the British opposition to the German monarch on the throne of England. The space of the court is doubly problematic in that it at once marks the restriction of a political liberty, gendered masculine, and the further loosening of a sexual liberty, gendered feminine; in doing so, it becomes the site of a fundamental disruption of an ordering taxonomy, threatening to privilege feminine sexual liberty at the expense of masculine political liberty.

Framed by these pamphlets in which the figure of the wild man generates a satire along the axes of race and gender, while locating as a site of anxiety those social spaces—particularly the Hanoverian court—where established orders are being called into question, Swift's contribution, *It cannot Rain but it Pours: or, London strow'd with Rarities,* refocuses attention squarely on Peter himself and engages directly the earlier representation of *An Enquiry.*[19] Although *An Enquiry* participates in a blurring of cultural boundaries—identifying Peter as the fulfillment of Lilly's astrological prophecy in light of the newsmongers' commodification of elite culture (opera, national politics, etc.) as vulgar entertainment—it does so unself-consciously and uncritically, adding to the profusion of boundary blurring in its representation of Peter. *It cannot Rain but it Pours: or, London strow'd with Rarities* (the second part, inadvertently published first) takes as its starting point this blurring of boundaries in developing its highly topical satire. In doing so, it blends satire and burlesque in a manner reminiscent of some of Swift's finest pieces.

In presenting the speculation that Peter had been suckled by a "She-Bear," the author of *An Enquiry* (as we have seen, a staunch believer in mother-infant bonding) discards the possibilities of Peter being raised by a wolf or a sow before concluding that "'tis not improbable, that if a Bear was brought to him, he would discover by some Action or other, that might naturally break out that that Creature had been no Stranger to him, and would confirm the Opinion of his being brought up by that Creature, rather than any other" (4). Swift begins his pamphlet by parodying the speculations of *An Enquiry.* He, too, invokes Romulus and Remus and Orson by way of introducing a variant of Lilly's prophecy and pretends that that which the author of *An Enquiry* had hoped for has come to pass, though with some difference in the outcome: "Observing Children to ask Blessing of their Mothers, one Day he fell down upon his Knees to a Sow, and mutter'd some Sounds in that humble Posture" (6).

Swift follows the enquirer in dismissing the widely considered possibility that Peter is of mixed generation ("he had a Father and Mother like one of us") and in supporting conjectures about his youth (he appears "to be about Twelve

or Thirteen"). Swift, however, turns these observations to a very different application with what ensues: "His being so young was the Occasion of the great
Disappointment of the Ladies, who came to the Drawing-Room in full Ex-
pectation of some Attempt upon their Chastity: So far is true that he endeavour'd to Kiss the young Lady W_____le, who for that reason is become the Envy
of the Circle; this being a Declaration of Nature, in favour of her superior
Beauty" (5).

Here again the figure of the wild man offers the opportunity for erotic fantasy that genders excessive sexual desire as feminine, but Swift subverts the
usual deployment of the trope. The fantasy suggested here is negated by the
youthful innocence of Peter even before it is articulated. Indeed, the fantasy
serves as a vehicle for introducing a more pointed satiric allusion that works in
quite a different direction. While Peter is a "great Disappointment" to the ladies
at court, he singles out for attention "the young Lady W[alpo]le." Capitalizing
on recent court scandal, this incident directly yokes political and moral corruption at court to the person of the prime minister.

Two years before, the ever ambitious Walpole, recognizing that his power
depended in no small degree on his control of the House of Commons, settled
for a vicarious promotion to the peerage by having his son, Robert, named
Baron Walpole. At the same time, he arranged for Robert's marriage to the
wealthy Margaret Rolle, daughter and heir to Samuel Rolle of Devon. Margaret
was, at the time, "aged fourteen and some months." A decade later, Margaret
Walpole would dispose of herself more happily (albeit scandalously) by running off to Europe with Samuel Sturgis, but in 1726 she was still very much the
acknowledged sexual property of the Walpole administration.[20] Lady Mary
Wortley Montague narrates to her sister the then-current court scandal surrounding the young Lady Walpole:

> I have so good an opinion of your taste, to believe Harlequin in person will never
> make you laugh so much as the Earl of S[tair]'s furious passion for Lady Walpole
> (aged fourteen and some months). Mrs. M[urray] undertook to bring the business
> to bear, and provided the opportunity (a great ingredient you'll say); but the young
> lady proved skittish. She did not only turn this heroic flame into present ridicule,
> but exposed all his generous sentiments, to divert her husband and father-in-law.[21]

The young Lady Walpole of fourteen who proves skittish in this story is nicely
matched with the twelve- or thirteen-year-old wild youth whose innocence

proves such a "great Disappointment" to the court Ladies. But, as Swift's pointed innuendo underlines, Peter's role as sexual plaything is imagined, while Margaret Rolle's was very real. All representations of Peter emphasize his youth and innocence, and generally they point to a vague contrast between innocent nature and social corruption. The specificity of Swift's allusion carries a much greater immediacy, however, by directing our attention to two children, one oblivious to sexuality and the other already exploited in the sexual politics of the court. In such a context, it is not women so much as the court—and its encouragement of exploitative self-interest—that must bear the brunt of the charge of moral corruption.

Swift's attack on morally suspect self-promotion at court is what most distinguishes his pamphlet from *An Enquiry,* and that distinction principally takes shape through the representation of Peter himself. In the former pamphlet, Peter is represented through his potential, the promise of upward mobility he offers. In *London Strow'd,* Swift deploys Peter as a sign of collapsing boundaries, the location where man and beast, courtier and commoner, share an intermingled identity that comments adversely on each. If *An Enquiry* is an instance of hucksterism, pandering in tabloid fashion to the public thirst for curiosities mixed with promises of royal preferment, *London Strow'd* is a satire that bites both the credulous mob at Bartholomew Fair and the equally credulous beau monde at court. Like most accounts, *An Enquiry* took the position that Peter was an object of curiosity, but however much potential he might exhibit, he was at the moment utterly savage and bestial. In some ways representative of this divided attitude is an account published in *Wye's Letter,* April 5, simultaneously noting his innate deference to royalty and his bestial behavior:

> He's supposed to be about 13 Years old, and scarce seems to have any Idea of Things; however, 'twas observed he took most Notice of His Majesty and the Princess, giving him her Glove, which he tried to put on his own Hand, and seemed much pleased, as also with a Gold Watch, which was held to strike at his Ear. They put on him blue Cloaths, but he seems uneasy to be obliged to wear any, and cannot be brought to lie on a Bed, but sits and sleeps in a Corner of the Room. Whence 'tis conjectured he used to sleep in a Tree, for security against wild Beasts; they having been obliged to sawe down one when he was taken. We hear he is to be committed to the Care of Dr. Arbuthnot, in order to try if he can be brought to the Use of Speech, and made a sociable Creature.

Swift turns this divided attitude on its head by finding in Peter's behavior evidence not of his beastly upbringing but of his innate humanity. Like the uncomfortable depictions of human behavior that we find in *Gulliver's Travels,* Peter's behavior is disturbingly human:

> Aristotle saith, That Man is the most Mimick of all Animals; which Opinion of that great Philosopher is strongly confirmed by the Behaviour of this Wild Gentleman, who is endow'd with that Quality to an extreme Degree. He receiv'd his first Impressions at Court: His Manners are, first to lick People's Hands, and then turn his Breech upon them; to thrust his Hand into every body's Pocket; to climb over People's Heads; and even to make use of the Royal Hand, to take what he has a mind to. At his first Appearance he seiz'd on the Lord Chamberlain's Staff, put on his Hat before the King; from whence some have conjectur'd, that he is either descended from a Grandee of Spain, of the Earls of Kingsale in Ireland. However, these are manifest Tokens of his innate Ambition; he is extremly tenacious of his own Property, and ready to invade that of other People.[22]

That lack of decorum, those violations of societal norms that serve in other representations of Peter as a token of his animalistic lack of humanity, become in Swift's version the very sign of his humanity, and in doing so, they reveal the corrupt actions belied by court hypocrisy. Thrusting one's hand into "every body's Pocket" may be a sign of social barbarity, but it may just as well serve as the identifying sign of a politician. One may make allowances for a poor brute, dependant on the charity of the king, when he takes whatever he has a mind to; but one might also see a criticism of the too-great allowances granted to a grasping prime minister, "extremely tenacious of his own Property, and ready to invade that of other People."

In a similar inversion, Swift represents Peter as adept at languages. Nearly universal among representations of Peter is the observation that he has little or no command of language, but Swift, more cagily, conveys the same information at once more accurately and with a different spin: "he distinguishes Objects by certain Sounds fram'd to himself, which Mr. *Rotenberg,* who brought him over, understands perfectly" (6). Peter's lack of command of the English language is at a stroke folded into the similar deficiency of the Hanoverian court. We are made aware at once of equal absurdities: measuring humanity by a knowledge of English and the English nation being ruled by a court that does not understand the national language.

In this fashion we discover one of those metaphoric lists to which Swift was partial: having been taken to a slaughterhouse, "ever since he calls Man by the same Sound which expresseth Wolf. A young Lady is a Peacock, old Women Magpyes and Owls; a Beau with a Toupee, a Monkey; Glass, Ice; Blue, Red, and Green Ribbons, he calls Rainbows; an Heap of Gold a Turd" (6–7). Notable in this list is the reference to blue, red, and green ribbons, a political swipe borrowed from *Gulliver's Travels*, where lately it has been questioned as not intended by Swift. In the context of a larger argument preferring the text of Motte's 1726 edition to Faulkner's 1735 edition of the *Travels*, F. P. Lock observes that in the first edition the threads for which dexterous Lilliputian politicians perform were colored purple, yellow, and white. Arguing against reading the first voyage as a political allegory, he rejects the long-standing view that the 1735 emendation to blue, red, and green was Swift's restoration of an original text corrupted by Motte, arguing instead that Swift is revising ("for the worse") a general satire into a particular one: "In 1726, the satiric point is general. The hierarchy of colours suggests silver, gold, and imperial purple in a natural progression that represents no particular system of honors" (79). The appearance of the three ribbons in this sequence in a pamphlet by Swift (one that made pointed allusion to the prime minister), published while he was overseeing the publication of *Gulliver's Travels*, would add credence to the view that those were the colors originally intended by Swift in 1726, and consequently that he had at least one eye on a topical political allegory.

What is most important in Swift's treatment of Peter is the way in which Peter becomes a sign, capable of multiple—even inconsistent—interpretations, one that can consequently serve the purposes of the satirist. For Swift, those purposes are the standard ones of satire: to ridicule the folly of those who credulously believe the unfortunate Peter to have been raised by animals and simultaneously to expose the corruption that lurks beneath the polish of the court. Peter draws together in common folly the mob and the king, but where in mass culture folly is ridiculous, among the powerful "cultural elite" its corruption is dangerous. Swift's satire on Lord Peter collapses the boundaries between high and low culture, revealing the necessary complicity of the curious and the credulous, the knave and the fool. It is the very liminality of the satyr figure of the wild man that licenses the transgressive challenge to boundaries that characterize the activity of satire.

The proliferation of voices that marks Peter's entrance into the public sphere opens up fundamental questions about the nature of that sphere. For if the enquirer panders (perhaps too vulgarly) to the bourgeois ambitions of his readers, the Scriblerians seek simultaneously to discredit equally the pretensions of the court and the bourgeois institutions associated with the public sphere (newsmongers, masqueraders, etc.). Does the public sphere that includes the *Spectator* and the coffeehouse also include the Anodyne Necklace and *Eronania*? Do the satirists who seek to discredit *both* court and bourgeois shapers of public opinion participate in the bourgeois public sphere in spite of themselves?[23] This latter question is particularly pertinent to the important role Habermas assigns to the Tory opposition. While most discussion of the category of bourgeois public sphere has tended to focus on the periodical essays of Addison and Steele, Habermas assigns the creation of "political journalism in the grand style" to the Scriblerians: "In the summer of 1726, inspired by Bolingbroke, there appeared as the 'long opposition's' literary prelude three pieces satirizing the times: Swift's *Gulliver,* Pope's *Dunciad,* and Gay's *Fables.* In November of the same year Bolingbroke brought out the first issue of the *Craftsman,* the publicist platform of the opposition until the editor's emigration to France in 1735" (60). Aside from Habermas's imprecision with dates (Gay's *Fables* was published in 1727; *The Dunciad* in 1728) and his willingness to see Bolingbroke behind every Tory satire, what is most interesting is his largely accurate perception that beginning in the summer of 1726, the Scriblerians mounted a sustained satiric salvo of several years' duration formalizinged the notion of public opposition that lies at the heart of his historical account of the bourgeois public sphere. Certainly, the opening shots in that salvo were fired in the pamphlets surrounding Peter in May of 1726.

The notion of the public sphere as a unitary origin of liberal democratic pluralism is compromised by critical attention to those markers of exclusion (class, race, gender, etc.) that determined the space of public discussion. Yet, as the case of Peter illustrates, the public sphere becomes most useful as a conceptual tool at the moment when it problematizes its own discursive identity. The salons, the coffeehouses, and the readership of periodical essays of Addison and Steele may have defined discussion through acts of exclusion, but by definition their boundaries were such that they could not be rigidly policed. Addison and Steele's readership overlapped with Dr. Francis Tanner and *The Practical Scheme;* frequenters of Button's coffeehouse also frequented The Sign of the Anodyne Necklace. At the same time, Scriblerian pamphlets attacking the erosion of hierarchical boundaries at court and the leveling pretensions of newspapers participated in the very discursive space of the public sphere that served to erode those boundaries. What marks the critical significance of this space is the degree to which it is defined by its own contradictions: silencing and excluding voices of those by whom it claims to be constituted, it also articulates the resistance of those who claim to oppose it.[24]

3

The Travels
of a Wild Youth

*wherein one castaway survives
four years alone on a desert island,
and another establishes an island
colony—with reflections as well
useful as diverting on language
instruction, agriculture, and goats*

In this chapter I engage in some further bibliographic discussion, this time offering evidence in support of retaining a little-known work about Peter, *Mere
Nature Delineated,* in the (notoriously suspect) Defoe canon. Discussing that
work and its relation to Defoe's demonstrable interest in deaf-language instruction and the "natural condition" of man serves to introduce discussion of
Defoe's famous castaway, Robinson Crusoe, and his relation to other real-life
castaways such as Alexander Selkirk. Beyond the already well-traveled ground
of the Selkirk-Crusoe affinity, this discussion locates both figures within a particular context of biogeography, in which both islands and their animal popu-
lations (particularly goats) carry special significance. One conventional context
for reading *Robinson Crusoe* overlaps with that which framed Peter's representations: the redemptive narrative of the prodigal son—a wild youth who runs
away and must survive alone. Crusoe, however, is ultimately doubly distinct
from the prodigal: his father dies long before his return, and he does not merely
survive, but flourishes. Examining the metonymic relation between castaways,

their islands, and the animal population on those islands enables us to locate Defoe's island fantasy within an emerging imperial discourse.

In the previous chapter, I mentioned only briefly two pamphlets occasioned by Peter's arrival in London: *The Most Wonderful Wonder that Ever Appeared* and *The Devil to Pay at St. James*. The latter has long been regarded as a highly dubious Scriblerian attribution. Published in 1727, it was included in the Glasgow 1751 edition of Arbuthnot's works that was immediately repudiated by the doctor's son. Like the pamphlets written by Swift, Gay, Arbuthnot, and Pope, this one offers a potpourri title page promising discussion of numerous surprising current events; unlike the other pamphlets, it then attempts such an organization, moving rapidly from one topic of current gossip to the next, including in passing the rumor that Peter, after being sent to Hempstead, had impregnated a dairy maid. Although the Scriblerian pamphlets promised a mélange of subjects on their title pages, each pamphlet developed a focused satire, in pointed opposition to the indiscriminate profusion of the title. *The Devil to Pay,* on the other hand, moves rapidly and indiscriminately through a range of "news" items: quarrels at the opera; Orator Henley; William Gibson, the Quaker; a carnival attraction known as "the flying man"; Peter, the wild boy; Mary Tofts, the rabbit breeder; the recent death of George I; the pending coronation of George II; the current popularity of the fabric "bumbazeen"; and, particularly, the recent return of Dean Swift to England and the Lilliputian pigs he is said to have brought with him.

Like *The Most Wonderful Wonder that Ever Appeared* (published in 1726), *The Devil to Pay at St. James* was printed by "A. More," a bookseller's phantom (probably Curll's) who often appears on the title page of pamphlets attempting to cash in on the popularity of the Scriblerians with spurious continuations. In 1723, "A. More" had printed *A Supplement to Dean Swift's Miscellanies,* "by the author"; a spurious *Memoirs of the Life of Scriblerus,* "by D. S_____t"; and— most pertinently—"Printed from the Original Copy from Dublin," *The Wonderful Wonder of Wonders: Or, the Hole-History of the Life and Actions of Mr. Breech.* In the same year, 1723, "A. More" was responsible for printing a surreptitious edition of Bishop Atterbury's speech to Parliament when he was imprisoned in the Tower. Of this edition, *The True Briton* reported that it "is surreptitiously printed, without the knowledge or consent of the Bishop, or any of his friends . . . it is spurious, it is very imperfect; several entire paragraphs being omitted, and many others vilely mangled." Pope similarly declared to Spence: "The Bishop of Rochester's speech as it is printed could not be as he spoke it"

(102). This phantom of Curll's is the object of the "Phantom More" episode of Pope's *Dunciad.* Clearly, no small part of "A. More"'s stock in trade was capitalizing on Swift's popularity; it is perfectly consistent to imagine "More" being used to imitate a popular series of pamphlets, understood to be Scriblerian. Alternatively, it is conceivable that the name is being used to publish a piracy cobbled together from working "hints" of the Scriblerian pamphlets.

The Devil to Pay at St. James, then, offers a particular opportunity to explore one of the charges often leveled against Habermas's formulation of a bourgeois public sphere—the claim that his treatment of the eighteenth century "doesn't look at 'penny dreadfuls,' lurid crime and scandal sheets, and other less than altogether rational-critical branches of the press or at the demagoguery of traveling orators, and glances only in passing at the relationship of crowds to political discourse" (Calhoun 33). This knockoff, Grubstreet production, stitched together out of the past year's oddities and news events and falsely attributed to currently popular writers is the sort of vulgar hackwork that Habermas tends to overlook. Its motley contents, however, may be seen in one sense as of a piece with the rational discourse of periodicals and coffeehouses on which he focuses. As the quick survey of those contents mentioned above suggests, *The Devil to Pay* insists on bringing together into common discourse street oratory and opera, the death of kings and the birth of rabbits.

Peter had been the fashionable attraction in London in the spring of 1726, and pamphlets about him at that time frequently set his visit next to that of Faustina Bordoni, the famous Italian singer who had also recently arrived. These two were in a sense rival spectacles, competing for fashionable attention. The competition was, however, short-lived, for Faustina—whose visit had been long anticipated—was rendered hoarse and unable to perform almost immediately after her arrival; Gay subsequently staged this disappointment in *Polly,* when the singer "Signora Crotchetta" enters complaining that she has a cold and cannot go on. Public fascination with Peter soon waned, and over the summer he was literally farmed out to a rural retirement in Hempstead. By that fall, Peter was all but forgotten in the fervent speculation surrounding Mary Toft, the rabbit breeder of Godalming, Surrey. She was brought to London, under the attention of court physicians and men midwives, and housed in Lacy's Bagnio in Leicester Fields. By the early months of 1727, Mary Toft had confessed to a hoax and been arraigned as a "Vile Cheat and Imposter," and Faustina was applauded by the opposition in her rivalry with Madame Cuzzoni, who enjoyed the support of the king.

Such politicizing of the opera was more or less a matter of course in the early eighteenth century, but this conflict took a surprising turn when the two rivals reportedly came to blows in the middle of a performance of Buononcini's *Astyanax* before the Princess of Wales, with all the accompaniments of screeching, hair pulling, scratching, and pummeling; in Gay's *Polly*, Signora Crotchetta exits "in a fury." The anonymous author of *Devil to Pay* opens his carnivalesque tour of the past year's entertainments by introducing the fight between Faustina and Cuzzoni with an extended simile, likening it to quarrels between mackerel sellers near London Bridge or mutton vendors in Covent Garden. Quickly the dispute becomes an excuse for preferring honest, protestant English entertainment to highbrow affectation for vaguely Jacobite, Italian performers. The conflict between Faustina and Cuzzoni is at once rendered as ridiculous and affected, and at the same time as exemplifying an excess of passion that is obscurely threatening. In this manner, the satire proceeds to hint at a vaguely scandalous conversion of the *castrato* Senesino by Orator Henley and a more plainly carnal desire inflamed in a certain anonymous Lady _____ by the Quaker William Gibson. This excessive passion serves as the transition to the latest rumor about Peter:

> But who would have thought that Peter, the Wild Boy, who appear'd so Sly and Serious, who, I say, would have thought that he of all People in the World, should have any Insight into the Trade of Basket-making? but it is certainly true, neither better or worse; for it seems he has play'd his Wild Pranks with a Dairy Maid at Harrow the Hill, whom he has got with Child. Now should she be brought to Bed of another wild Boy, Lord have Mercy upon us! what shall we do? Or how shall we catch him? He will certainly be as fleet as a Hare the Minute he is born, as his Father was before him. And if the Child should run away and be lost in the Woods, what a deal of Amusement will the Town lose. But they say the Dairy Maid is to be brought forthwith to Town, to Lacy's Bagnio, and to have the Rabbet-Woman's Apartment fitted up for her. She is Daily to be attended by Men-Midwifes, and narrowly to be watch'd by Constables. If so, we are like to have some Diversion, however, this Summer: and no doubt she will be visited by a great deal of good Company. But how can People mind Diversions, or any Thing else, when there is Mourning going forwards; and how can they think of Mourning for the Coronation, or of the Coronation for the Birth-Day? (*Devil to Pay* 218–19)

In this topsy-turvy narrative, Peter's muteness is read (through the lens of social convention) as a pose, an affectation: a "Sly and Serious" demeanor masking the animal passion of his "Wild Pranks" that promises to generate monsters "as fleet as a Hare" that in turn call up the recent delivery of Mary Toft's stillborn rabbits, all of which, like the opera, is offered by way of diversion to the official state celebrations of "Mourning," "Coronation," and "Birth-Day." Explicitly, this passage codes two of the defining tropes associated with Peter—passion and language—as linked, and it does so by associating him with the current vogue for opera.

Defoe, if he is the author, had made a similar move in a somewhat different register in *Mere Nature Delineated*. That book, published in the summer of 1726, before Peter was retired to Hempstead and thus also before the outbreak of the Faustina-Cuzzoni grudge match, similarly brings into play questions of language, passion, opera, and violent spectacle, but with respect to an instance of domestic violence that also competed for London's attention during the spring of Peter's arrival. Among the many other anonymous works often attributed to Defoe, two in particular bear on *Mere Nature Delineated: The Life and Adventures of Duncan Campbell* and *The Deaf and Dumb Philosopher*. Although I am inclined to accept the attribution of *Mere Nature Delineated* to Defoe (some of my reasons are given below), I am persuaded by the arguments of Rodney Baine that Defoe wrote neither of the other works. Whether or not any of these works are Defoe's, all share a common interest in the problem of teaching language to the deaf, and they do so in ways that share a common evaluation of the project and a common concern over the role of language in distinguishing the limits of human identity. Moreover—and here their interests intersect with the jumble of activities noted in *The Devil to Pay*—the problem of teaching language to the deaf resides on the border that separates passionate spectacle from rational speculation. Nicholas Mirzoeff calls our attention to the need to reexamine the place of the deaf in early modern culture: "I have been concerned to try to write deaf history, as a case study not of pathology but of the cultural construction of 'centers' and 'margins' and of how certain groups came to be excluded from the ranks of the civilized. . . . Many Enlightenment thinkers regarded the deaf as machines, incapable of independent thought. One of Kant's less celebrated universals was the necessity of speech to reason. Thus he argued that a deaf person 'can never achieve more than an analogue of reason'" (78). From Kant's perspective, the deaf, like other quasi-human brutes, remain trapped within a private interiority of passion cut off from public discourse. Yet that separation simultaneously protects their innocence, forever shielding them from the corruption endemic to society that can be communicated only through language. Language instruction—like Peter, Duncan Campbell, and the orang-outangs—is figured ambivalently: at once beyond all human art and a despoiling of natural purity. Repeatedly, in *Mere Nature Delineated*, Defoe returns to questions of deafness and the instruction of the deaf that seemed to have fascinated him elsewhere as well, but in one particularly provocative passage he, too, remarks on this coupling of wildness and culture, language and passion, social violence and innocent solitude:

> Had he seen the late Mrs. Hayes burnt alive at a Stake it would not have been at all any Surprize to him, or have given him any Ideas differing from a Dance or the Theatre.
>
> Thus of his Hearing: I believe he would no more have been moved with her Screiches in the Fire, than he would have been with the charming Faustina, singing in an Opera; and this, not that he could not hear both, but that, like a Horse, or any other Fellow Brute, his Ear could convey no Notions to his Understanding, of the Things he heard, or of the Difference between them; and all for want of Instruction. (33–34)

Now there is, of course, much that demands clarification here, but one place to begin may well be with the English resistance to Italian opera. The passage speaks, as such passages often did, of Peter's sensory deprivations, of being unable to distinguish between the cries of Mrs. Hayes and the singing of Faustina. But the explanation offered—that the ear can convey nothing meaningful to the understanding—is precisely what was true for any Englishman listening to Faustina perform in Italian opera.[1] It is, however, impossible to read this passage without shuddering at the way this vivid description of a woman being burned alive is located within popular debate over *opera seria;* the effect is indeed a good deal like Swift's description of a woman flayed. Doing justice to that incongruity requires a brief retelling of the case of Mrs. Hayes.

In February 1726, shortly before Peter's arrival, a human head was found floating in the Thames. The unidentified head was placed on display in Westminster, and newspapers encouraged Londoners to see if anyone could identify the face. Within several days, the head was identified as belonging to a Mr. Hayes, and Catherine Hayes and two accomplices were shortly arrested. The story that emerged over the next several weeks depicted the Hayes marriage as consisting of two decades of alcoholism and abuse. On the night of the murder, Hayes had gone to bed drunk while Catherine remained up, drinking and talking with two men in their early twenties (one of whom was reported in some accounts to be her eldest son; Catherine had given birth to a dozen children). Together, they had planned to end Hayes's abuse of Catherine by murdering him in his bed. After the murder, his body had been dismembered and locked in a trunk that they dropped in a pond outside London; the head they threw into the Thames. In one widely circulated version of the story, the murder of husband culminated in incestuous relations between mother and son. The two young men were sentenced to death by hanging for the capital offense of murder, but Catherine Hayes—who maintained her innocence to the end—was convicted of petit treason in the murder of her husband and therefore sentenced to be bound at the stake and burned alive. Sentence was carried out in April of 1726. When all was in readiness, the executioner set fire to the kindling. The intense heat, however, caused him to drop the rope intended to strangle Mrs. Hayes, and she fell into the flames. There, her screams and cries caused great uneasiness in the crowd, until someone picked up a large block of wood and struck her in the head, ending her cries and their torment.

The delineator's belief that Peter "would no more have been moved with her Screiches in the Fire, than he would have been with the charming Faustina, singing in an opera" directs our attention to what it means to be moved, to the appalling distance between the genuine passion of Mrs. Hayes's suffering and the feigned passion of Grand Opera. That distance, of course, is belied in the implicit parallel that Gay developed the next year in *The Beggar's Opera,* suggesting a connection between the vulgar spectacle at Tyburn and the elite spectacle staged at Haymarket. Yet the Hayes affair is redolent of other ironies as well: that Catherine Hayes's execution must be staged more elaborately (and thus, more disastrously) as a crime against the state, rather than against a person; that her botched execution makes her (in some sense) an object of public pity in a way that a life of domestic abuse could not; that this particular public presentation of justice requires one grotesquerie after another, from the public exhibition of the severed head to the botching of her execution. For the delineator, there is something equivalently mysterious in the fascination with opera and the fascination with Mrs. Hayes, in each case a public staging of passion that does not communicate to the understanding.

This is the connection that both opera and execution have to Peter, then, the inability to communicate to the understanding. The delineator, who several times alludes disparagingly to an earlier pamphlet by Swift, on this point simply lifts Swift's ironic fiction and retails it as fact: "it is said, A certain Lady looking gravely upon him, shook her Head, and added, *'Tis pity he is not a little older, he would make an admirable _____ for he could tell no Tales*" (31). What in Swift's pamphlet is pointed away from Peter and directed to the liberties taken at court, is for the delineator, the confluence of passion and noncommunication. One of the stronger arguments in support of Defoe's identity as the delineator is the repeated allusions made to "the ingenious Mr. Baker" as one who may be uniquely qualified to teach Peter to communicate. Henry Baker, who would in 1727 marry Defoe's favorite daughter, Sophia, had developed his own system for teaching language to the deaf through gestural signs. In the manner of the time, Baker required as a condition of treatment that his clients agree not to divulge for seven years his method of instruction, enabling him to develop a reputation as a miracle worker. The delineator repeatedly makes the case for entrusting Peter to the care of Mr. Baker, as most qualified for this kind of instruction: "we have seen some, who have attained to the Power of expressing themselves articulately, and in Words, which those that stand by, can both hear and understand, though that Person so speaking, cannot hear the Sound he makes. The ingenious Mr. Baker, is a living witness of this, who is eminently known for a surprizing Dexterity in Teaching such as have been born Deaf and Dumb, both to speak, and understand what is said when others speak to them" (39).

Indeed, this issue becomes the central focus of the delineator's account, returning in various forms of philosophical prose, satiric prose, narrative account, and even verse to the problem of how to teach language to the deaf. The poem, a 223-line composition, "On the Deaf and Dumb being taught to Speak," explicitly returns to the question of passion's relation to language and in doing so chooses in the end for the state of innocence that a lack of language guarantees: "O! who, that knows himself in full extent, / Would not, like them, be Dumb and Innocent" (134–35). While the work of Jean Marc Itard with Victor of Aveyron is usually credited with establishing the modern field of special education, that work in fact marks a culmination of interest signaled by the delineator's description of Peter:

> He is now, as I have said, in a State of Meer Nature, and that, indeed in the literal Sense of it. Let us delineate his Condition, if we can: He seems to be the very Creature which the learned World have, for many Years past, pretended to wish for, *viz.* one that being kept entirely from human society, so as never to have heard any one speak, must therefore either not speak at all, or, if he did form any Speech to himself, then they should know what Language Nature would first form for Mankind. (17)

Perhaps not surprisingly, there is considerable traffic between historical accounts of feral children and histories of deaf language instruction. Certainly one of the most influential historians in both areas has been Harlan Lane, author of *When the Mind Hears: A History of the Deaf* and *The Wild Boy of Aveyron*.[2] As Lane has established, the foundation of modern instruction of the deaf was laid by Jean Marc Itard and his work with Victor, the wild boy of Aveyron, following the principles of his predecessors M. de l'Epée and M. Sicard. As Lane remarks, histories of deaf education have long been concerned with "the oralist/sign debate"—the question of whether the deaf should be instructed through gestural language and sign, or rather be compelled to learn speech and lipreading. Itard, Lane notes, would seem to be an ardent oralist: in teaching six pupils from 1805 to 1808 he never learned to sign, he frequently said that he would prohibit signing among his pupils if he could enforce it, and he never attempted to teach Victor to sign. Yet, as Lane goes on to observe, by the end of his career he "came to believe profoundly that sign language was 'the natural language of the deaf'" (207). From the perspective of the historian of deaf education, this question is indeed a persistent and important one, and Lane is an important advocate for the revisionist claim that only recognition of sign as "the natural language of the deaf" can liberate deaf people from the linguistic colonialism of the hearing community. This revisionist history points to the limited success of the oralist approach and the manipulative practices imposed by hearing people on the deaf in the early history of oralist instruction of deaf pupils by hearing instructors.

In this revisionist paradigm, the British tradition of Wallis, Holder, Baker, and Braidwood is identified as oralist and repressive and is contrasted to the French sign tradition of Sicard, de l'Epée, and Itard. Although I would not dispute the colonialist implications of Lane's argument, it may be worth considering where the British tradition is located within an emerging natural history. Emphasis on speech instruction in England derived ultimately from a pre-Darwinian collision of religion and natural history: as it was the *logos* that distinguishes humans from the rest of the brute creation, not only spiritual salvation of the deaf but even their salvation as human beings depended on their being capable of being brought to language. On this point, Alan Bewell writes: "Unlike the New Testament, Enlightenment philosophy did not seek to lessen the separation of these individuals from society. It did just the opposite, as it emphasized and accentuated their difference in order to increase their speculative value" (29). As I believe the passages in Defoe's poem indicate, this is something of a misleading oversimplification. The "speculative value" of the deaf themselves paled next to the "speculative value" of the "miraculous" powers of salvation practiced by deaf language instructors, such as Henry Baker and Thomas Braidwood. To recognize gestural language as a "natural language" for the deaf defied the taxonomic criteria that distinguished human from beast on the basis of spoken language. Thus, while Lane and others trace the oralist movement in England back to Wallis, in doing so they often overlook or downplay the ideological commitment to empiricism that framed those endeavors.

A closer look at Wallis's method reveals first of all that he was not the rigid oralist he is sometimes made out to be, but advocated the use of sign as a complement to oral instruction. Furthermore, it becomes clear that Wallis's pedagogic goal was itself shaped by a commitment to the Royal Society's taxonomic construction of knowledge. Wallis's method begins by presuming sign to be the basic means of communication between teacher and pupil and builds on that initial semiotic exchange by formalizing a gestural alphabet that may be correlated to the written alphabet and through which the deaf pupil may learn both to write and to sign the names of certain objects. From that stage, Wallis proceeds through an elaborate, step-by-step progression to teach language as a direct corollary of teaching the world, via taxonomy: "Thus, in one paper, under the title "Mankind," may be placed, not confusedly, but in decent order, man, woman, child (boy, girl). In another paper, under the title "Body," may be written, in like convenient order, head (hair, skin, ear), face, forehead, eye (eyelid, eyebrow)" (32). And so on. The organization of knowledge in this fashion continues through a variety of such classificatory schemes and returns to the importance of signing: "It will be convenient all along to have pen, ink, and paper, ready at hand, to write down in a word what you signify to him by signs, and cause him to write, or show how to write, what he signifies by signs, which way of signifying their mind by signs deaf persons are often very good at; and we must endeavor to learn their language, if I may so call it, in order to teach them ours, by showing what words answer to their signs" (40).

In spite of the tendency to associate Wallis and his British successors with the "oralist school," this notion of deaf language instruction was predicated on a basis of signed communication that explicitly considered such gestural communication a kind of language. Thus, at the level of communicative agency, Wallis may be seen as recognizing a form of cultural difference not unlike what Mirzoeff imagines between the deaf and "the majority, phonocentric culture" (78). Within, however, a framework of a natural history that defines "humanity" in part by vocal capacity, the perceived need to translate from "gestural language" to spoken language takes on the familiar colonialist garb of the missionary. Gestural language might be recognized as sufficient to communication, while still remaining insufficiently "human," according to taxonomy that privileged speech.

Wallis's method of instruction for bringing the deaf from gestures to the privileged realm of speech is remarkably similar to the one Robinson Crusoe follows with Friday. In the first few pages after Friday's rescue, almost all of the communication between the two is carried out by signs, and these signs are remarkably expressive: in the first three pages we observe them to communicate by signs: "to come forward," "of encouragement," "swearing to be a slave forever," "to lend him my sword," "of triumph," "to let him go," "that more might come after him," "to go lie down and sleep," "of a humble, thankful Disposition," "of subjection, servitude, and Submission," "it was very good for him," "that we should dig them up again, and eat them." Notwithstanding the pronounced tendency here to equate communication with the negotiation of political relations, this is a surprisingly rich and varied gestural vocabulary, one that appears to be capable of even greater nuance on the following page when Friday signs the following message: "that they brought over four Prisoners to feast upon; that three of them were eaten up, and that he, pointing to himself, was the fourth. That there had been a great Battle between them, and their next King, whose Subjects it seems he had been one of; and that they had taken a great Number of Prisoners, all which were carry'd to several Places by those that had taken them in the Fight, in order to feast upon them, as was done here by these Wretches upon those they brought hither" (150).

I confess myself unable to imagine the gestures necessary for such a narrative, but with such communication already possible, it seems a shame that Friday must soon be reduced to the creole speech on which Charles Gildon remarked. In his caustic response to *Robinson Crusoe*, Gildon has Friday and Crusoe arraign their author for injustices committed upon them: "Have injure me, to make me such Blockhead, so much contradiction, as to be able to speak *English tolerably well* in a Month or two, and not to speak it better in twelve Years after" (71). Nonetheless, Crusoe's education of Friday begins with language instruction, and if—like Wallis and Baker—it builds on a basis of gestural communication, it—also like those two—follows the empiricist taxonomy that organizes things with their names in a nominative taxonomy compatible with the Royal Society motto of *Res et Verba:* "Friday began to talk pretty well, and understand the Names of almost every Thing I had occasion to call for, and of every Place I had to send him to" (154). Clearly, language is here figured as a fundamentally Adamic tool (enabling the naming of the world), but just as clearly, its social function is to delineate a clear relationship between sovereign and subject—Crusoe's language classes never proceed far beyond their first lesson: "I likewise taught him to say *Master,* and then let him know, that was to be my Name" (149).

We think of Crusoe on a desert island, perhaps in the cartoon image of a bearded castaway in rags beneath a solitary palm tree, but "desert" had very different connotations in the eighteenth century than it does today. Its primary sense meant "depopulated" and hence "uncultivated"; Johnson's dictionary makes no mention of aridity, defining the word as "A wilderness; solitude; waste country; uninhabited place." Peter, discovered in the wilds of the German Black Forest, was described as found in a desert. Where there is no human population, and hence no agriculture, no cultivation, there is wild desert. But such a desert need not mean barren desolation; it can instead be a rich, fertile, even fecund habitat that wants only human cultivation to bring forth its treasures. Such an "uncultivated desert" can appear in the sense of a lost Eden, still maintaining a pristine innocence; in this sense it is the extreme opposite of the doubly lost location of urban life that is at once tainted with human experience but barren and uncultivated. Characteristic of what Latour has labeled "Modern Purification" is the impulse to distinguish nature as that which is external to culture; the realm of the nonhuman, distinct from the realm of the human. Such a purification is always accompanied by an ambivalence that idealizes what it denigrates. David Lewis's poem "The Savage," occasioned by Peter's arrival at court, articulates this ambivalence in ways that underline the reinforcing dichotomies of reason/passion, human/beast, civilized/wild, and so forth, only to destabilize that ideology with the unsettling pair of corruption/innocence. He first charges the court,

> Receive this Youth, unform'd, untaught,
> From solitary Desarts brought
>
> . . . .
> . . . and with tender Care,
> For Reason's use his mind prepare
>
> . . . .
> And civilize him into Man. (ll. 5–6, 9–10, 14)

But, Lewis goes on to warn, if you only instruct him in language so that he may learn hypocrisy and disingenuousness, it would be better to send him back silent, innocent, and free to the deserts from whence he came. The poem concludes with the proper moral—one that, like Defoe's poem "On the Deaf and Dumb being Taught to Speak," imagines mute innocence preferable to the potential corruption of rational exchange:

> He, whose lustful, lawless Mind
> Is to Reason's Guidance blind,
> Ever slavish to obey,
> Each imperious Passion's sway,
> Smooth and Courtly tho' he be,
> He's the Savage, only he. (ll. 29–34)

Although Crusoe's island has figured prominently in recent discussions of Western imperialism, relatively little attention has been paid to its relation to contemporary science and ecological imperialism.[3] For Defoe and his contemporaries, one sign of wildness was a fertile abundance that awaited only human cultivation to pour forth its bounty. Thus in the various accounts that inform Defoe's narrative, European species (rats, cats, and goats, in particular) explode on the island of Juan Fernández. The proliferation of imported species marks the island's reproductive potential. William Dampier's account of the island goes into some detail respecting its potential for cultivation[4]:

> Goats were first put on the island by John Fernando . . . it was in his second voyage hither that he set ashore 3 or 4 Goats, which have since, by their increase, so well stock'd the whole Island. But he could never get a patent for it, therefore it lies still destitute of Inhabitants, tho' doubtless capable of maintaining 4 or 500 Families, by what may be produced off the Land only . . . for the Savannahs would at present feed 1000 Head of Cattle besides Goats, and the Land being cultivated would probably bear Corn, or Wheat, and good Pease, Yams, or Potatoes; for the Land in their Valleys and sides of the Mountains, is of a good black fruitful Mould. (247)

In reality, of course, such species activity often signals the destruction of one ecosystem by an imported species. The island on which Selkirk was cast away (Robinson Crusoe Island) now serves as a university lab site for the study of paleoecology and evolutionary biology. The lush island that proved so fertile for Crusoe's goats has been devastated by the omnivorous grazing and burrowing of another European import, rabbits, who first arrived in 1935; Alexander Selkirk Island has been reduced to a barren, desolate, rocky desert island. For only part of the year, it is home to a few dozen fishermen. The colony of "4 or

500 families" supported by "the land only" that Dampier imagined never materialized. Today, the entire population of Robinson Crusoe Island hovers between five and six hundred individuals, clinging to the coastline, supporting themselves by fishing for the lobsters that were so ubiquitous when Selkirk arrived and are today ever more scarce. There is virtually no agricultural economy on the archipelago, but the effects of attempts to cultivate the island are still felt:

> The introduction of domesticated animals and their transition to the feral condition began to place tremendous pressures on the native vegetation. Feral dogs, pigs, and goats have roamed in quantity, especially during 1574–1765 (Wester, 1991). The former two pests have largely disappeared from the Islands, but feral goats abound, particularly on Alejandro Selkirk, where 5,000–10,000 individuals roam the higher reaches of the island [Bourne et al. 1992]. The coati mundi, introduced as a pet to the village, has escaped and is beginning to cause some damage to the vegetation, especially from its burrowing habit that loosens the soil and accelerates erosion. (Natural History Museum)

The greatest "pest" identified by Cambridge University, however, is not an animal but a plant, one closely identified with English agriculture. When, at the end of the eighteenth century, William Wordsworth famously returned to the banks of the Wye River to review the definitive prospect of Romantic Nature, he saw "these hedgerows, hardly hedgerows, little lines / Of sportive wood run wild" that might mark "some Hermit's cave, where by his fire / The Hermit sits alone" ("Tintern Abbey," 15–16, 21–22). Throughout the seventeenth and eighteenth centuries, English agriculture was increasingly identified with the practice of enclosing fields for cultivation, a practice Carolyn Merchant identifies with the transformation from feudal to market economy: "enclosure represented for the English the most prevalent method of entering the market economy" (55).[5] The picturesque English countryside of Wordsworth's Romantic landscape is bound up with Cambridge University's late-twentieth-century study of ecological imperialism in a thorny tangle that includes Defoe's *Robinson Crusoe* in its ironic circulation of literature and life.

Richard Grove's excellent study of the origins of environmentalism, *Green Imperialism*, has made the case for a more complex theorizing than "the hypothesis of a purely destructive environmental imperialism" (7) in which Europeans project Edenic fantasies onto a New World waiting to be despoiled. Particularly in his discussion of *Robinson Crusoe*, Grove attends to how Utopian fantasies of paradise are intertwined with the theme of desert island survival, its attendant anxieties of extinction, and the commercial themes of economic expansion. Observing how the various accounts of Selkirk's survival that accompanied his return to England contribute to this emerging discourse, he also argues for a contextualizing of Defoe's novel that attends to its Caribbean location, with its associations of cannibalism and economic empire. In doing so, Grove resurrects an argument dating from the 1930s that Crusoe's island alludes not to Juan Fernández but to the Caribbean island of Tobago. Interestingly enough, the Tobago argument was originally pursued in part by a campaign to develop tourism in Tobago, a campaign that had included in 1893 a display at the Chicago Exhibition, sponsored by the governor of Tobago, that included an old he-goat (impossibly) identified as the one made famous in Defoe's novel. At the time that this Tobago hypothesis was put forward, the critical question was merely one of literary influence and source study, and Juan Fernández was known simply as "Mas-a-Tierra." Now, of course, a Chilean tourism industry as imaginative as any Tobago has ever known has renamed the large island for Robinson Crusoe and the smaller one for Alexander Selkirk. The imaginative commodification of both "island paradises" nicely illustrates the need that Grove insists on in complicating our understanding of environmental imperialism. This is where his analysis differs significantly from the earlier proponents of Tobago as a "source" for Defoe.

Grove's argument, ultimately, is not that the island of Tobago (rather than the island of Juan Fernández) provided the original raw material for the creative imagination of the Englishman Defoe, but rather that if one context in which to read Crusoe's castaway narrative is the desert island survival story popularized by the drama of Alexander Selkirk, that context should also be supplemented by John Poyntz's *The Present Prospect of the Famous and Fertile Island of Tobago* (1683). Without questioning the importance of locating *Robinson Crusoe* in the context of the economic expansion advertised by Poyntz (and feeding into the South Sea company's developing influence), as well as in the explicitly Caribbean context of European discourse of cannibalism, I would also make note of a possible imaginative conflation in Defoe's locating his castaway off the coast of Brazil.[6]

Robinson Crusoe was first published in April 1719 and sold rapidly, with a fourth edition coming out in August. That fourth edition was the first to include a folding "map of the world with the latest Discoveries, on which is delineated the Voyage of Robinson Crusoe." The map in question was a variant of the map made by Herman Moll that had appeared in Woodes Rogers's *Cruising*

Voyage round the World, in which Selkirk's story had been told. The most significant change in the two maps is that where the latter had charted Rogers's course with a dotted line, the former charted Crusoe's course. The course "delineated" on the Crusoe map does not stop at Tobago or any other island, but it does chart a course that would have intersected with an archipelago depicted on Moll's map but removed for *Robinson Crusoe*. That archipelago, off "C. Roque," is known as "Fernando de Noronha," and in subsequent editions of *Robinson Crusoe* it was restored to the map and simply labeled "Fernandes Is." Could Defoe, in creating his imaginary island, have conflated Juan Fernández Island off the coast of Chile in the Pacific with "Fernández Island" off the coast of Brazil in the Atlantic?

Clearly Defoe knew of Fernando de Noronha, because on his ill-fated voyage, Crusoe's ship "steer'd as if we was bound for the Isle *Fernand de Noronha* holding our Course N. E. by N. and leaving those Isles on the East" (31). It is immediately after this that the ship encounters the first hurricane in the series that eventually shipwrecks him, and the locations provided in the intervening paragraphs indicate that his ship has moved north and west into the Caribbean. On the other hand, Woodes Rogers also refers to this island, but confusingly under the name "Juan Fernández." Thus the same account that tells the story (pp. 91–96) of Alexander Selkirk on Juan Fernández has also located "the island of Juan Fernández" north and east of Rio de Janeiro in the Atlantic (36). Perhaps, then, Defoe conflated these two islands of Juan Fernández.

Without insisting on an identification of Crusoe's fictive island with the island of Tobago that Poyntz was so aggressively marketing for colonial development, one can agree with Grove that Poyntz's marketing of Tobago, like the attempts to market Juan Fernández, contributed to Defoe's representation of Crusoe's economic development project on his desert island. Manuel Schonhorn seeks to identify Crusoe's discussions of "hedges" with political rhetoric (143–44). While his argument is attractive in seeking a connection between agricultural theory and political metaphor, it still seems most plausible to me that Crusoe's agricultural practice has more to do with Defoe's thinking about agriculture than his thinking about politics—even though I believe it makes sense to see those modes of thinking as compatible. In particular, Schonhorn looks past the fact that the precedents he cites for a political rhetoric of "fencing" and "hedging" are at odds with Defoe's own uses. That is, in the earlier instances, the king or prince serves as a hedge or fence, protecting his subjects; in those political works attributed to Defoe where the figure appears, it is either

Lockean law or the "double fence" of "the Law and the People" that protects king and country. What seems more relevant to Defoe's novel is the way in which the agricultural technology of the hedge is becoming the principal mechanism for economic development. Here, Poyntz's pamphlet advertising Tobago offers a particularly adept proposal whereby an Englishman could profitably cultivate the untapped resources of the Caribbean by clearing and hedging farmland. As Douglas Chambers has argued persuasively, early-eighteenth-century agricultural theorists did not associate "enclosure" with the depredations of large landholders in the way that people have after Goldsmith's "Deserted Village." Instead, writers such as Bradley, Houghton, and Worlidge advocated enclosure as the tool of the small farmer, benefiting the ordinary husbandman: "for it is not to be doubted, but that land enclos'd and till'd, yieldeth a far greater increase to the husbandman than lands open and untill'd" (Houghton 144).

The proliferating goats that signaled natural fecundity in the accounts of Selkirk's stay on Juan Fernández called out for the civilizing touch of European cultivation. In Defoe's narrative, Crusoe steps in to play the part of the English landed gentleman, cultivating his wild paradise with eighteenth-century agriculture. While agriculture is for the most part foreign to Crusoe's background (a deficiency he remarks on several times), he is indefatigable in fencing in and enclosing his lands. Once he ventures into the middle of the island and is charmed by its natural beauty, he sets about fencing in a portion of it and describes his actions in rhetoric that unmistakably identifies himself with the estate holder: "I built me a little kind of bower and surrounded it at a distance with a strong fence, being a double hedge as high as I could reach, well staked and filled between with brushwood; . . . I fancied now I had my country house and my seacoast house" (75). Subsequently, he again constructs another hedge to enclose his original dwelling; then protects his corn crop from predators "by making an enclosure about it with a hedge" (85); and finally culminates in his most extensive enclosure project in which he eventually encloses five separate feeder lots with holding pens for what becomes a considerable goat farm (107).

Crusoe's career as a farmer follows the paradigm of cultivating by enclosing and employs the English agricultural technology of the hedge. Two observations on his career are worth making at this point: first, Crusoe's enclosing hedges always protect a vulnerable domestic space of cultivation from a threatening external wildness lurking just beyond the horizon; and second, Crusoe had his followers among eighteenth-century attempts to settle Juan Fernández.

Crusoe's final elaborate enclosure project was prompted by his desire to domesticate a portion of the proliferating wild goat population: "it presently occurred to me that I must keep the tame from the wild, or else they would always run wild when they grew up, and the only way for this was to have some enclosed piece of ground . . . that those within might not break out, or those without break in" (106). The idea of "domestic space" in the eighteenth century has an interestingly double quality, one that is particularly pertinent to *Robinson Crusoe*. It may be useful in thinking of Crusoe's domestication of island life to consider Johnson's definitions of "domesticate" ("to make domestick; to withdraw from the publick"). On the one hand, that which is domesticated is no longer wild, but it is also that which is no longer public. In one sense, Crusoe's stay on the island constitutes a curious balancing act in which he is withdrawn from the public realm, without actually degenerating into wildness, and his return to society is brought about by his ability to reconstitute a viable public within his solitary realm, a process that begins with his domestication of his environment. Faced with Crusoe's dilemma of separating "wild" and "tame," early settlers of Juan Fernández attempted his solution, importing blackberry vines to reinforce the hedgerows. If life here imitated literature in the attempt, it fell woefully short in the event. The goats, from all accounts, seem to have been relatively unimpeded by the resulting hedges. Long after the settlers threw up their hands and abandoned the island, the blackberry vines flourish everywhere, choking out indigenous plant life and leaving the island an impenetrable thicket—"sportive wood run wild" with a vengeance.

A long and valuable tradition of Crusoe criticism locates a significant component of the book's enduring appeal in the central character's ambivalent relation to his island home. Sometimes the island is his "little Kingdom (100)," at other times his "desolate solitary Island (101)." John Richetti captures well the centrality of this ambivalent attitude to both Crusoe's religious and phenomenological appeal:

> His conversion enables Crusoe to leave his paranoid seclusion and to convert his island from a prison into a garden. From this point on Crusoe turns to the island itself, exploring it, domesticating it, and indeed enjoying it in various ways. The self, liberated from survival by a reciprocal relationship with an 'other', is free to gratify itself. . . . That detail [drying grapes into raisins] of Crusoe's Eden can stand as a perfect example of Crusoe's new condition: . . . He is able to speak jauntily of 'my reign or my captivity, which you please' (100). (363–64)

The divided condition of Crusoe's own mental habits is, as Leopold Damrosch argues, indicative of a Puritan psychology that swung between poles of submission and self-assertion and left itself open to charges of hypocrisy. The impulse to self-aggrandizement is never far below the surface in Defoe's novel, and Gildon was prompt to notice that some measure of that self-promotion might be traced to Defoe's own door. The full title page of *Robinson Crusoe* links Crusoe's identity to his island habitat ("who lived eight and twenty years all alone in an uninhabited island"); Gildon's parodic title page at once identifies Crusoe with Defoe and his island with England: "The Life and Strange Surprising Adventures of Mr. D_____ De F_____ of London, Hosier, who has lived above Fifty years by himself, in the Kingdoms of North and South Britain." Just as Crusoe's doubled identity as subject/sovereign takes on a special metaphoric importance for an eighteenth-century English reader, so, too, does the doubled prison/paradise identity of the island itself become a landscape for national projection.

The island's divided condition (prison or paradise) is nowhere remarked on in "Providence Display'd," the original pamphlet account of Selkirk's isolation (which is largely reproduced in Woodes Rogers's account); nor is it given much attention in the other contemporary accounts—Dampier's account suggests something of the island paradise but gives no hint of its prison identity. When Steele devoted an issue of *The Englishman* to Selkirk, he introduced the transformative moment when captivity is turned to deliverance by the mediation of religious conversion:

> He grew dejected, languid, and melancholy, scarce able to refrain from doing himself Violence, till by Degrees, by the Force of Reason, and Frequent reading of the Scriptures, and turning his Thoughts upon the Study of Navigation, after the Space of eighteen Months, he grew thoroughly reconciled to his Condition. When he had made this Conquest, the Vigour of his Health, Disengagement from the World, a constant, chearful, serene Sky, and a temperate Air, made his Life one continual Feast, and his Being much more joyful than it had before been irksome. (236–37)

Steele's account may actually be closer to Richetti's characterization than is Defoe's, for in *Robinson Crusoe* the jaunty expression "my reign or my captivity, what you please" does not indicate a complete liberation from his island prison; instead, Crusoe continues to swing between the poles of terror and omnipotence. Certainly, however, in the aftermath of Crusoe's novel, the island of Juan Fernández comes to be identified through this bifurcated lens of prison/

paradise. In the middle of the eighteenth century, as Captain Anson wandered the South Pacific, the island's double identity is suggested in his narrative. Lost, with his men dying of scurvy, Anson desperately retraces his course, looking for land, and finally finds Juan Fernández, where they make shore. The island is their salvation, but one that arrives so late that half of his five hundred men perish from disease before he is able to resume his voyage. While the captain is looking for the island, a cabin boy is swept overboard and abandoned at sea to die in the storm-tossed waves of the Pacific; famously, this victim becomes the central figure in Cowper's haunting poem "The Castaway," which pursues the same vein of sublime terror of abandonment that *Robinson Crusoe* mines. Moreover, by the nineteenth century, the island quite literally becomes a prison, and the caves that sheltered Selkirk are converted to housing prisoners of the Chilean government.

Yet, even through this stage in its history, the island also continues its reputation as "an island paradise." Today, that double identity is strongly in evidence. As "Robinson Crusoe Islands," the three islands—Robinson Crusoe (where Selkirk was abandoned), Santa Clara (a very small island separated from Robinson Crusoe by an inlet and designated "Goat Island" on Captain Anson's map), and Selkirk Island (which corresponds to Friday's home island in the novel)—constitute an important part of the Chilean tourist industry, although so far they do not seem to have caught on as much as the government would hope. Nonetheless, contemporary references to the islands almost invariably include some allusion to their status as "island paradises," an identity conferred upon them since the publication of Anson's *A voyage round the World*":

> Some particular spots occurred in these vallies, where the shade and fragrance
> of the contiguous woods, the loftiness of the overhanging rocks, and the trans-
> parency and frequent falls of the neighboring streams, presented scenes of such
> elegance and dignity, as would perhaps with difficulty be rivalled in any other part
> of the globe. It is in this place, perhaps, that the simple productions of unassisted
> nature may be said to excell all the fictitious descriptions of the most animated
> imagination.[7]

Johnson's *Dictionary* offers us a useful reminder of the twinned associations of wildness that the Juan Fernández Islands rather conveniently embody. "Feral" Johnson defines as "funeral; mournful"—the sense those islands would have conveyed when Anson and his debilitated crew struggled to shore, as surely as it did to Crusoe when he came to mourn his desolate condition: "I had a dismal Prospect of my Condition, for as I was not cast away upon that Island without being driven . . . some Hundreds of Leagues out of the ordinary Course of the Trade of Mankind, I had great Reason to consider it as a Determination of Heaven that in this desolate Place, and in this desolate Manner I should end my life" (46–47). "Feracity," on the other hand, Johnson defines as "fruitful-ness, fertility"—the sense that dominates accounts of the islands in Rogers's and Selkirk's accounts, as well as the latter days of Crusoe's stay on his island. My point here is not to contend against those voices (Grove, Seidel, Hunter, etc.) who have quarreled with the explicit identification of Crusoe's Caribbean island with Selkirk's South Pacific Island; rather, it is to attend to how certain characteristics attach equally to the real and the fictive locations as semiotic markers of "wildness." The wildness of the island location metonymically asso-ciated with Crusoe is reinforced by his (and the islands') metonymic identi-fication with goats.

Not only are goats the markers of an ecological imperialism blind to its own depredations; they also mark in this novel the stark antithesis of wild and do-mestic, savage and tame. Indeed, one of the important ways in which Crusoe does not degenerate is that he exercises his dominion over the brute creation of his island, taming the wild goats, who in their turn fulfill their role as do-mesticated flock. Of course, when Crusoe arrives on the island it is not goats but more predatory beasts that his imagination conjures up. Throughout his twenty-eight years on the island, goats are as wild as it gets. Before he reaches the island—in Africa—and again after he leaves the island—in Europe—Crusoe encounters wild carnivores as well as herbivores. The contrast between the island's goats and the lions, leopards, bears, and wolves that Crusoe en-counters is striking.[8] The goats that populated Selkirk's island refuge, and which Crusoe domesticates, represented in eighteenth-century natural history a limi-nal creature between wild and tame, savage and domestic. In an emerging dis-course of species, the identity of goats was as vexed as the identity of the wild man—perhaps a degenerated production of an originally domestic species; perhaps a primitive original from which, by cultivation, the domestic sheep had been improved; perhaps a hybrid production, half-wild, half-domesticated. Goats were, for the eighteenth-century European, something of a puzzle, bor-der creatures whose identity was as puzzling in its own way as were those trou-bling orang-outangs. Johnson, again, provides us with a useful indicator of the ordinary, nonscientific understanding of the term; a goat, he tells us, is "a ruminant animal that seems a middle species between deer and sheep." Johnson's brevity neatly articulates the border identity that Buffon enlarges on:

> Though the species of animals are separated from each other by an interval which nature cannot overleap, yet some species approach so near to others, and their mutual relations are so numerous, that space is only left for a bare line of distinction. When we compare these neighboring species, and consider them in relation to ourselves, some appear to hold the first rank for utility, and others seem to be only auxiliary species, which might in many respects supply the place of the first. Thus the ass might nearly supply the place of the horse, and the goat that of the sheep. . . . These auxiliary species are more rustic and robust than the principals; the ass and the goat require not near so much attention as the horse and the sheep. They every where find means of subsistence, eating almost indiscriminately the grossest as well as the most delicate plants. They are less affected by the influence of climate, and can better dispense with the aid of man. The less they depend on us, the more they seem to belong to nature; and instead of regarding these subaltern species as degenerated productions of the principal species, instead of considering the ass as a degenerated horse, it would be more consonant with reason to say that the horse is an improved ass; that the sheep is a more delicate kind of goat, which we have trained, raised to greater perfection, and propagated for our own use; and, in general, that the most perfect species, especially among domestic animals, derive their origin from those wild and less perfect kinds which make the nearest approach to the former. (1:347)

Buffon's discussion proceeds from here to address the possibility (which he does not dismiss) of mixed generation: "No intermediate species has been formed between the goat and sheep. The two species are distinct, and still remain at the same distance from each other. No change has been effected by these mixtures; they have given rise to no new or middle race of animals; they have only produced individual differences, which have no influence on the unity of each primitive species, but, on the contrary, confirm the reality of their characteristic and essential distinction" (1:347–48). The discussion that develops, however (one laced with cross-references to horses and mules, and humans and apes), remains undetermined on the critical question of species identity, and experimentation is, in his opinion, called for to resolve the matter:

> In the mean time we wander in darkness, perplexed between probabilities and prejudices, ignorant even of possibilities, and every moment confounding the opinions

9. A woodcut from *Robinson Crusoe* (1719), showing Crusoe
metonymically swallowed up in his goatskin garb.

of men with the operations of nature. Examples are innumerable: but without leaving our subject, we know that the he-goat and ewe, and the ram and she-goat pro-
create together: we have still to learn, however, whether the mules produced by this
commixtures be barren or fruitful. . . . The truth of these facts [that such mules will
be barren], which obscure the real distinction of animals, as well as the theory of
generation, should be either confirmed or destroyed. (1:348)

Shortly before the moment when he recounts the discovery of a solitary
footprint, Crusoe interrupts his narrative to provide a "sketch of [his] figure"
that has become iconic through its numerous illustrations:

I had a great high shapeless Cap, made of a Goat's Skin, with a Flap hanging down
behind . . . I had a short Jacket of Goat-Skin, the Skirts coming down to about the
middle of my Thighs; and a Pair of open-knee'd Breeches of the same, the Breeches
were made of the Skin of an old *He-goat,* whose Hair hung down such a Length on

either Side, that like *Pantaloons* it reach'd to the middle of my Legs; Stockings and Shoes I had none, but had made me a Pair of somethings, . . . of a most barbarous Shape, as indeed were all the rest of my Cloaths. I had on a broad Belt of Goat's-Skin dry'd, which I drew together with two Thongs of the same . . . I had another Belt not so broad, and fasten'd in the same Manner, which hung over my Shoulder; and at the end of it, under my left Arm, hung two Pouches, both made of Goat's-Skin too; in one of which hung my Powder, in the other my Shot . . . and over my Head a great clumsy ugly Goat-Skin Umbrella. . . My beard I had once suffer'd to grow till it was about a Quarter of a Yard long; but as I had both Scissars and Razors sufficient, I had cut it pretty short, except what grew on my upper Lip, which I had trimm'd into a large Pair of Mahometan Whiskers . . . I will not say they were long enough to hang my Hat upon them; but they were of a Length and Shape monstrous enough, and such as in England would have pass'd for frightful. (108–9)

Crusoe's self-portrait has become famous as an icon of the castaway, but it also operates within enlightenment discourse to establish his self-identification as wild, monstrous, degenerated, liminal man. Quite literally, the passage locates Crusoe within the ancient cross-cultural romance tradition that Margaret Doody has commented on as "The Man in Skins."[9] Crusoe describes himself variously as "barbrous," "monstrous," and "frightful." Moreover, those adjectives describe always his hirsuteness; although he trims his whiskers, he does not shave in the European style but rather as "Mahometan." This instance is symptomatic of a larger ambivalent rhythm that we see at work in *Robinson Crusoe,* in which Defoe sets out to present a portrait of man degenerating in solitude, but he then finds it necessary to compromise the vision. Quite literally, Crusoe is swallowed up in the description of his goatskins. He begins his self-portrait with the following words: "Be pleas'd to take a Sketch of my Figure as follows" (108). After devoting several paragraphs to his goatskin wardrobe, he then erases the body within by concluding "as to my Figure, I had so few to observe me, that it was no manner of Consequence; so I say no more to that part" (109).

The novel's concern with cultivation and domestication of the wild leads inevitably to its concerns with the acquisition of language and particularly its relation to systems of power. Defoe's novel begins as his hoped-for experiment in degeneration, but he is unable to allow his Englishman to degenerate. Unlike Peter Serrano, the Moskito Indians, and Alexander Selkirk, Crusoe cannot abandon his written language and thus never loses his civilization or, by extension, his national identity as "a true-born Englishman." For Defoe, such an experiment proves ultimately untellable, and the failure of first-person narration to articulate degeneration prompts the introduction of a second character, Friday. A first-person narration cannot, after all, lapse into the loss of language; on the other hand, Friday's narrative must be mediated by a teller, and Friday is thus reduced to the status of colonized other. Friday must be brought almost immediately to language, but in a dependent relation he is never able to leave (as Gildon commented on the book's publication). Friday's acquisition of language bears some significant parallels to Wallis's system for teaching language to the deaf (as well as to Swift's projectors). For all of these, language is primarily nominative, and the emphasis is on the names of things, without any significant development of relational articulations. Yet, for Crusoe, the function of language is power and its mediation—specifically, the articulation of oaths. *Crusoe* is a Williamite's novel of the absolute dependency of oaths. The psychological verisimilitude of the novel depends on the main character's violation of oaths at the beginning, especially his broken pledges to God. Yet the novel's ultimate resolution—and Crusoe's deliverance—depends on the happy sufficiency of the oaths of Crusoe's colonial subjects, extracted under duress but utterly binding.

Crusoe's language retention may, in part, be attributed to his commitment to language use. When Woodes Rogers described the rescue of Alexander Selkirk, his narrative conformed to the accepted pattern of degeneration in all particulars, including Selkirk's loss of fluency: "At his first coming on board us, he had so much forgot his language, for want of use, that we could scarce understand him, for he seemed to speak his words by halves" (334). By the time Steele recounts the narrative, Selkirk's linguistic ability has been saved by Christianity: "It was his manner to use stated hours and places for exercises of devotion, which he performed aloud, in order to keep up the faculties of speech, and to utter himself with great energy" (339). Crusoe steers a course closer to Steele's Selkirk than to Rogers's, for he retains a remarkably active verbal life for one who is in solitude for over twenty years. After his conversion, Crusoe (like Selkirk) prays aloud: "immediately I kneel'd down and gave God thanks aloud, for my Recovery from my Sickness. . . . I cry'd out aloud, 'Jesus, thou Son of David, Jesus, thou exalted Prince and Saviour, give me Repentance'" (70–71). But clearly Crusoe also keeps his conversational skills alive with the help of his parrot, Poll: "just in such bemoaning Language I had used to talk to him, and teach him; and he had learn'd it so perfectly, that he would sit upon my Finger, and lay his Bill close to my Face, and cry, 'Poor Robin Crusoe, Where are you? Where have you been? How come you here? And such things as I had taught him" (104). In spite of his twenty years alone, Crusoe remains verbally active; if orang-outangs and feral children lack both speech and writing, Crusoe is one castaway who continues both habits of civilization. Crusoe's commitment to speech suggests one type of sociability that blends private domesticity with state politics:

> It would have made a Stoick smile to have seen me and my little Family sit down to Dinner; there was my Majesty the Prince and Lord of the whole Island; I had the lives of all my Subjects at my absolute Command. . . . Then to see how like a King I din'd too all alone, attended by my Servants; Poll, as if he had been my Favourite, was the only Person permitted to talk to me. (108)

But the blending of public and private, political and domestic, is also present in Crusoe's commitment to written language, particularly in the journal that he keeps. A number of readers have commented on various aspects of Crusoe's journal and particularly on the way in which the clearly drawn boundary between retrospective narrative and the immediate present tense of the journal keeps dissolving. Journal writing is a particularly private mode, a style in which the writer may choose to turn inward and explore the interior world of the self or record those elements of the external world that register on a particular psyche. Narrative, by contrast, always presumes an external audience to whom a story is addressed and for whom it is shaped. As others have noted before, Crusoe's shifts in narrative mode allow Defoe to mine both veins: the journal draws the reader in to Crusoe's subjective experience, even as his retrospective narrative shapes and orders those experiences as they are related. The rhetorical pattern, then, of Robinson Crusoe is ultimately social, not solitary. From the very beginning of his stay on the island, the private and solitary mode of journal writing exceeds its bounds and spills over into public narrative. In this respect, Crusoe's experience stands in stark contrast with those of other real castaways.

In April 1992, Christopher McCandless hiked into the wilderness north of Mt. McKinley; in September of that year, his remains were discovered in an abandoned bus. Whether (like his critics) one views McCandless as a naively self-centered youth unprepared for the real challenges posed by the wild, or (like his apologists) one views him as a daring but not foolhardy young man who accidentally poisoned himself just as he was about to return from his solitary excursion, the journal he left behind bears striking similarities to and important departures from the model of Crusoe's journal. In the early days of his solitude the entries of McCandless, like those of Crusoe, swing between mundane particulars of recording food items to more expansive entries in which he draws some significant moral reflection. One such reflection occurs in the margin of a passage in Thoreau's *Walden*. McCandless had recently killed a moose, only to discover that most of the meat spoiled before he could preserve it; commenting on a passage where Thoreau laments that the fish he has caught have not fed him "essentially," McCandless reflects: "It is hard to provide and cook so simple and clean a diet as will not offend the imagination; but this I think is to be fed when we feed the body; they should both sit down at the same table" (qtd. in Krakaeur 167). The line almost quaintly echoes the Thoreau McCandless has been reading, but it also belongs to the genre of Crusoe's reflections. Rhetorically, such a sentence illustrates the peculiar liminal space of journal writing, addressing an audience at once intensely private and anonymously public. When we read such a sentence we simultaneously experience two quite different aesthetics: we are reading someone's thoughts, notes to himself for later consideration; but we are also encountering a vatic utterance that presents itself as maxim, a truism, some transcendent general truth. The importance of this mode to *Robinson Crusoe* is illustrated by the popularity of "The Serious Reflections of Robinson Crusoe," published the same year. It is, however, the castaway narrative itself that famously contains those reflections on how easily satisfied are our true desires. If, however, McCandless's journal follows some of Crusoe's precedents, it also departs from Crusoe's in striking ways. Even from the outset, we realize that McCandless's concern with food seems obsessive by Crusoe's standards. Day after day, virtually nothing commands his attention beyond feeding his body; in contrast, although food is of primary importance to Crusoe, the journal quickly broadens to include what seems by any standards a remarkably rich and active vocational life.

The difference in scope between the journals of McCandless and Crusoe is accentuated when we look at McCandless's final entries. Krakaeur plausibly suggests that McCandless had inadvertently poisoned himself in the last weeks of July; certainly his entry for July 30 indicates his illness and his own belief that it was due to the potato seeds he had eaten: "extremely weak. Fault of pot. seed." In the next week, there is only a single entry ("Aug. 2 Terrible Wind") before he records an important milestone: "Aug. 5 Day 100! MADE IT! But in weakest condition of life. Death looms as a serious threat. Too weak to walk out. Have literally become trapped in the wild.—No Game" (195). Perhaps that last articulation speaks to the seriousness of his plight, or perhaps it records the absence of food. In either case, the journal contains no entries for the next three days.

On the 9th, he shoots at a bear but misses; on the 10th, he sees a caribou but fails to get a shot off; he does, however, kill five squirrels. The next day, he kills and eats a ptarmigan. On the 12th, he drags himself out of the bus to search for berries, leaving a sign describing his distress. For the 13th through the 18th, his journal records nothing more than a mute calendar of the days. Sometime during this week he wrote his final message: "I have had a happy life and thank the Lord. Goodbye and may God bless all!" (199).

In his final, almost celebratory, message McCandless returns to a public rhetoric, speaking now clearly beyond himself to an imagined audience manifestly not present. But in the weeks leading up to that final declaration, the journal records a rhetorical starvation that accompanies his embodied plight. As the horizons of his world contract to the urgent demands of bodily nourishment, the journal similarly contracts to a literally bare-bones recording of lack. In the particularly pathetic aesthetic of such narratives, it is the mute testimony of the final week in which nothing is recorded beyond the passing of empty days that is most moving.

If the fiction of *Robinson Crusoe* pretends to the danger of such starvation, it is a danger manifestly belied by the journal's rhetoric of excess. Where the entries in McCandless's journal seem to forget about an audience "out there," as the journal writer focuses his energy and attention on feeding the private body, Crusoe cannot keep to himself, and his journal famously and repeatedly spills over into retrospective narrative, thereby reminding us insistently of his survival. Although I think both the parallels and departures between the journals of Crusoe and McCandless are worth noting, it may be even more pertinent to consider the case of a Dutch sailor set ashore on Ascension Island in 1725.[10] This anonymous Dutch sailor was set ashore for sodomy ("making use of my fellow-creature to satisfy my desire, whom the Almighty Creator had ordained another sex for"), and his diary records the daily struggle for sustenance from May 5 to mid-October, when it trails away. The journal was found in his tent by sailors who landed on the island the following January.

There are several affinities between this sailor's plight and that of Crusoe. Cast ashore on a barren island populated with goats, he first sets up his tent "on the beach, near a rock," and later shifts his habitation several times, fencing it around with stones and eventually relocating into a cave. He prays repeatedly both for delivery from his miserable condition and in gratitude for those blessings which Providence bestows upon him. He plants a meager crop (peas and calavances), which is devoured by vermin before he can harvest it. He is unable to capture or kill the goats, for they are too fleet for him; and his diet is constrained to turtles and turtle eggs, which (as Crusoe feared) occasion a looseness and flux. He is visited with visions that strike him with the utmost terror during one week in July, where night after night the same apparition comes to him, "conversed with me like a human creature, and touched me so sensibly of the sins of my past life" that he is moved to repentance. For this sailor, however, there is no Providential redemption. Throughout his stay, he is unable to locate a reliable source of fresh water, and his physical condition steadily deteriorates as he searches vainly, digging a well of more than twenty feet at one point. Eventually, he is forced to the extremities of drinking the blood and urine of turtles and, eventually, himself. As in the case of McCandless, the diary, which in its early entries offered to an imagined public audience moral and spiritual reflections (the lengthy memorial of his first vision concludes "I cannot afford paper enough to set down every particular of this unhappy day), in the end narrows to an entirely private record of the failure to sustain the body and trails away into a mute tallying of the final days, where poignancy arises from a profound silence:

> The 4th [Sept.], drank the last of the blood, which was well settled, and a little sour. The 5th, 6th, 7th, and 8th, I lived upon the turtles blood and eggs; but my strength decays so, that it will be impossible I should live long. I resign myself wholly to Providence, being hardly able to kill a turtle. The 9th, 10th, and 11th, I am so much decayed, that I am a perfect skeleton, and cannot write the particulars, my hand shakes so. The 12th, 13th, 14th, 15th, 16th, and 17th, lived as before. I am in a declining condition. The 18th, 19th, 20th, 21st, 22nd, 23rd, 24th, 25th, 26th, 27th, 28th, 29th, 30th. October the 1st, 2nd, 3rd, 4th, 5th, and 6th, all as before.
>
> The 7th, my wood is all gone, so that I am forced to eat raw flesh and salted fowls. I cannot live long, and I hope the Lord will have mercy on my soul. The 8th, drank my own urine, and eat raw flesh.
>
> The 9th, 10th, 11th, 12th, 13th, and 14th, all as before. (207–8)

The terrible mute testimony of that final silent week stands in sharp contrast to the volubility of Crusoe's happy deliverance. In the end, Crusoe's deliverance (however much it may be assigned to the active intervention of Providence) depends heavily on the political efficacy of oaths. Lamb offers a particularly helpful context in which to read this dependence: "In the 'real' South Seas, the larger of the two islands of Juan Fernández provided the focus not only of an imagined staging post for British expeditions, but also a site for mutinies and utopian gambles, where void contracts and pretenses combine to expand the minds of individuals and fill them with dreams of power and plenty" (174). In the ensuing pages, as Lamb's discussion of "void contracts" unfolds, we are confronted with how deeply the history of Juan Fernández was associated with broken vows. For any writer as familiar with this history as Defoe would have been, the mechanism of reliable oath-taking on which Crusoe's deliverance depends would have been miraculous indeed. For a narrative that has been as dominated by soliloquy as *Robinson Crusoe,* the final weeks of Crusoe's captivity comprise a veritable orgy of oath taking. Just as the initial sign-language communication between Crusoe and Friday was preoccupied with negotiating their political relationship, their ultimate deliverance from the island depends on the negotiation of a series of verbal contracts, establishing Crusoe's political sovereignty. After Crusoe and Friday rescue Friday's father and a Spaniard, the island becomes a model polity based on good Lockean principles of contractually limited monarchical authority. Like Defoe's vision of William's authority, the rule of the monarch, however dependent on the oaths of his subjects, is—once those oaths are exercised—supreme: "My island was now peopled, and I thought my self very rich in Subjects; and it was a merry Reflection which I frequently made, How like a King I look'd. First of all, the whole Country was my own meer Property; so that I had an undoubted Right of Dominion. 2dly, My People were perfectly subjected: I was absolute Lord and Lawgiver; they all owed their lives to me, and were ready to lay down their Lives, *if there had been Occasion for it,* for me" (174). The oaths of these subjects bear more than a passing similarity to Defoe's position in *The True-Born Englishman* that the oaths of allegiance at the time of William's accession require complete subjection to the new monarch. But this particular instance of a Restoration settlement is only a prelude to the far more dramatic set of contractual negotiations that will bring about simultaneously Crusoe's deliverance and his establishment of a working colony.

Shortly after the loyal Spaniard departs to recruit sixteen more Spanish subjects (all of whom must first swear their loyalty to Crusoe, a figure whose existence is at the moment unknown to them), Crusoe's island is visited by a set of English mutineers. The ensuing dramatic rescue scenario involves bloodshed, narrowly avoided executions, and clever military stratagems, but it is, in the final analysis, remarkably long on oaths of subjection. Crusoe's first step is to require complete allegiance from those who were the victim of the mutiny; this is easily obtained, since as the Captain says he "would owe his Life to me, and

acknowledge it upon all Occasions as long as he liv'd" (184). Soon two of the
mutineers are admitted into Crusoe's service on the Captain's recommendation
and "their solemnly engaging to live and die with us" (188). The next step is to
capture the two men left behind with the boat; these two are "easily perswaded,
not only to yield, but afterwards to joyn very sincerely with us" (191). Of the remainder, two are quickly killed; the rest surrender, "appear'd very penitent, and
begg'd hard for their lives." From this collection, Crusoe retains five hostages
and assembles the remainder into a boarding party that under the original Captain's leadership kills the leader of the mutiny and retakes the ship. Of the five
hostages, all are left behind to establish a colony and await the return of the
Spaniards, but after the first night, two desperate for their survival swim out to
the ship and beg to be taken in. After "solemn promises of amendment, they
were taken on Board, and were some time after soundly whipp'd and pickl'd;
after which they prov'd very honest and quiet fellows" (200). The return voyage is uneventful.

What I find most ironic in this deliverance is the importance of exchanging
liberty for life in the form of an oath by those who have established a poor basis for credibility. Certainly, it is fortuitous at the very least; and, indeed, the
chain of sustained conversions to Crusoe's cause is even more remarkable than
those defections from the armies of James II that enabled the "glorious revolution" of Defoe's royal patron, William. In fact, for many readers, the sequence
that enables Crusoe and Friday to effectively commandeer an entire ship under
hostile command and arrange their deliverance is a remarkable breach of narrative decorum, one that ushers in the wildly improbable final section of the
novel that seems so at odds with the painstaking detail that lent Crusoe's island
stay its tantalizing air of plausibility. Readers who admire the small touches of
Crusoe's failed pots avert their eyes in order to tolerate the ever-increasing im-
probabilities that accompany Crusoe's rescue and his subsequent return to England. Yet the mechanism of effective oaths, on which so much of Crusoe's rescue depends, runs directly counter to a very early moment in the narrative that
plays a crucial role in earning Crusoe the reader's credibility. When Crusoe first
goes to sea, he is in fear of his life and prays for his deliverance, promising God
that he will return home if he makes it to land. Make it to land, of course, he
does; but his improving condition makes short work of his repentance: "in a
word, as the Sea was returned to its Smoothness of Surface and settled Calm-
ness by the Abatement of that Storm, so the Hurry of my Thoughts being over,
my Fears and Apprehensions of being swallow'd up by the Sea being forgotten,

and the current of my former Desires return'd, I entirely forgot the Vows and Promises that I made in my Distress" (8–9).

This confession of Crusoe's is, I would suggest, pivotal in establishing his credibility. Few readers, indeed, would be those who cannot identify with widespread—perhaps universal—propensity for retracting, when at liberty, the promises made when one's life was threatened. Yet that is, paradoxically, the very mechanism on which Crusoe's salvation ultimately depends, that those mutineers (who, by definition, have already violated one oath) will remain bound by an oath elicited from them under threat of death. Moreover, it seems to me no accident that these diametrically opposed attitudes toward oaths that frame Crusoe's narrative entail quite different initial conditions—a difference that can perhaps best be characterized as the difference between public and private. The oath Crusoe violates at the beginning of the novel is among the most private there is, the promise of prayer; the oaths that underwrite Crusoe's success as the island's "Governour" are explicitly political oaths. Crusoe's betrayal of his private oath renders him empathetic; we tend not only to forgive the lie, but in fact to place our confidence in his narrative. At the novel's conclusion, we swallow the unlikely acquiescence of his newfound subjects as the necessary narrative price for an ending that will enable the fiction's political fantasy. In this respect, *Robinson Crusoe* stands as a warning against non-juring, for the private tribulations brought about by Robinson's betrayal are remedied only by a political mechanism that rests on the fantasy that the subjects' loyalty can be meaningfully extracted by an oath.

The oaths required for Crusoe's deliverance may be necessary, but they are not sufficient, to a happy resolution of the narrative. To that end, Crusoe must undergo a return journey from his island prison-paradise (cultivated into a little England) to his original homeland. That journey is characterized by dangers even more incredibly hyperbolic than any posed by his reformed mutineer rescuers. Crossing the Pyrenees on his return voyage, he is entertained by a comic demonstration of bear hunting by Friday and then almost overcome by an organized attack of several dozen bloodthirsty wolves. Here Defoe loses touch with a twentieth-century reader's understanding of natural history on several counts (though both his comic slow-witted bear and his demonically bloodthirsty wolves have ample correlatives in eighteenth-century natural history). One explanation for this rhetorical excess is that the episode of crossing the Pyrenees functions as a liminal transition between wild and civilization that explicitly echoes the earlier African encounters with lions and leopards involving Xury. Crusoe himself encourages us to note the parallel by remarking that "the Howling of Wolves run much in my Head; and indeed, except the noise I once heard on the Shore of Africa, of which I have said something already, I never heard any thing that filled me with so much Horrour" (214). There Xury, under Crusoe's tutelage, had dispatched the lion in much the way Friday instructs Crusoe on the proper way to kill a bear: "coming close to the Creature, put the Muzzle of the Piece to his Ear, and shot him into the Head again which dispatch'd him quite" (22). That Friday should have experience in the handling of bears and wolves is perhaps even more surprising than that Xury should require Crusoe's instruction. While Crusoe's island had been populated with nothing more ominous than goats, it turns out that Friday's island was home not only to contesting tribes of cannibals but to bears and wolves as well. Famously, of course, Friday remarks, "laughing himself very loud; 'so we kill bear in my country'" (214). Crusoe takes issue with this, not by doubting a sufficient quantity of bears but by pointing out that Friday's people have no firearms—a minor inconvenience that is explained away by the alternative technology of the "great much long arrow" (214). Friday's hunting expertise and experience has already, by this time, been featured in repulsing the first wolf attack: "It was happy for the poor Man, that it was my Man Friday; for he having been us'd to that kind of Creature in his Country, had no Fear upon him; but went close up to him, and shot him as above; whereas any of us, would have fir'd at a farther Distance, and have perhaps either miss'd the Wolf, or endanger'd shooting the Man" (210).

Of course, whether one imagines Friday's island in the Pacific or the Atlantic, no island off the coast of South America has ever been home to any species of wolf or bear. These two predators, however, do share the distinction of being carnivores once native to Crusoe's island—not his adopted homeland, but his native England, though both species had long since been eradicated there, the last wolf apparently being destroyed in the sixteenth century. The wild mountains that form the backdrop for this perilous land crossing enjoyed in Defoe's time a reputation for unusual wildness. Not only were these regions home to the fiercely independent Basque population, but in the year of *Robinson Crusoe*'s publication—1719—they were also the scene of one of the most widely reproduced (though sketchily reported) sightings of feral children. Virtually every discussion of feral children in the eighteenth century alludes to the pair of wild children seen—but not captured—in the Pyrenees that year. Crusoe's final crossing, then, constitutes a figurative translation back through the wild to the civilization he had left behind in his youth. If the prodigal Crusoe, born into civilization, was a wild youth who rejected his heritage to run off into the wild

world, and if his experiences led him to the despair of solitude, which was remedied by first cultivating his island and then populating his dominion, now his
return to his natural habitat of civilization requires one final over-the-top
crossing of the wild border that marks the frontier of European civilization.

The meandering course of this chapter has been indirect, perhaps even dis-
orienting. The island ecology of *Robinson Crusoe* keeps melting and dissolving
as "real" accounts of "real" flora and fauna on "real" islands bleed and dissolve
into "imaginary" accounts of "imaginary" flora and fauna on "imaginary" islands. Crusoe's island keeps switching oceans impossibly, while real accounts,
both prior to and subsequent to the novel, authenticate and validate the particular fantasies of human encounters with a figurative wild environment that are
mobilized by Defoe's narrative. What is being constructed is a "virtual ecology"
that underwrites a particular colonialist ideology, but that virtual ecology is not
being constructed "by Defoe" so much as it is by the interactive fantasy in which
Defoe's narrative is one significant, but not solitary, voice. Moreover, at the level
of the recurrent trope of wildness and liminal border identities, the virtual ecology of *Robinson Crusoe* enables a reading of problematic human identity in the
narrative that undermines the conventional reading of *Crusoe* as a heroic novel
of the triumph of "economic individualism." This is not to say that the novel
does not assert such a doctrine—I continue to think that it does (notwithstanding those who see Defoe undercutting Crusoe's claims to sovereignty); but
rather that even as it asserts the stabilizing doctrine of the triumph of economic
man, it also (inadvertently, as it were) compromises its own doctrine by calling
into question the very wild/civilized dualism it seeks to establish in a clear economic relation. The problematic status of human identity within this virtual
ecology seeks authorization in a traditional source for both religious and political sovereignty—language. Crusoe's language retention in his desolate condition, as well as his mobilization of his environment to that end (Bibles, journals,
parrots, etc.), marks his failure to degenerate, and when he is confronted with
wild (i.e., degenerate) man Friday, his language instruction not only redeems
Friday by making (i.e., constructing) him human, but it does so in a way that
authorizes Crusoe's sovereignty—a sovereignty that is subsequently testified to
via the mediation of oaths of allegiance facilitating Crusoe's deliverance. In such
a reading, language is the defining sign of humanity and simultaneously the
mechanism of deliverance and of imperialism. This reading of language *within*
the novel, however, also focuses attention on how that language operates re-
cursively as the technology *of* the novel. Those readers who come to share an

imagined community discover within the virtual ecology of the narrative a particular narrative construction of the "human," in which such identity is troped by a colonialist power relation between wild and civilized that naturalizes such a relation largely by virtue of the very technology whereby the reader enters the virtual.

Narratives about Peter tended to center on the trope of abandoned innocence and how his exclusion from language left him trapped in a passionate interiority that forever exiled him from rational society. Crusoe's narrative, instead, deploys the trope of the prodigal's exile and return, a return that requires first his acts of cultivation and then his ability to deploy language in the service of a rational sociability and political government. The next chapter considers the travels and trials of another castaway, whose relation to language and passion conforms to neither of these models, and whose political reflections move in quite different directions. Before proceeding there immediately, however, it may be helpful to step back and review where we have been. Our "nonmodern" insistence that the wild man is not safely "other" than the citizen—but is instead one of those troubling, necessary hybrids in part constitutive of an emergent public sphere—has required us to shuttle back and forth between high and low culture, bourgeois and plebian spaces, the savage and the civilized. Following his peregrinations allows us to contribute to a mapping of "how certain groups came to be excluded from the ranks of the civilized" (Mirzoeff 78). And yet, in organizing each of the foregoing chapters, I have tried to foreground the range of wild alternatives to the citizen of the public sphere by emphasizing in each chapter a different aspect of what constitutes this wild "other." If we think again of the grid I have loosely adapted from Greimas, we might locate the contents of the foregoing chapters as follows:

Social/Passionate	*Social/Rational*
(Tea-drinking, cane-wielding chimps of chapter 1) Traveling from the New World to the Royal Society via the fair booth	(Fellow of the Royal Society, quality and gentry at court, European civilization)

Solitary/Passionate	*Solitary/Rational*
(Peter the wild youth of chapter 2) Traveling from the wilds of the Black Forest to court	(Castaways, real and fictitious, of chapter 3) Traveling from the wild island back to civilization

In the chapters that follow, the movement and oscillation across these boundaries and frontiers may grow more rapid and complex, and the focus in some respects reverses itself, for we may consider each of the next three chapters as following representatives of the public sphere on their journeys away from civilization to encounter those wild men, who in some respects complete their construction of the human. In various ways, the comforting illusion of relational separation that is still maintained, however tenuously, in the grid above becomes increasingly difficult to maintain as the traffic between these environs accelerates. Accompanying that process is an intensification of the overlapping of discourses of nation and species, as a particular model of distinctly British liberty comes under stress.

4

Unimaginable Communities

in which a castaway makes
several voyages and encounters
a variety of pygmies, dwarfs,
apes, and orangs

Apes, feral children, and castaways are each a kind of wild man, but no wild man has left a more lasting literary impression than those Yahoos Gulliver encounters in his final voyage. Indeed, it is impossible to continue our consideration of the wild man in the public sphere without turning our attention not only to those Yahoos encountered by Gulliver but also to the remarkable alacrity with which they permeate the public sphere as soon as they are conjured up by Swift's narrative. Few books have entered as entirely or as immediately into the discursive space of public opinion as has *Gulliver's Travels*, and no single aspect of that book has had a more dramatic or lasting impact on public opinion than the troubling kinship between Gulliver and his "fellow Yahoos." More than any other single feature, this has been seen as the success of Swift's design to "vex the world, rather than divert it."

When Swift arrived in England in the spring of 1726, he was at the peak of his political celebrity. The £300 bounty offered for the identity of the Drapier had lapsed the previous spring, and in the session of Parliament that fall, the patent for Wood's halfpence had been repealed. As an exemplary case of how letters and literature can operate within the public sphere to mobilize public opinion as a viable opposition to state authority, one could not offer a better model. As "the Copper-farthing Dean," his movements were now the topic of newspaper and coffeehouse discussion. Arriving in London in mid-March, he dined with Walpole sometime before April 16 (when he first saw the wild youth), and through the intercession of the Earl of Peterborough, he arranged a private meeting with the prime minister for the morning of Wednesday, April 27. Whatever hopes may have existed on either side for some accommodation between these political opponents, Swift's letter to Peterborough the following day (in which he lays out those Irish concerns that he had attempted to present to Walpole) makes it clear that this meeting put an end to all such hopes: "I failed very much in my design; for, I saw, he had conceived opinions from the examples and practices of the present and some former governors, which I could not reconcile to the notions I had of liberty, a possession always understood by the *British* nation to be the inheritance of a human creature" (*Correspondence* 3:132).

Swift's characterization of the meeting in his letter to Peterborough is as significant as the meeting itself. The rise of a sustained literary opposition to the Walpole administration during the summer of 1726 may be seen as properly beginning with the opposition to Wood's halfpence in Ireland and should be expanded to include the Scriblerian pamphlets occasioned by Peter's arrival that appeared in the weeks immediately following Swift's meeting with Walpole.[1] Equally important for the purposes of this chapter is Swift's characterization to the Whig Lord Peterborough of the grounds on which the Tory dean distinguishes himself from the Whig prime minister. The key term is, of course, "liberty"; and in Swift's rhetoric it is here explicitly deployed to trade on a particular construction of British nationalism that enables a traffic between the discourses of nation and species. That traffic provides the focus for the ensuing discussion of *Gulliver's Travels*. The paradox here is a delicate one that certainly could not be sustained indefinitely; yet it operated with a remarkable force from the time of the Civil War at least until the American war of independence, and with some convenient modifications it aided considerably in underwriting nineteenth-century British imperialism. Priding itself on its identity as a nation of liberty, in contradistinction to its European neighbors in France and Spain, Britain claims uniquely to value the notion of "liberty" as an inalienable human right: thus what is claimed to be common to peoples everywhere is at the same moment denominated a property of the British.

In the following consideration of how the discourses of nation and species engage one another in *Gulliver's Travels,* I want to subject Terry Castle's famous "Why the Houyhnhnms Don't Write" to two complementary revisions: in one version, we may think about "why the Yahoos don't speak," and by doing so, attend to how the voyage foregrounds an emerging discourse of speciation. Castle, who posed her query when deconstruction was new, answered herself by deciding that the Houyhnhnms don't write because Swift is a graphophobe, and so are his Houyhnhnms. What if, however, we approach Castle's question from the other end: "what follows from the fact that the Houyhnhnms don't write?" In these days, the corollary answer must be that if they do not write, they cannot participate in print capitalism, and hence, following Benedict Anderson, they cannot constitute for themselves a national identity. These are, in one respect, playful word games, but I believe that they also enable a serious point to be raised about language, writing, and national identity in *Gulliver's Travels.* In his important contribution to the study of the origins of national identity, Anderson articulates a crucial triple role performed by print capitalism:

> These print-languages laid the bases for national consciousness in three distinct ways. First and foremost, they created unified fields of exchange and communication below Latin and above the spoken vernaculars. . . . Second, print-capitalism gave a new fixity to language, which in the long run helped to build that image of antiquity so central to the subjective idea of the nation. . . . Third, print-capitalism created languages-of-power of a kind different from the older administrative vernaculars. Certain dialects inevitably were "closer" to each print-language and dominated their final forms. (44–45)

As Anderson unfolds these three roles, print language created the possibility of imagining a shared sense of community across space that did not require membership in an international elite of clerics and scholars (the community where Latin was the common tongue), enabling a notion of shared identity relatively looser in class associations. This identity is marked by a distinction from those of neighboring communities where a different language is spoken. At the same time, print language enabled the collective imagining of a shared identity backward in time with earlier generations, enabling (and requiring) a myth of historical continuity. Even as these constructs of shared identity were coming into being, they were also creating new hierarchies that would identify access to power with linguistic features.

One may observe that Anderson's tripled formation nicely describes the mechanism of the Drapier's rhetorical success in fashioning a language of national opposition that remains widely accessible while rising above common vernacular; at the same time, the Drapier repeatedly emphasizes the bond that unites loyal subjects to their earlier ancestors by hammering away at the historical precedents that limit the royal prerogative; finally, some of the most successful rhetorical flourishes are achieved by using the language of Wood as a means to undermine his pretensions to exert royal authority. After developing these themes through the first three letters, the fourth letter of the Drapier (which earned a bounty on the head of the author) culminates in an ironic *tour de force* in which Swift manipulates those linguistic features of power to which Anderson alludes in such a way as simultaneously to intertwine the identities of Wood and Walpole, while at the same time sinking both beneath the honorable resistance of loyal Irish subjects:

> In another printed paper of [Wood's] contriving, it is roundly expressed, that Mr. Walpole will cram his Brass down our throats. Sometimes it is given out, that we must either take these Half-pence or eat our brogues. And in another News-Letter, but of Yesterday, we read, that the same great Man hath sworn to make us swallow his Coin in Fire-Balls. . . .
>
> What vile Words are these to put into the Mouth of a great Counsellor, in high Trust with his Majesty, and looked upon as a Prime Minister? If Mr. Wood hath no better a Manner of representing his Patrons; when I come to be a Great Man, he shall never be suffered to attend at my Levee. This is not the Style of a Great Minister; it savours too much of the Kettle and the Furnace; and came entirely out of Wood's Forge. (315)

The explicitly political occasion for the *Drapier's Letters* mark that text as particularly opportune for considerations of public sphere discourse. This is, indeed, the principal reason that criticism, while long admiring Swift's rhetorical control and his satiric touches, has left the *Drapier's Letters* on the periphery of the literary canon; this text is too avowedly concerned with public discourse, political resistance, and social action to meet even relaxed belletristic standards. *Gulliver's Travels,* whose composition was interrupted by Wood's halfpence, has always enjoyed a more complex reputation as working simultaneously in the topical arena of public discourse and the timeless arena of imaginative creation. The linguistic features of print capitalism that Anderson identifies, and that can be seen so readily in Swift's avowedly political writing, echo in a more minor key in *Gulliver's Travels.* The voyage to Lilliput has long been recognized as most closely concerned with events that shadow the contemporary politics of Europe, and so it is perhaps not surprising to find correlations between Anderson's theory of the emergence of national identity and the role of print language in Lilliput. Gulliver originally attempts to communicate with the Lilliputians in a European tongue: "I spoke to them in as many languages as I had the least smattering of, which were High and Low Dutch, Latin, French, Spanish, Italian, and Lingua Franca, but all to no purpose" (*Prose* 11:31). In spite of this initial failure, Gulliver's own remarkable felicity in mastering new languages allows him to acquire enough Lilliputian to be understood in a very few weeks. The language Gulliver masters is, like the various European tongues, a significant marker in distinguishing Lilliputian and Blefescudian identities: "It is to be observed that these [Blefescudian] Ambassadors spoke to me by an Interpreter; the Languages of both Empires differing as much from each other as any two in Europe, and each Nation priding itself upon the Antiquity, Beauty, and Energy of their own Tongues, with an avowed Contempt for that of their Neighbor" (11:55). This observation of Gulliver's rather neatly encapsulates Anderson's argument with respect to both linguistic pride in national difference and historical continuity, but it may be worth noting that Gulliver goes on to remark how "from the great Intercourse of Trade and Commerce between both Realms; from the continual Reception of Exiles, which is mutual among them; and from the custom in each Empire to send their young Nobility and richer Gentry to the other, . . . there are few Peers of Distinction, or Merchants, or Seamen, who dwell in the Maritime Parts, but what can hold Conversation in both Tongues" (11:55). Like so much else in Lilliput and Blefescu, language seems to follow a European model in enabling the emergence of national identities, and Gulliver's account seems to lay stress on the correlation between different languages and national difference.

In the second voyage, however, Gulliver's characterization of Brobdingnagian language emphasizes rather a different component, but one also addressed by Anderson's formulation. Unlike the florid style of the Lilliputians (and the English), Brobdingnagian style follows a simple Swiftian precept ("proper words in proper places"): "clear, masculine and smooth, but not florid; for they avoid nothing more than multiplying unnecessary Words, or using various Expressions" (11:137). They are economical, not only with words, but with books themselves—with the king's library numbering no more than a thousand volumes, one cannot imagine a flourishing Grub Street industry. However few books they possess, their literature does provide the sort of historical continuity that Anderson remarks upon, for "they have had the Art of Printing, as well as the Chinese, Time out of Mind" (11:136). If print capitalism in Brobdingnag has no rival nation against which to define itself, it does offer a source of historically grounded national identity—and it also offers a normative dialect of power against which vernaculars can be—and are—measured. When the king first interviews Gulliver, he is impressed to receive "rational Answers, no otherwise defective than by Foreign Accent, and an imperfect Knowledge in the Language; with some rustick Phrases which I had learned at the Farmer's House, and did not suit the polite Style of a Court" (11:103).

Castle suggests a reading of Gulliver's fourth voyage that identifies the logocentric myth of the fall from oral innocence into literary sin at its narrative heart. She contrasts the Houyhnhnms' otherwise inexplicable lack of letters with the Yahoos' scribbling potential: "their enthusiastic and decorative shit-smearing seem, anthropologically speaking, on the way to the discovery of a script" (393). Perhaps. But I think Castle grants too quickly the leap from scatological dabbling to literature. The Yahoos are at first appearance considerably distinct from the human race; only as the narrative progresses does Gulliver come to see an "exact" resemblance between himself and Yahoos, in accordance with his Houyhnhnm master's observations. What continues to distinguish Gulliver from the Yahoos is his facility with languages—the Houyhnhnm decision to send Gulliver into exile turns on their interpreting this as a difference of degree and not of kind. Yahoos may lack language but, like Tyson's pygmy, not the capacity for speech, for they are frequently described in terms of their "roaring" (11:224), "lamenting" (11:261), "groaning" (11:263), "squalling" (11:265), "horrible Howlings" (11:272), and in a word they amount to "the most filthy, noisome . . . Animal which Nature ever produced" (11:271). In this respect they reproduce qualities identified with recently discovered nonhuman primates who physically resemble humans, even insofar as their vocal capacity, yet who are distinguished from humans primarily on the grounds that while they might possess the physical capacity for speech, they do not possess the moral capacity for speech. As natural philosophy insisted that such a distinction was a difference of kind, not merely degree, the Houyhnhnms' wisdom here poses a difficult dilemma for those who would contend Swift idealizes their wisdom: hard school interpretations would place Swift in the camp of late-twentieth-century radical ethologists, denying a species difference between human and nonhuman primates.

Linnaeus, of course, had not yet published his first attempt at a *General System of Nature* when Swift was writing *Gulliver's Travels*. The leading taxonomy of the time was John Ray's *Synopsis Methodica Animalium Quadrapedum*. Man nowhere appears in that volume; when Linnaeus included man among the quadrupeds in 1735, the backlash was sufficiently strong that he reorganized the category to "mammal" on the grounds that although we may dispute whether we walk on two legs or four, all must concede that we are nursed as infants. Privately, Linnaeus continued to maintain that bipedalism was an acquired cultural trait rather than an innate natural condition. Without man, foremost in Ray's *Synopsis* is the horse, identified in superlatives: "the strongest, swiftest, comeliest, and most docile Animal" (62). Throughout the fourth voyage Swift seems to have one eye on Ray; in conversation with his *Houyhnhnm* master, Gulliver reports "that the *Houyhnhnms* among us, whom we called *Horses*, were the most generous and comely Animal we had; that they excelled in Strength and Swiftness" (11:241). Similarly, descriptions of *Houyhnhnms* echo natural philosophy's descriptions of horses: the first mare Gulliver meets is "very comely" (11:229); "Strength is chiefly valued in the Male, and Comeliness in the Female; not upon the Account of Love, but to preserve the Race from degenerating: For, where a Female happens to excel in Strength, a Consort is chosen with regard to Comeliness" (11:268–69); they "train up their Youth to Strength, Speed, and Hardiness" (11:269); "I admired the Strength, Comeliness and Speed of the Inhabitants" (11:278). It is, of course, not surprising that *Houyhnhnms* are described in the terms contemporary science used to describe horses. In a book that emphasizes perspectivalism as much as this one, however, it is worth attending to how the "naturalizing" effect of such descriptions helps enable a crucial slippage in our reading of the categories of natural history so central to the drama of the fourth voyage.

For just as Swift deploys the language of natural philosophy in his descriptions of horses and Houyhnhnms, so he borrows from natural philosophy in his descriptions of humans and Yahoos. Certainly, central to these descriptions are the terms used to describe orang-outang, wild men, and feral children. Perhaps as importantly, however, is the way these descriptive categories are themselves framed by an equine perspective: repeatedly, descriptions of Gulliver and the Yahoos are filtered through the lens of Ray's foremost quadruped, the horse. Particularly relevant here is the term "docillimum." Ray's description of the horse consists entirely of superlatives; none of those superlatives is more important than this last-mentioned term, which defines the horse as the most domesticated animal. It is the ranking of "most docile," in its etymological sense of "most easily taught or trained" that operates most vividly in book 4. Natural philosophy did not accord a particularly high rank to the horse for intelligence, per se, but did accord it highest honors for being easily taught. One of the ironies of book 4 hinges on the ease with which Gulliver is taught (more accurately, trained) by Houyhnhnms, while the Houyhnhnms themselves remain stubbornly resistant to learning from Gulliver anything that contradicts what they already "know." Frequently in the fourth voyage, human and Yahoo reason is questioned in terms of the equine/Houyhnhnm category of "docillimum."

When the Houyhnhnms are first introduced to Gulliver, they are struck by this intellectual difference that they discern between him and the Yahoos, whom they think he resembles. When Gulliver apes their speech (without comprehension), the Houyhnhnms "appeared amazed at [his] Capacity" (11:227). His successful efforts to learn their language quickly bring them to see him "as a Prodigy, that a brute Animal should discover such Marks of a Rational Creature" (11:234). Thus, even as Gulliver's descriptions of Yahoos point us toward those fascinating creatures that Linnaeus teaches us to label "nonhuman primates," the Houyhnhnm descriptions of Gulliver come more and more to resemble European descriptions of wild men—Gulliver is remarkable to the Houyhnhnms in much the same way that Peter was remarkable to the court of George I. Moreover, the Houyhnhnms clearly try to frame him in their own system of natural philosophy, only to be troubled by this quality. For in Houyhnhnm natural philosophy, the Yahoo is not so much an ape or orangoutang, but is instead a "nonhorse": Gulliver "must be a Yahoo, but my Teachableness, Civility and Cleanliness astonished him; which were qualities altogether so opposite to those animals" (11:234). In time, of course, Gulliver's prodigious docility enables him to learn here—as he does everywhere—not only the master's language but his conceptual scheme as well: "By what I could discover, the *Yahoos* appear to be the most unteachable of all Animals, their Capacities never reaching higher than to draw or carry Burthens" (11:266).

Some have contended that in book 4, Gulliver is confronted with a blinding revelation (like the denizens of Plato's cave when they venture into the light), and that the perfect but unattainable virtues of the Houyhnhnms unhinge his sanity. I think they are wrong. Gulliver does undergo a conversion experience in his fourth voyage, I would argue, and one that renders him unfit for human society, but less because of Houyhnhnm teaching than because of Yahoo action. Before this conversion experience, Gulliver's descriptions of the Yahoos bear a striking affinity to contemporary travelers' accounts of other primates, alien to his own species identity; after his conversion, Gulliver adopts a Houyhnhnm doctrine of speciation in which all humans are Yahoos. The species boundary that was as important to Tyson as to Buffon disappears for Gulliver. Even as Tyson had presented his anatomy of "a pygmy" in explicit opposition to the theory of "mixed generation," his text had insisted on the reproduction of such "impossible" species-confounding narratives. And the remarkable residual persistence of such narratives extended deep into the eighteenth century, including (among others) one of Linnaeus's most trusted correspondents, the Swedish traveler Keoping, who claimed to have seen "a child of an Oran Outan by a woman" (Burnett 133 n.). While such stories operated primarily anecdotally, they were so frequently cited as to be almost ubiquitous. It is difficult to encounter a discussion of primate speciation conducted by an Enlightenment philosopher that does not retail at least one narrative of hybridous reproduction, and although a certain amount of repetition is encountered, it is surprising how many variations of this single story are encountered. Londa Schiebinger has noted that although there are multiple variants of this story, one motif seems paradigmatic: "In these accounts it is invariably the male ape who forced himself on the human female. To my knowledge there was not one account in this period of a female ape taking a man or even of intercourse between a female ape and a male human" (95).

Although Schiebinger is right to stress the near ubiquity of the gendered configuration of the hybrid coupling, a rule-proving exception may be found in this incident that forms the crucial moment of self-identification in *Gulliver's Travels*. Here Gulliver, who has until this moment strenuously denied any connection to the bestial Yahoos, tells us he was bathing in a river when "a young female Yahoo . . . inflamed by desire . . . came running with all speed and leaped into the water within five yards of the place where I bathed. . . . She embraced me after a most fulsome manner" (11:250). This event is a "mortification" to Gulliver, "for now I could no longer deny that I was a real Yahoo in every limb and feature since the females had a natural propensity to me as one of their own species" (11:267).[2] From the text's opening pun on "masturbation," Gulliver's alienation from his fellow humans has in part been signaled through sexual innuendo, a point not lost on his friend Alexander Pope, whose minor epistle on the occasion of the publication of *Gulliver's Travels* ("Mary Gulliver to Capt. Lemuel Gulliver") responds in kind: "*Where sleeps my* Gulliver? *O tell me where?* / The Neighbors answer, *With the Sorrel Mare*" (486–88).[3] Gulliver's mistaken epiphany returns with full force at the conclusion of his narrative when he articulates most clearly his self-deluded state: "yet my Memory and Imaginations were perpetually filled with the Virtues and Ideas of those exalted

Houyhnhnms. And when I began to consider, that by copulating with one of the Yahoo-Species, I had become a Parent of more; it struck me with the utmost Shame, Confusion, and Horror" (11:289).

Although it is often remarked that the obsession with Houyhnhnm virtues repeats a common eighteenth-century formula for madness (the "perpetual fixation" of the faculties of "memory" and "imagination"), it goes largely unremarked that that formula is directly linked to Gulliver's subsequent confusion of embodied identities. Yet Gulliver's confusion over his own species identity echoes in a darkly comic vein the very confusion present in Tyson's *Anatomy.* On the one hand, Tyson insisted that the very test of species identity was reproductive potential, and so the creature he anatomized could not be a product of "mixed generation"; yet even as he made that claim, he continued to reproduce species-confounding stories of human-ape reproduction. Gulliver, in Houyhnhnmland, distinguishes himself from the bestial Yahoos, until the moment when he becomes the object of Yahoo sexual desire; that moment overthrows his prior commitment to a species barrier separating human and Yahoo, and he conflates the two. On his return to England, the material evidence of his human identity (i.e., his reproductive breeding potential with the human species) serves not to return him to a sense of his own human identity but instead convinces him of the Yahoo identity of all humans, at precisely the same moment that he most clearly articulates his delusive obsession with Houyhnhnm virtue.

Better known than the species confounding assault in Gulliver's fourth voyage is a related moment in the second voyage. Here in an anticipation of King Kong, Gulliver in Brobdingnag (where everything is twelve times the scale we are accustomed to) is seized by an ape and carried, like Fay Wray, to the top of a tall building. Before he is rescued, he must suffer the trauma of being force-fed by the maternal male primate: "he took me up in his right Fore-foot, and held me as a Nurse does a Child she is going to suckle; just as I have seen the same Sort of Creature do with a Kitten in *Europe*" (11:122). Although this scene has provided considerable material for biographical and psychoanalytic critics (Swift, a posthumous child, had been abducted by his nursemaid while an infant), Dennis Todd notes that Gulliver's allusion refers to an interspecies drama staged as public spectacle that Swift is likely to have witnessed in London. Ned Ward's *London Spy* contains a description of the show alluded to; in our own time, a comparable spectacle is the children's picture book of *Koko's Kitten.*[4] Francine Patterson has been faulted for anthropomorphizing Koko, and Charis

Cussins's story "Confessions of a Bioterrorist" slyly alludes to Koko's reproductive difficulties aping those of her affluent human alter egos (201). Swift's narrative, with its ironic overtones, conceals as much as it reveals about Swift's own attitude: is Gulliver a helpless human in the hands of a giant beast, or does the narrative remind us of a kinship between nurturer and nurtured, desired and desiring? Whatever Swift's attitude, the display Ned Ward described operates in a visual economy exactly the same as the one Francine Patterson promotes through *Koko's Kitten:* viewers are fascinated by the mix of similarity and difference in another primate's appearance, especially as that creature's behavior seems to reproduce our "nature."

In one very important sense, of course, the fair-booth exhibit described by Ned Ward highlights the tension between anatomist and naturalist conceptions of "nonhuman primates": the spectacle is that the ape apes not only a human form but a human nature as well. When, in Swift's version, Gulliver is introduced into the role played by a kitten, species identities cross boundaries in unsettling ways. Recall that the common explanation for Peter's survival in the forests of Hanover depended on a universalized maternal instinct that crossed species barriers; such an explanation could rationalize the behavior of Gulliver's monkey and Ned Ward's ape by subsuming "human" nature to a transcendent "maternal" nature. But to do so requires denigrating Gulliver's identity to that of the helpless kitten as the generically animal "pseudo-infant." As Dennis Todd has observed, this is the crucial dissonance that animates what he terms the "internal economy" of monster exhibits and of *Gulliver's Travels;* wherever Gulliver travels, he is always both a monster (or "*lusus naturae*") and a good Baconian viewer of monsters.[5]

It is worth remarking that virtually all critical discussion of Gulliver's fourth voyage from Swift's day to the present proceeds from a consideration of Yahoo and human identities as they are represented by Gulliver relative to one another after his conversion, and virtually no attention is paid to Gulliver's initial description of the Yahoos. Thus critical discussion begins from the presumption that Yahoo identity is *in some way* human, whereas Gulliver's initial perception is directly antithetical to this:

> At last I beheld several Animals in a Field, and one or two of the same Kind sitting in Trees. . . . Their Heads and Breasts were covered with a thick Hair, some frizzled and others lank; they had Beards like Goats, and a Long Ridge of Hair down their Backs, and the fore Parts of their Legs and Feet; but the rest of their Bodies were

bare so that I might see their Skins, which were of a brown Buff Colour. They had no Tails, nor any Hair at all on their Buttocks, except about the *Anus.* (11:223)

Such a description, emphasizing the animality of the Yahoos, codes the creatures as animal—and hence, nonhuman, for in spite of Aristotelian definitions of "rational animal," we still inherit a Christian tradition distinguishing humans from the rest of the "brute creation," a tradition much more forcefully in place when Swift wrote. This description, for instance, would fit comfortably alongside Gauthier Schoutten's description of orang-outangs: "nearly of the same figure and size with men, only their back and reins are covered with hair, though there is no hair on the fore part of their bodies" (in Buffon, 47). Indeed, Gulliver's first encounter with a "herd" of Yahoos, "howling and making odious faces," culminates with "several of this cursed Brood getting hold of the Branches behind, leapt up into the Tree, from whence they began to discharge their Excrements on my head" (11:224). Few readers today, or in Swift's time, are prepared to identify Yahoos with humans at this point, but indeed another candidate may very well present itself in contemporary descriptions of recently discovered species of New World monkey known today as howlers. Linnaeus termed the red-haired howler "seniculus" (from "old man of the woods") and the black-haired howler "belzebul" (for the pandemonium it raised). Marcgrave was among the first to describe the fierce cries and noxious behavior of this creature, and his description was endorsed by Dampier: "When we approached they all assembled together, uttered loud and frightful cries, and threw at us dried branches which they broke off from the trees. Some of them voided their excrements in their hands, and threw them at our heads" (in Buffon, 70).

In his initial description, Gulliver notes that "they climbed high Trees, as nimbly as a Squirrel, for they had strong extended Claws before and behind, terminating in sharp Points, and hooked" (11:223). Later, he adds the observation that "they are prodigiously nimble from infancy" (265); these characterizations are not only frequently present in descriptions of monkeys and orang-outangs, but constitute one of the staples of descriptions of feral children as well. Peter, for instance, who was represented in the triptych clambering through trees is described in one pamphlet as one who "could clamber and climb up the trees with an agility scarce to be conceived" (*Enquiry* 2). News accounts likened him "to a squirrel" at the time of his capture, as did accounts of Mlle. Memmie Le Blanc, when she was taken in the forest of Soigny.[6]

Yahoos, then, based on Gulliver's initial description, belong to that enormously vexing category of "pre-primate primatology" that includes such quasi-humans as Tyson's pygmy. It is only under Houyhnhnm tutelage that Gulliver begins to discern a human resemblance, albeit one that differs from his own European countenance in accordance with contemporary accounts of other cultures:

> My Horror and Astonishment are not to be described, when I observed, in this abominable Animal, a perfect human Figure; the Face of it indeed was flat and broad, the Nose depressed, the Lips large, and the Mouth wide: but these Differences are common to all savage Nations, where the Lineaments of the Countenance are distorted by the Natives suffering the Infants to lie grovelling on the Earth, or by carrying them on their Backs, nuzzling with their Face against the Mother's Shoulders. (11:229–30)

What is mortifying to Gulliver at this point is the Houyhnhnm's leveling use of the word "Yahoo." The European explanation of differences in physiognomy between European and other cultures enabled a consoling slippage between recognition of similarity and recognition of difference. Creatures such as the Khoi-San (or Hottentots) could be identified as human, even while national difference is naturalized to a degree that approximates a species distinction. Gould reports that one derivation of the term "bushmen" for the Khoi-San was as a variation of "orang-outang" or "wild man of the woods." This is part of the logic that underwrites the racist economy of slavery articulated by Edward Long and others at the end of the century—a logic in which one branch of a species is "naturally" subordinate to another. This is the paradoxical logic of British nationalism neatly summarized by Swift at the close of his letter to Lord Peterborough. If the British nation is right to see liberty as the natural inheritance of every human creature, then there is, of course, nothing to distinguish an Englishman from any other human beyond a self-recognition that his natural condition is a state of liberty. The cynical counterpart, of course, is that if only the English know themselves to be "naturally free," then all others are fit to be enslaved. This particular moment of mortification, when the Houyhnhnms assert a common Yahoo species identity where Gulliver perceives a cultural distinction between savage and European, puts into play the fundamental and troubling question of the fourth voyage: to what extent is our conception of human identity natural, and to what extent is it cultural?

If, in Houyhnhnmland, Gulliver's Baconian descriptive prowess is challenged by the presence of monstrous quasi-humans who threaten by resembling him too closely; we should not lose sight of the fact that here, as much as anywhere, even Brobdingnag, Gulliver is himself on display as a monster and a prodigy. When one considers the considerable effort expended on teaching Peter language, and the dramatically conflicting reports as to his successes and failures (not to mention the challenge that faces each generation in recognizing when their offspring begin to speak intelligibly, if not yet purposefully), it is no surprise that the omnifluent Gulliver first commands the admiration of the Houyhnhnms through his facility with language. His ability to imitate (without comprehension) their pronunciations of first "Yahoo" and then "Houyhnhnm" surprises his hosts, who "appeared amazed at my Capacity" (11:227). Indeed, the Houyhnhnm puzzlement over Gulliver is patterned on European difficulties in "pre-primate primatology." Just as that discourse was divided between the camps of the anatomists and the naturalists, contending with one another as to whether physical form or essential nature provided the basis for species identity, so Gulliver's identity proves similarly troubling to the Houyhnhnms. Gulliver's prodigious command of language and "some glimmerings of reason" recommend him as a monster by violating the expectations of his Yahoo nature. Houyhnhnm characterizations of Yahoo nature frequently echo the naturalist assessments of apes, who while possessing a human form fall well down on the scale of nature.

Defoe's similitude, "like a Horse, or any other Fellow Brute, his Ear could convey no Notions to his Understanding, of the Things he heard, or of the Difference between them; and all for want of Instruction," written in the summer of 1726, speaks directly to the central issue of Gulliver's fourth voyage, published later that fall. Defoe's purpose, of course, is to illustrate the brute nature of the Yahoo-like wild child; the horse, that paragon of docile educability, serves to represent the utter inability of the brute creation to communicate sense to understanding. Having established the brute similarity of wild child and domestic horse, Defoe's satiric twist reminds us that indulgence in spectacles of passionate excess in which the ear can convey nothing meaningful to the understanding—executions and Italian operas—is as much a staple of human culture as of mere uncomprehending animals.

The experiment that Peter represented, and that Defoe had earlier alluded to, was the dream of learning our natural condition: if a child, found raised in nature, utterly removed from human culture, could be instructed in language, what would he tell us about his experience of his early life in nature? Some speculated that he would be able to communicate the truth of who we are; others speculated that he would be able to tell us nothing of his experience prior to language, because without language, his understanding would not have been able to form ideas. Defoe's satire at once insists on our linguistic separation from the animal world and reminds us of our propensity to disown that separation. Swift's satire imagines a slightly more complicated experiment: imagine a race of such wild children, utterly removed from human culture and utterly unable to be instructed; further imagine a race of horse, exactly like those we domesticate, except that these are endowed with language. What would they tell us about their natural condition and our own? We cannot be sure what Swift thought of the former experiment; his comments clearly indicate that he did not consider Peter the appropriate vehicle: "I can hardly think him wild in the sense they report him." I presume he shared this view with Arbuthnot, who at first attempted but soon abandoned the task of teaching Peter a language. The fourth voyage attests, however, that in the latter experiment, Swift imagines that what counts as "natural" condition will be determined by the language in which that condition is described. The Houyhnhnm language Gulliver adopts dictates the world he perceives, including himself.

One long-standing view of the fourth voyage contends that when Gulliver is forced to confront the disparity between human practice and those rational ideals that the Houyhnhnms embody, his sense of identity is destroyed, and he is rendered mad. In most versions of this reading, Houyhnhnms represent an idealized rationality, whether attainable or not, and Yahoos epitomize the passionate nature of man that all our claims to rationality cannot erase. In broad strokes, such a reading makes sense to me, but only with the strong proviso that neither Houyhnhnm nor Yahoo—purely rational being nor merely passionate being—can substitute happily for our own mixed and contradictory condition. Whether or not rational Houyhnhnm behavior is attainable, it is not desirable. The so-called hard reading of book 4 argued—against comic interpretations—that in this voyage Houyhnhnms were not a comic foil, but a daunting and inescapable measure of human failure. At times, I am inclined to agree, but I am always chuckling as I do so. If Houyhnhnm virtue reminds me of my failure to live up to some ideal human potential, then Houyhnhnm sanctimonious self-importance reminds me of my glorious human capacity to laugh at absurdity, particularly within my species, broadly conceived. Of the many virtues we may imagine the Houyhnhnms capable of attaining, an appreciation of Swiftian satire seems entirely beyond them, for they are utterly incapable of sustaining paradox and contradiction.

Such a comic reading of Houyhnhnm virtue is recorded in a letter by one of

Swift's contemporaries—the very Lord Peterborough cited at the outset of this chapter. Peterborough (who four years earlier had secretly married Anastasia Robinson, then the foremost diva in England) begins his letter to Swift of November 29, 1726, with the following allusion to the difficulties of Houyhnhnm language:

> I was endeavouring to give an answer to yours in a new dialect which most of us are very fond of, I depended much upon a Lady [i.e., Robinson] who had a good Ear and a pliant Tongue, in hopes she might have taught me to draw sounds out of consonants, but she being a profest friend to the Italian speech & vowels would give me no assistance, & so I am forced to write to you in the yahoo language.
>
> The new one in fashion is much studied, and great pains taken about the pronunciation, Every body (since a new Turn) approves of it, but the women seem most satisfied, who declare for a few words, & Horse performance, itt suffices to lett you know, that there is a Neighing Duetto appointed for the next Opera. (*Correspondence* 3:191)

While Peterborough's allusion praises Houyhnhnm language, his letter clearly views the idealized Houyhnhnms as fundamentally comic, and subsequent passages continue in that vein: "others expect an Oration equall to any of Cicero's finest from an Eloquent Barb, and some take the braying of an Asse for the Emperor's speech in favour of the Vienna alliance" (3:191). Like Swift's other correspondents that winter, Peterborough is "forced to write . . . in the Yahoo language." Those other correspondents are, of course, members of the political opposition: either Swift's usual friends (Pope, Gay, Arbuthnot, etc.), or, like Peterborough, politically influential Whigs who hoped that the succession of the current prince would bring about a change in ministry.[7] Foremost among this latter group, certainly, was Princess Caroline herself, who had her maid of honour, Mrs. Howard (subsequently Lady Masham), correspond with Swift on her behalf. Mrs. Howard signs the bantering letter that initiates that correspondence with the self-deprecating, "Sieve Yahoo."[8] The entire correspondence that ensues is rich in witty sexual innuendo, feigned innocence, and clever manipulation of conventional professions of political civility on both sides.

Certainly, however, Caroline was as adept at spinning political symbolism, and the content of the correspondence is adroitly managed to keep the political opposition in hopeful suspense. Swift had given his friend, Mrs. Howard, a gift of Irish wool plaid before he left England. Pope, with a mixture of savvy admiration and friendly skepticism, correctly analyzed the situation in a November 16 letter: "Are you determin'd to be National in every thing, even in your civilities? You are the greatest Politician in Europe at this rate; but as you are a rational politician, there's no great fear of you, you will never succeed" (3:181). As Swift must have hoped, the princess had appropriated the gift and requested more, a request with which Swift immediately set about complying. Effectively, the princess chooses to appear in Swift's livery, extending a tacit approbation to *Gulliver's Travels;* this is explicitly the reading of the political situation that Peterborough offers in his letter. The obscure parenthetical phrase, "since a new Turn," alludes to this intervention, for his letter describes in fanciful ways how the "scribbling Magitian" was in danger of political reprisals until "the greatest Lady in the nation . . . takes vi et Armis the plad from the Lady it was sent to, which is soon to appear upon her Royall person" (3:192).

Clearly, the opposition read (as Caroline no doubt wished them to) the episode of the royal plaid as a hopeful sign in the winter of 1726. But it is particularly worth noting how the correspondence of that winter repeatedly wraps the serious interpretations of changing political climate within a fundamentally comic bantering surface humor—one that repeatedly deployed Houyhnhnms and Yahoos as comic terms. In these letters, the term "Yahoo" is not shorthand for a misanthropic distortion of human frailty but is repeatedly deployed (as Mrs. Howard and Peterborough use the term) in comic self-deprecation of the type required in the elaborate rhetoric of civility. Correspondingly, the Houyhnhnm virtues that Peterborough and others admire (and find lacking in the current ministry) cannot escape the taint of absurdity promised by the "Neighing Duetto appointed for the next Opera." As one of the directors of the opera, Peterborough must have had in mind when he wrote this the long-awaited performance of *Astyanax,* in which Faustina and Madame Cuzzoni appear onstage together, with the unfortunate consequences discussed in the previous chapter.

Peterborough's observations on the similarities between incomprehensible Houyhnhnm language and incomprehensible opera remind us of how Defoe drew equally on equines and opera to describe Peter's passionate noncomprehension. In *Mere Nature Delineated,* Defoe had leaned heavily on Swift's treatment of Peter, even if he had insisted that his own consideration would not be "*a la buffoon,* as has been thought proper by a learned Author of Brains and Brass (for he calls himself *The Copper-Farthing Author*)" (29). Although he borrows several features from Swift, perhaps most notable is the idea that all animals—not humans alone—speak. In his poem "On the Deaf and Dumb being taught to speak," he writes, "They all can speak, know what to speak, and when / Tho' we *in scoff* pretend to call them Mutes, / They've all *a Voice,* we find no silent brutes" (2–4). The borrowing is from Swift's radical claim that Peter "understands perfectly the Language of all Beasts and Birds, and is not, like them, confin'd to that of one Species" (7). This observation immediately precedes two anecdotes that would certainly take on added point if in fact Swift is the author. The first of these is simply a sentence that sounds not unlike the way Swift might choose to allegorize his own role in the recent resistance to Wood's halfpence: "One Day he warn'd a Flock of Sheep that were driving to the Shambles, of their Danger, and upon uttering some Sounds, they all fled" (7). Such an allegory would contain that distinctly Swiftian cadence of ambivalence, both about himself (at once heroic and represented by an ultimately pathetic figure) and about the Irish he found it so frustrating to try and assist. In any case, the incident that follows takes on an added dimension after the publication of *Gulliver's Travels* five months later: "He takes vast Pleasure in Conversation with Horses; and going to the Meuse to converse with Two of his intimate Acquaintances in the King's Stable. . . . He expresseth his Joy most commonly by Neighing; and whatever the Philosophers may talk of their Risibility, neighing is a more noble Expression of that Passion than Laughing, which seems to me to have something Silly in it; and besides is often attended with Tears" (7–8).

Certainly, in the figure of Peter conversing with two of the king's horses, we should see a foreshadowing of Gulliver's decision on his return to purchase "two young stone-horses" with which he may converse in amity and friendship. But we may also want to admire for a moment how precious an irony this must have appeared to Swift. After conceiving of this conclusion to his satiric fable, he journeys to London only to discover that the principal admiration of the court is directed to a youth whose vocalizations would seem to approximate the very ideal his satiric hero advocates. Even as we relish this irony, we may also wish to give some attention to the phrase that "neighing is a more noble expression of that passion" of risibility, for it has its echo in a statement of Gulliver's that turns our attention directly to the question of Houyhnhnm language and the relation of reason and passion.

The stark polarities dividing Houyhnhnm and Yahoo, on which hard-school readings depend, collapse when language is introduced: "I plainly observed, that their Language expressed the Passions very well" (11:226). It is not the Yahoos but the Houyhnhnms whose language express passion. In some respects, of course, the language of the Houyhnhnms is explicitly linked to Ancient Greek, and in this context, their nonliteracy points to the idealized pre-Homeric Golden Age. The observation, however, that "their Language expressed the Passions very well" is in some respects an odd observation, for it is not one of the common criteria for evaluating languages in the period. Typically, Greek was esteemed as excelling all other languages, and the reason given was usually for its capacity for expression. It was, however, most often praised for excelling in expressing ideas. Most relevant to the fourth voyage, however, may well be Pope's observations in the preface to Homer: "whoever will but consult the Tune of his Verses even without understanding them (with the same sort of Diligence as we daily see practis'd in the Case of *Italian Opera*'s) will find more Sweetness, Variety and Majesty of Sound, than in any other Language or Poetry. . . . Indeed the *Greek* has some Advantages both from the natural *Sound* of its *Words,* and the Turn and *Cadence* of its *Verse,* which agree with the Genius of no other Language" (11). The parenthetical irony at the expense of courtly preference for opera is of a piece with the double application of Houyhnhnm language. This is all the more remarkable when we consider the famous moment at the end of the nineteenth book of the *Iliad,* when Achilles, roused to action by the death of Patroclus, arms himself and mounts his chariot. As he does so, he faults his horses for leaving Patroclus behind, only to have them turn on him—in a surprising moment—discursively:

> Xanthus and Balius! Of Podarges' strain,
> (Unless ye boast that heav'nly Race in vain)
> Be swift, be mindful of the Load ye bear,
> And learn to make your Master more your Care:
> Thro' falling Squadrons bear my slaught'ring Sword,
> Nor, as ye left Patroclus, leave your Lord.
>   The gen'rous Xanthus, as the Words he said,
> Seem'd sensible of Woe, and droop'd his Head:
> Trembling he stood before the golden Wain,
> And bow'd to Dust the Honours of his Mane,
> When strange to tell! (So Juno will'd) he broke
> Eternal Silence, and portentous spoke.
>   Achilles! yes! this Day at least we bear
> Thy rage in safety thro' the Files of War:
> But come it will, the fatal Time must come,
> Nor ours the Fault, but God decrees thy Doom.
> Nor thro' our Crime, or Slowness in the Course;
> Fell thy Patroclus, but by heav'nly Force.
> The bright far-shooting God who gilds the Day,

(Confest we saw him) tore his Arms away.
No—could our Swiftness o'er the Winds prevail,
Or beat the Pinions of the Western Gale,
All were in Vain—The Fates thy Death demand,
Due to a mortal and immortal Hand.
  Then ceas'd for ever, by the Furies ty'd,
His fate-ful Voice. Th'intrepid Chief reply'd
With unabated Rage—So let it be!
Portents and Prodigies are lost on me.
I know my Fates: To die, to see no more
My much lov'd Parents, and my native Shore—
Enough—When Heav'n ordains, I sink in Night,
Now perish Troy! He said, and rush'd to Fight. (19:441–72)

In his note to this surprising passage, Pope quotes from memory a translation of Oppian by Fenton:

Of all the prone Creation, none display
A friendlier Sense of Man's superior Sway:
Some in the silent Pomp of Grief complain,
For the brave Chief, by Doom of Battel slain:
And when young Peleus in his rapid Car
Rush'd on, to rouze the Thunder of the War,
With human Voice inspir'd, his Steed deplor'd
The Fate impending dreadful o'er his Lord. (19:452 n.)

Whatever we are to make of the affinity between the Houyhnhnm language and Pope's representation of the Greek in terms of expressing the passions, or of the affinity between its nasal qualities and those pronounced by the Hanoverian court—whatever these affinities may suggest, they are explicitly set against particular excellencies of modern European languages, which are to express ideas and rational thought. In fact, the received interpretation of book 4 as dramatizing an internal human conflict between passion and reason depends on projecting human passion onto the Yahoos and human reason onto the Houyhnhnms. Nowhere, however, is the Houyhnhnm language exalted for expressing reason—quite the opposite. In all those areas where the operation of judgment and reason are required, the Houyhnhnms are hopelessly at sea, cut off from comprehension by their own linguistic insufficiency. Their language excels at expressing the passions and must be supplemented for even describing—much less practicing—rational debate.

The ambivalence here surrounding Houyhnhnm language may well be of a piece with the "ancient" attitudes Swift and Pope shared toward language. On the one hand, the Golden Age was an idealized, pre-literate, pre-Homeric Greek whose language expressed the passions directly. At the same time, the contemporary age of lead, whose corrupt, illiterate culture stooped to a language of passionate expression, unhinged from communication. At either end human language borders on animal utterance, but where the "barbaric" language of the ancient Greeks approximated a divine original, the beastly language of contemporary England settles into a corrupt confusion. Thus, the nonliterate Houyhnhnms are explicitly linked to the "illiterate" Germans currently running the English court. That satiric link simultaneously attacks the court and undermines the ostensible idealization of the Houyhnhnms. If the passionate expressions of Houyhnhnm language betray their rational pretensions, so they also return us to narrowly topical political satire, for in another place Swift glances ironically at the current Hanoverian court: "In speaking, they pronounce through the Nose and Throat, and their Language approaches nearest to the *High Dutch* or *German,* of any I know in *Europe;* but is much more graceful and significant. The Emperor *Charles V.* made almost the same Observation when he said, That if he were to speak to his Horse, it should be in *High Dutch*" (11:234). The emperor's comment, of course, had been delivered as a derisive sneer directed to the Hanoverian court. Swift appropriates Gulliver's idealization of the Houyhnhnms in order to repeat, and indeed intensify, the slander. If Charles would speak to his horse in High Dutch, Gulliver notes that equine speech is "more graceful and significant." There would seem an inconsistency here in Gulliver's twin characterizations of Houyhnhnm speech. On the one hand, "their language expressed the passions very well," but at the same time, their language closely approximates the High Dutch of the Hanoverian court. Now, no one particularly singled out High Dutch for its excellence in expressing the passions, nor would it seem in keeping with Swift's satiric project to linguistically align the court of George I with his rational ideals. I think, in fact, that this problematic aspect of Houyhnhnm language points to one of the critical ways Swift undercuts Gulliver's idealization of them and does so in ways that link the satire to his earlier satire on Peter, the wild boy.

For in May, after observing Peter, Swift had published a satire that differed significantly from usual representations with respect to language. If usually

Peter was depicted as without language or perhaps able to learn only a few words, Swift represents him as perfectly fluent in a language that is not generally comprehended. In this way, he accurately captures Peter's capacity for verbal utterance, but he also folds that capacity into a satire on the Hanoverian court. For although those utterances are usually perceived to be inarticulate gibberish, in Swift's treatise they are understood by his sponsor and the king's minister Rautenberg. Houyhnhnm language, at once expressive of passion and approximating that found at court, echoes the cries Swift heard from Peter in the spring of 1726. As much as that language, in Gulliver's representation, epitomizes the rational discourse of an idealized Habermasian public sphere, it also remains a provincial, barbaric language utterly distanced from the communicative cosmopolitan world of print capitalism. Houyhnhnm culture is primitive culture, for better and for worse, and its language, as Castle reminds us, is pre-literate.

Swift, however, as much as he was an ancient, did not merely praise all things primitive and lament the coming of modernity. Poets may have been banished from Plato's republic, but letters and literature were deeply valued by Swift. When he retells the taunt of Charles V, just as when he likens Peter's gibberish to the language of the royal court, we can detect that part of the sting for Swift (as for Pope) of the Hanoverian succession was that England had come to be governed by a barely articulate, much less literate, backwater provincial family, scorned by the politer courts of Europe, void of literary heritage, and entirely unable to enter into the larger European conversation. When all is said and done, Gulliver's linguistic facility stands in stark opposition to the monarch who could not speak to the people he ruled in their own language. From Swift's perspective, England under George I had suffered a significant linguistic reversal and was in danger of becoming within the European community, like Houyhnhnmland, an isolated island cut off from and oblivious to a larger world. For Houyhnhnmland is ultimately an isolationist nightmare realm, certain of the perfection of their own citizens, unable and unwilling to learn from others, speaking a language that cannot be written and that no one else can speak.

That characterization of Houyhnhnmland seems, at first, directly contrary to those frequent panegyrics offered by Gulliver on behalf of Houyhnhnm virtues. Those virtues are generally traits of sociability and generosity: "Friendship and Benevolence are the two principal Virtues among the Houyhnhnm; and these not confined to particular Objects, but universal to the whole Race" (11:268). But beyond Gulliver's perspective, we are also granted glimpses of the

Houyhnhnms' isolationist indifference to a larger world. They have no conception of a land beyond the boundaries of their own island, and when Gulliver
departs, he heads for a small island, which can be seen even before he raises his
telescope, "but it appeared to the Sorrel Nag to be only a blue Cloud: For as he
had no Conception of any Country beside his own, so he could not be as expert
in distinguishing remote Objects at Sea" (11:281). If Houyhnhnms are suscepti-
ble to the temptations of isolationism, they are at least not quite so far gone in
that regard as their chief disciple, Gulliver. For when he leaves the island, his
only goal is to seek out a desert island to serve as a refuge, such as those encountered by Alexander Selkirk or Robinson Crusoe: "My Design was, if possible, to discover some small Island uninhabited, yet sufficient by my Labour to
furnish me with the Necessaries of Life. . . . For in such Solitude as I desired, I
could at least enjoy my own Thoughts, and reflect with Delight on the Virtues
of those inimitable Houyhnhnms, without any Opportunity of degenerating
into the Vices and Corruption of my own Species" (11:283).

This is misinterpretation with a vengeance, since those "virtues" on which
Gulliver wishes to reflect (i.e., friendship, benevolence, generosity, etc.) are all
distinctly social virtues—both meaningless and impossible in isolation.[9] Nor,
whatever "hard-school" critics may like to assert, is this a misinterpretation
likely to have been lost on Swift. As much as he embraced withdrawal and retreat, that tendency was always tempered by a clear recognition of the value and
virtue of active friendship. Moreover, Gulliver's desire to retreat into solitude in
order to avoid the "opportunity of degenerating" is a merely stoic resistance,
such as Swift famously ridiculed. Those virtues that the Houyhnhnms practice
are difficult for the same reason that they are necessary: if people were different
than what they are, it would be easier—and less important—to practice those
social virtues that Gulliver prefers to contemplate in isolated serenity.

Finally, now, it may be helpful to consider some of the echoes that resonate
between *Gulliver's Travels* and the pamphlets occasioned by Peter's appearance
in the spring; frequently, topical allusions in both satires score at the expense
of the court surrounding the king. In Brobdingnag, two or three of Gulliver's
more desperate adventures involve the animosity of the Royal Dwarf, who
is mortified to discover someone so much smaller than himself. The troublesome nature of this dwarf—on one occasion he shakes a Dwarf apple tree while
Gulliver is beneath it; another time he wedges Gulliver into a marrow bone; and
a third time, he drops Gulliver into a bowl of cream—causes no lasting dam-
age to Gulliver but incurs royal displeasure. Although he is pardoned due to

Gulliver's intercession in the affair of the apple tree, he is soundly whipped on the other two occasions and forced to drink the cream; soon after these events, and as a direct result of them, he loses favor with the queen, who gives him away. Gulliver would provoke this Royal Page (the official function of the Dwarf) by calling him "Brother" (11:108).

Now the Brobdingnagian Dwarf had a counterpart in the court of George I, and one who played a significant role in the opposition concerns about the royal court. Officially, Christian Ulrich Jorry was a Royal Page, but unofficially he was one of three confidantes of George I, who not only spoke privately with the king in German but who was native to neither England nor Hanover. Frequently referred to as the "Young Turk," Jorry was clearly a favorite of the king's, with elaborate clothes made for him by the Royal Tailor, among other marks of royal favor. He also seems to have had a petulant temper given to violent and vocal tantrums that on more than one occasion incurred royal displeasure and left him vulnerable to opposition representations as the most ridiculous representative of George's German Court.[10] The two parts of *It cannot Rain but it Pours* each make allusions to this Royal Dwarf; in the second part (published first) he is identified simply as "U_____," while in the first part (published last) he is "U****k." In both texts, Maurice Johnson has identified this figure as "Urrik, His Majesties Page." In the second part, while writing of Peter, the author (Swift?) writes: "It has been commonly thought, that he is U_____'s natural Brother, because of some resemblance of Manners, and the officious Care of U_____ about him; but the Superiority of the Parts and Genius in *Peter,* demonstrates this to be impossible" (6). When the first part appeared, its title page promised among other things, "A full and true account of a fierce and Wild Indian Deer that beat the breath out of Mr. U****k's Body." Before the text itself, an advertisement for a "Third Part of This Book" (which was never printed) promises, among other things, "how Mr. U***k is recovered, and learns to Sing: With a Vindication of the Wild Gentleman from being his Brother, or bearing any Resemblance at all to him." The text itself offers only one paragraph on Jorry: "As for Mr. U***k (who according to Method should have been spoken of first) we are inform'd from very good Authority, that he was Blooded in like manner [as Faustina, who was seeking to recover her voice from a cold], but it is to be hoped it will not have the same Effect upon him; I mean of giving him a stronger Voice, since should there be any Addition made to his Vociferation it really might endanger the Royal Palace" (4).

If Gulliver is no more the brother of the Queen's Dwarf in Brobdingnag than

10. A panel from the King's Staircase at Kensington Palace, painted by William Kent in 1726–27, with Peter holding the oak leaf cluster. (Reproduced by permission of Historic Royal Palaces under licence from the Controller of Her Majesty's Stationery Office.)

11. Another panel from the King's Staircase at Kensington Palace: the Royal Dwarf, Ulrich Jorry, satirized in the pamphlets about Peter discussed in chapter 2 and satirized again by Swift in the figure of the Royal Dwarf in Brobdingnag, is shown standing outside the painted railing. (Reproduced by permission of Historic Royal Palaces under licence from the Controller of Her Majesty's Stationery Office.)

12. A third panel from the King's Staircase at Kensington Palace: George I's trusted Turkish advisers, Mehemet (keeper of the Privy Purse) and Mustapha, are depicted at the railing. (Reproduced by permission of Historic Royal Palaces under licence from the Controller of Her Majesty's Stationery Office.)

Peter is the "natural brother" of George's Royal Page, we might still wish to remember that contemporary readers of *Gulliver's Travels* would be invited to think of Ulrich when they read of Gulliver's antagonist. Moreover, the first part of *It cannot Rain but it Pours* proceeded to an association that had more serious political implications for an opposition audience. That pamphlet, after dispensing with Ulrich, had proceeded to detail the visit of the two Moroccan ambassadors, Mahomet and Bo-Ally. In introducing these two the following caution is given: "not that the Courteous Reader must think we mean Mr. Mahomet the Christian." With that stroke the satire collapses the two visiting Moroccan dignitaries into two of George I's most trusted personal advisers and gentlemen ushers, Mehemet and Mustapha. When George commissioned William Kent to paint the grand staircase at Kensington Palace with figures from the royal court, the panels included in the scene Mehemet and Mustapha, as well as Ulrich, and even Peter, the wild youth.[11] Mehemet is alluded to as "Mr. Mahomet the Christian," for he had converted to Christianity and had been christened Ludwig Maximilian Mehemet. More importantly, from the opposition perspective, "as well as being a groom of the king's chamber and keeper of the closet (and perhaps the closest servant to the king), Mehemet was also in fact though not in name, keeper of the privy purse. In this reign about half of the £30,000 a year provided for the privy purse was used to pay the expenses of the German court in London. This was technically illegal but it could never be discovered because the privy purse was private and the expenditure did not have to be accounted for" (J. M. Beattie 260).

Collectively, then, one can see how the allusions to Ulrich and the Moroccan ambassadors in the two parts of *It cannot Rain but it Pours* tie the parody of a quack remedy pamphlet occasioned by Peter to the foreign influence dominating the court of George I, a favorite opposition theme. The petulant behavior that marked Ulrich Jorry as the most ridiculous emissary of George's court also stood in dramatic contrast to both the benevolent humanity of the King of Brobdingnag and those Houyhnhnm virtues of friendship and benevolence, whose necessary social dimension is utterly lost on a Gulliver prepared to contemplate them in private isolation. In *Gulliver's Travels,* the more thinly veiled allusions of the pamphlet satire are dispensed with, but some of the same concerns emerge, and both Swift's satiric masterpiece and the more ephemeral pamphlet literature work together in the service of an opposition cause. Ultimately, the figure of the wild man offers a rallying perspective for the opposition. Clearly, Swift's offhand description to Tickell ("I can hardly think him wild in the sense they report him") indicates that he did not actually find Peter a particularly interesting challenge to normative constructions of human identity—in this respect, Peter is little more than Arbuthnot's "merry pupil." But the discursive strategies of the opposition mobilize this figure as the crisis point that tests "the notions I had of liberty, a possession always understood by the British nation to be the inheritance of a human creature." In the various guises he adopts within opposition satires of 1726, and in the manner in which he "apes" material actors at the court of George I, the wild man tests the limits of liberty as a defining trait of nation and species.

5

Walk Scotland and Carry a Big Stick

*in which the orang-outang is brought
before the bench of Public Opinion, a
Judge pleads his case while a lexicographer contends against him; and how the
learned lexicographer is brought closer
to the judge's view by a tour of Scotland.*

In 1726, Peter was rusticated.

That is a locution we no longer have, and the ironies of its application in this context are worth pursuing. "To rusticate," Johnson tells us, is "to banish into the country." It is obviously cognate to the adjectival "rustical—rough, savage, boisterous, brutal, rude," and the more widely used "rustick: rural, country; rude, untaught, inelegant; brutal, savage; artless, honest, simple; plain, un- adorned." There is an inconsistency in these usages that dramatizes the com- plexity of judgments surrounding class and sophistication. On the one hand, educated, urban sophistication is privileged over the rude, untaught behavior of rural folk; at the same time, however, particularly in university settings, the wild and indecorous behavior of students indicated that they had lost those virtues of innocence associated with the pastoral: "artless, honest, simple, plain, un- adorned." The remedy was rustication. When Bishop Burnet's son indulged too freely in the various tempting delights that Cambridge offered, he was "sent down" (in the common phrase for rustication) to Gillingham in Dorset.[1]

Peter, when he first arrived in England, was all the rage in London among the haute monde, and all of fashionable society flocked to see him at court. He was for some months entrusted to the care of Dr. Arbuthnot, the Royal Physician, who resided in Piccadilly, adjoining Lord Burlington's Palladian estate. During this time, he failed to progress in his studies, and his rude, savage, boisterous behavior that at first entertained the aristocracy (and, in the representations of the Tory satirists, mimicked the behavior of his hosts at court) soon lost its charm. In six months a royal pension was established for his maintenance, and he entered rural retirement at Harrow-the-Hill in Hempstead. What does the rustication of Peter mean? Certainly, his banishment is a convenience—he has outlived his entertainment value for the court; Arbuthnot despairs of success in teaching him and can hardly be bothered with such a "merry pupil"; a royal pension is a small price to be rid of such a nuisance. When a wayward son of the aristocracy failed in his studies and ran wild in his social life, rustication was the prescription to return him to those moral values and virtues that his culture (no less than William Bennet) considered foundational for responsible citizenship. Bishop Burnet's son never returned to Cambridge, but he did become a fellow of the Royal Society and spent a long career as colonial governor of New York and Massachusetts—thus combining civic responsibility with savage banishment. Was there a belief that Peter's banishment, while not only convenient, might effectively aid in the project of civilizing him? Repeatedly, in all the ways that the satirists saw—and more—English society found itself indistinguishable from Peter.

Peter's life in retirement would seem to be the end of his narrative—the terminus to his Warholian fifteen minutes of fame. Yet that is not the case. At the end of the century, and the dawn of anthropology, he is rediscovered in his second incarnation as rural, romantic sage. His history and his representations belong to new genres. Admittedly, I may be accused of exaggeration in claiming for Peter the identity of "sage," but it is an exaggeration that is in fact encouraged by the contexts in which he appears. Peter as old man, who sits for his portrait and is visited by philosophers, is described (albeit unflatteringly) in comparison to Socrates: "Though his head, as Mr. Wedgewood and many others had remarked, resembled that of Socrates, he was an idiot" (Edgeworth and Edgeworth 95). The Socrates joke is something of a staple in literature surrounding the figure of the wild man.[2] The charge of idiocy is championed most strongly by Blumenbach in deliberate opposition to the opinion of James Burnett, Lord Monboddo, who mounted a vigorous case for Peter as natural man: "He was a man in mind as well as body, as I have been informed by a person

13. A rusticated Peter in old age (1811), where he is visited in retirement by *philosophes.*

who lived for a considerable time in the neighborhood of a farmer's house where he was kept, and had an opportunity of seeing him almost every day; not an idiot, as he has been represented by some" (*Origin* 174).[3]

Now any eighteenth-century scholar who finds himself in the position of citing Monboddo for support must do so with great trepidation. For Monboddo is little known, and what reputation he has acquired has generally been in the categories of "eccentric, crank, buffoon, etc." He repeatedly and steadfastly maintained a belief in the kinship of humans and apes, a proposition more startling then than now (and perhaps more startling now than we would care to admit), but it was his equally vigorous adherence to the quirky extensions of such belief that damaged his credibility: he believed that mankind had once had tails (and he offered as an exemplary case a schoolteacher in Inverness). Even if the state of Enlightenment anatomy enabled one to make a plausible claim for a vestigial tail in the form of the coccyx, this is not the sort of opinion calculated to enhance one's reputation. Johnson—typically—summarizes Monboddo's reputation: "Other people have strange notions, but they conceal them. If they have tails, they hide them; but Monboddo is as jealous of his tail as a squirrel" (Boswell 5:111).

Johnson's scorn, followed quickly by Blumenbach's full-scale attack, damaged Monboddo's reputation irretrievably (and not entirely unfairly). The

gradual, but nearly complete, triumph of Darwinian evolutionary theory between *The Origin of Species* and the Scopes "monkey trial" prepared the ground
for an attempt early in this century to resuscitate that reputation. A. O. Lovejoy
found Monboddo important as early evolutionist, anticipating Darwin on primate kinship and distancing himself from enlightenment primitivism. My own
view tends to locate him somewhere between these two extremes: eccentric and
opinionated, but not as easily dismissed as Johnson might like; genuinely open-
minded and inquisitive pertaining to questions of human identity, yet far closer
to Aristotle than Darwin when it comes to scientific reasoning. Anthropologist
Alan Barnard provides a useful guide to Monboddo's historical significance:
"The common notion that Monboddo may have been the first person to see the
'true' relation between apes and humans is not of much interest in itself, and
indeed neither accurate nor particularly meaningful. Rather, what is of significance is the fact that current debates in both social and biological anthropology
and in linguistics mirror debates in the eighteenth century" (72).[4] Monboddo's
consideration of "Orang Outang" required him to move repeatedly from instances of what we would now term "nonhuman primates" to feral children
such as Peter and the wild girl of Soigny, to Europeans and back again. Barnard
identifies the degree to which Monboddo's consideration of the wild man is implicated in his ideology of the citizen:

> His Orang Outang bears close resemblance to the "natural man" of Rousseau's *Sec-*
> *ond Discourse.* He is akin to the imaginary inhabitants of Hobbes's "state of nature"
> too. These 'natural' beings are, quite possibly, little more than heuristic devices. In
> order to understand the true nature of Man, their authors had to invent a natural
> state which could not possibly exist except in the mind. Yet it did have to exist in
> that locus, for the definition of civilized humanity as conceived by Hobbes de-
> pended upon the presumption of an opposing, uncivilized form and that of Rous-
> seau on a pre-civil, natural ideal. Their theories would be impossible without such
> imagined exemplars. Similarly, Monboddo's Orang Outang can be seen as an
> ideal type which exists in Monboddo's thought, and whose existence is necessary
> in order to define Man as Monboddo wants to define him.
>
> . . . A feral child might be more human in appearance, but by definition he or
> she lacks sociality and culture. The Orang Outang, in contrast, was reported to be
> gregarious, though Orang Outang society was not yet developed enough to need
> language. . . . a hierarchy of classification as Monboddo appears to see it [exists] be-
> tween politics (or sociality), rationality, and language. (73, 76)

Barnard, I believe, is right in identifying the various existences of "wild men" in Enlightenment philosophy with preexisting concerns with the "citizen." And I believe he is also right to locate the relationship between those semiotic-material actors as sometimes opposing and sometimes complementary. Most of all, I believe he is right in finding Monboddo particularly useful in revealing how those relations are bound up with considerations of sociality and rational language. Precisely because Monboddo returns obsessively to the criterion of language, and at the same time triangulates the figures of the feral child, orangoutang, and the citizen, he reminds us of the interplay between the quadrants of our semiotic square:

Orang-outang	*Citizen*
(passionate sounds, domesticated brutes, herds)	(express ideas, teachable, public societies)

Feral child	*Castaway*
(inarticulate cries, anarchic solitude)	(contemplative, withdrawn exercise of liberty and reflection)

Monboddo returns to Peter repeatedly both in *Origin and Progress of Language* and in *Antient Metaphysics;* when he does so, he retells those descriptions that accompanied Peter's original appearance in England, but he also seeks to update those accounts with descriptions of Peter as an old man. One of the defining markers of "wildness" was the flight reflex: early accounts of Peter and the wild girl of Soigny, and subsequent accounts of Victor of Aveyron, all reinforce the "wildness" of the child by emphasizing a propensity to flee human society. When Monboddo narrates Peter's life in retirement, then, his emphasis on the cessation of that reflex operates as a sign of Peter's significant, albeit limited, domestication: "About twenty years ago, he was in use to elope, and to be amissing for several days; and once as I was told, he wandered as far as Norfolk: But, of late, he has been quite tame, and either keeps the house, or saunters about the farm" (*Antient Metaphysics* 3:63).

In an appendix, Monboddo provides the text of a letter sent to him by a student who had visited Peter at Monboddo's request. There, Peter's original wildness and more recent domestication are located within a narrative of political romance: "He has run away several times since he has been at Broadway [the name of the farm where he lived], but not since he has been with his present master. He was taken up for spy in Scotland, in 1745, or 1746: As he was unable to speak, they supposed him obstinate, and he was going to be confined, and was threatened with punishment for contumacy; but a Lady who had seen him in England, told them who it was, and directed them where to send him. Some say he was found at Norfolk" (*Antient Metaphysics* 3:372).

Blumenbach offers a variation of this narrative: "He probably lost himself several times in the neighborhood during the first ten years of his residence in England; but at all events one day, in 1746, he unwittingly strayed a long way, and at last got as far as Norfolk, where he was brought before a justice of the peace as the suspicious Unknown—this was at the time when there was look-out for the supposed emissaries of the Pretender. As he did not speak, he was committed for the moment to the great prison-house in Norwich for safe custody. A great fire broke out there on that night, so that the prison was opened as soon as possible, and the detained were let out. When after the first fright the prisoners were counted up, the most important of them all was missing, the dumb Unknown. A warder rushed through the flames of the wide prison, and found Peter sitting quietly at the back in his corner; he was enjoying the illumination and the agreeable warmth, and it was not without difficulty that he could be dragged forth: and soon afterwards, from the advertisements for lost things he was recognized as the innocent Peter and forwarded to his farmer again. Briefly, as an end to the tale, this pretended ideal of pure human nature, to which later sophists have elevated the wild Peter, was altogether nothing more than a dumb imbecile idiot" (qtd. in Singh and Zingg 187).

Neither Monboddo nor Blumenbach are writing satire, nor indeed would their considerations of Peter be ordinarily considered literary. Both, however, interpolate into their philosophic narratives an anecdote that blends irony and political romance, albeit for different ends. In doing so, they elaborate and transform the satiric representations of Peter that marked his arrival in England. On his arrival, Peter's muteness marked his significance; then, as in the subsequent representations of Monboddo and Blumenbach, that muteness was overwritten as craft and manipulation. In the earlier narrations, the pose of silence he affected ("sly and serious") was read as the cunning ploy of a lover, a screen for erotic fantasy. The political satire of these earlier representations emerged out of the fantasies of erotic transgression marked by his silence. The narratives of Monboddo and Blumenbach displace this erotic transgression onto the political realm of the Jacobite rebellion.[5]

It is worth noting that when Monboddo originally recounts this political romance, he subordinates it to three important arguments he is putting forward at the time. First, Monboddo insists on a species intercourse that identifies human and orang-outang, and for Monboddo, Peter is the necessary term shuttling between the two: thus, the account of Peter in which this narrative appears is introduced with the claim that "the case of the Orang Outang, I think, it is impossible to distinguish from the case of Peter the Wild Boy" (367). Second, the function of the interpolated narrative in Monboddo's handling is to emphasize his growing domesticity and to locate his penchant for wild flight in the past. That serves to reinforce the important third claim that, even with minimal education late in life, Peter's humanity is confirmed by his acquisition of language, however limited. Within the context of this larger argument, the political narrative reinforces the claim that Peter (and by extension, the orang-outang) is human.

Surprisingly, Blumenbach, seeking to discredit the fanciful theories of Monboddo (and Rousseau) with the solid evidence of scientific reasoning, resorts to an even more highly elaborated version of the political romance, in which Peter is elevated from political spy to one of the many legendary stand-ins for the Pretender himself. Blumenbach's scornful conclusion as to Peter's status as "imbecile idiot" reflects on the political frenzy of the Jacobite rebellion of 1745 that could allow even Peter to be mistaken for the Pretender. For Monboddo, confusing Peter with the Pretender comically confirms his claim to humanity; for Blumenbach, such confusion confirms only a Swiftian scorn spread equally among those who fear the Pretender and those who consider Peter their equal. In attacking Monboddo (and Rousseau), Blumenbach (and later his disciple, Lawrence) embraces a degeneration theory of variation within the human species that privileges Caucasian man as the primitive variety from which all others are degenerated. Such a theory retains the fixity of species and accounts for differentiation only within species. Monboddo, often identified as an "evolutionist," can be claimed as one only with respect to man; he, too, acknowledges the fixity of species throughout the animal kingdom—with the single exception of man. There, like Rousseau, who focused on what he termed "perfectibility" or "potential," Monboddo finds man alone defined not by his natural attributes, but by his capacities. So, although Blumenbach shares with Swift a scorn that unites political intrigue with the case of an idiot boy, it is Monboddo who shares with Swift a belief that man is by nature *not* a rational animal, but only an animal capable of reason.

Nor is this mere semantic hairsplitting, as Blumenbach would like to have it, for the question is not only germane but also central to any attempt at a natural history of man. Monboddo's modified evolutionist paradigm identifies man with a parabolic history of rise and fall, in which mankind evolved from an original wild state to attain its fulfillment in classical Greek civilization from which it has subsequently been degenerating. Alternatively Blumenbach's degenerative paradigm identifies primitive man with a Caucasian original that has degenerated as the original dispersed and where physical degeneration accompanies moral and cultural progress. In Blumenbach's model, language and the rationality it signifies distinguish man from animal; in Monboddo's model, language emerges only as a historical phenomenon subsequent to a prior political or social organization, as he summarizes a description of orang-outangs: "they are so far advanced towards the political life, as to herd together, and to communicate together, by a chattering guttural noise, which, I am persuaded, led the way among all people to articulation and the use of speech" (4:30).

If we imagine for a moment our semiotic square, we can see that Blumenbach's model emphasizes the vertical separation marking language acquisition, whereas Monboddo's emphasizes the horizontal separation marking social organization. Blumenbach's response to Monboddo ultimately takes the form of denying the humanity of the wild man on the basis of "wildness" itself. When Peter first arrived in England, Defoe had heralded his arrival as offering decisive evidence on the natural condition of man:

> He is now, as I have said, in a State of Mere Nature, and that, indeed in the literal Sense of it. Let us delineate his Condition, if we can: He seems to be the very Creature which the learned World have, for many Years past, pretended to wish for, *viz.* one that being kept entirely from human society, so as never to have heard any one speak, must therefore either not speak at all, or, if he did form any Speech to himself, then they should know what Language Nature would first form for Mankind.
> (*Mere Nature* 17)

Blumenbach's repudiation of the evolutionist tendencies of Monboddo, Rousseau, and Linnaeus leads him to reverse the terms of this thought experiment. Far from being conclusive evidence as to man's natural condition, Peter is by virtue of his wildness excluded from that natural condition; instead, Blumenbach insists that man alone in the animal kingdom is naturally domestic: "Man is a domestic animal. But in order that other animals might be made domestic about him, individuals of their species were first of all torn from their wild condition, and made to live under cover, and become tame; whereas he on the contrary was born and appointed by nature the most completely domesticated animal" (qtd. in Singh and Zingg 190–91). According to this view, domesticated animals such as horses and dogs degenerate to their original wild condition when they enter the wild, but humans having no such original wild condition vary enormously from case to case. Peter, then, does not represent a primitive condition of natural man, prior to both language and society, as Monboddo claims, but is instead only a pathetic individual, probably driven from society because of particular impairments of reason, speech, or both. Blumenbach is certainly not the first to view Peter this way; Swift's judgment— "I can hardly think him wild in the Sense they report him"—suggests a similar view. The test for Monboddo, however, comes less from Blumenbach's response than it does from Samuel Johnson.

When Monboddo first began to publish his reflections on wild children, the orang-outang, and man, it would have been hard to find a more widely recognized representative of the triumph of civil society than Samuel Johnson. Johnson's *Journey to the Western Isles of Scotland* serves to stage a staple of Enlightenment conversation: the confrontation between civilization and the savage. Several years earlier, Boswell, recently returned from his tour of Europe, would champion Rousseau in an effort to provoke Johnson; this seems to have been a topic on which Boswell could rely in setting Johnson off: "I attempted to argue for the superior happiness of the savage life, upon the usual fanciful topicks" (2:73). Johnson's rebuke has all the earmarks of a long-rehearsed position in a familiar exchange, and it served at once to align Monboddo with Rousseau and to dismiss him from serious consideration: "No, Sir; you are not to talk such paradox: let me have no more on't. It cannot entertain, far less can it instruct. Lord Monboddo, one of your Scotch Judges, talked a great deal of such nonsense. I suffered him, but I will not suffer you. . . . Rousseau knows he is talking nonsense, and laughs at the world for staring at him. . . . But I am afraid (chuckling and laughing), Monboddo does not know that he is talking nonsense" (2:73–74). Nothing was more injurious to Monboddo's reputation in his lifetime and afterward than this bon mot; in particular, that parenthetical chuckle is hard to overcome.

When, at long last, Boswell succeeded in his efforts to bring Johnson to Scotland, their tour began and ended in Edinburgh. MacPherson's *Ossian* had appeared only a few years earlier, and throughout his tour of Scotland, Johnson frequently engages in contentious discussion over the poem's merit and origins.

That England's most renowned critic would be frequently engaged in discussion of a poem that claimed to establish a national poetry in Gaelic is not surprising.[6] From the beginning of the tour, however, discussion of MacPherson's *Ossian* (and the nationalist subtext to that discussion) is collapsed into discussions of Monboddo's *Origin and Progress* (and the species subtext to that discussion).

In May 1773, Boswell journeyed to London and confirmed Johnson's plans to join him in Edinburgh when the Court of Session rose in August. Monboddo's *Origin and Progress,* proposing that the existence of orang-outangs living in so- cially organized herds without language constituted evidence for a similar stage in the development of human society, provoked Johnson's dismissal: "He at- tacked Lord Monboddo's strange speculation on the primitive state of human nature; observing, 'Sir, it is all conjecture about a thing useless, even were it known to be true. Knowledge of all kinds is good. Conjecture, as to things use- ful, is good; but conjecture as to what it would be useless to know, such as whether men went upon all four, is very idle" (2:259–60). This, then, may be taken as Johnson's attitude when he set out on his journey; in Scotland, he hoped to see many things, but certainly he expected to encounter men who flat- tered the nationalist pretensions of a poem he maintained to be a forgery and who indulged the philosophical pretensions of one who courted singularity rather than truth. Both expectations played to the governing trope of the civi- lized English citizen confronting a savage race; Johnson in Scotland would be bringing "nurture" to "nature."

On his arrival, almost before the journey had begun, this opposition is staged. Johnson arrived in Edinburgh on August 14; on Monday the 16th, he met Sir Adolphus Oughton, "who was not only an excellent officer," Boswell writes, "but one of the most universal scholars I ever knew, had learned the Erse language, and expressed his belief in the authenticity of Ossian's Poetry" (5:45). Boswell fears from Johnson's reply that "the dispute would have run high be- tween them. But Sir Adolphus, who had a very sweet temper, changed the dis- course, grew playful, laughed at Lord Monboddo's notion of men having tails, and called him a Judge *a posteriori,* which amused Dr. Johnson, and thus hos- tilities were prevented" (5:45). Poor Monboddo; he seems destined for these bon mots. There is something paradigmatic in this juxtaposition: the con- troversy of MacPherson will always carry an unmistakable intensity that threat- ens to break out in conflict, famously in the episode of the threatening letter from MacPherson and Johnson's "courageous" reply; at the same time, Mon- boddo will be trotted out periodically, almost as jester or fool, to lessen tensions and ease hostilities.[7] Yet, oddly enough, our own attitudes tend to persist in these veins, even while evidence has reversed the poles: debate over the authenticity of MacPherson is at an end—no one today seeks the Ur text of a Gaelic epic; Monboddo's "conjecture" comprises one of the most important branches of modern science and remains far more vexed than Johnson could have imagined.

Later that evening, Monboddo's belief that the orang-outang may be taught to speak arises again and is again brought down by Johnson's ridicule. Basing his position on the anatomical conclusions of Tyson and others that the orang-outang was physically capable of speech, Monboddo reasoned (*posse, ergo esse*) that a speaking animal was an animal capable of speech, and that if man was deemed rational because he was capable of reason, then an orang-outang who was capable of speech was a speaking animal who had merely not *yet* learned his potential. Just as Swift's satire had problematized distinguishing man from beast on the grounds of reason, Monboddo challenged our distinction from orangs on the basis of speech. Johnson notes (favoring rhetoric over anatomy) that it is at least as possible that the orang-outang cannot speak as he can, but he yields that point in favor of the witticism: "I should have thought it not possible to find a Monboddo; yet *he* exists" (46). Johnson's arrival in Edinburgh, then, is marked by satiric wit: he will expose the knavery of imposture in the case of MacPherson and ridicule the folly of false reason in the case of Monboddo. In the recurrent debate of Enlightenment philosophers, what Boswell repeatedly calls "the familiar topick"—whether to prefer the savage or civilized state—satire is the triumphant mark of civilization, folly and knavery the sign of the savage.

Yet, for all of that, there is, as John Wain rightly notes, another side to Johnson's journey that reveals itself as soon as he sets out from Edinburgh:

> there are signs that Johnson was impatient, inwardly, for new experiences that should mark a total change from his accustomed life. He was hungry for wildness, solitude, the untamed. . . . On their very first day, crossing the Firth of Forth, he caught sight of the tiny island of Inch Keith and insisted that they land and explore it. Considering how many islands and how much exploration he was to encounter before the trip was over, his insistence points to a hankering to get in among wild nature from the very beginning. (306)

Inch Keith is that thoroughly constructed "wild nature" that we are familiar with in the form of metro parks; "small beer," as Wain puts it. This is not yet

Johnson in the sublime, but Dr. Johnson's summer vacation. In Boswell's narrative, it serves to mark a passage, from Edinburgh into Scotland, from culture into nature; in Johnson's *Journey,* it marks the beginning, the opening site. Its sublime elements—"shattered crags" and "unfrequented coasts" that have never "afforded to man or beast a permanent habitation"—operate in the service of the picturesque: "a small herd of cows grazes annually upon it in the summer" (3). Most notably, upon departure, the doctor evaluates its worth as cultural commodity: "if it had been placed at the same distance from London, with the same facility of approach; with what emulation of price a few rocky acres would have been purchased, and with what expensive industry they would have been cultivated and adorned" (4).[8]

The journey now begun soon brings together the English critic and the Scottish judge. On the third day, Boswell contemplates the opportunity of staging one of those confrontations that so pleased him: "I doubted much which road to take, whether to go by the coast, or by Laurence Kirk and Monboddo. I knew Lord Monboddo and Dr. Johnson did not love each other: yet I was unwilling not to visit his lordship; and was also curious to see them together" (5:74). In Johnson's *Journey,* the meeting is slightly mentioned, almost disregarded: "Early in the afternoon Mr. Boswell observed that we were at no great distance from the house of Lord Monboddo. The magnetism of his conversation easily drew us out of our way, and the entertainment which we received would have been a sufficient recompence for a much greater deviation" (12).

Boswell, typically, provides a fuller description of the meeting, filtered, of course, through his own ambivalence about potential fireworks. Monboddo was a close friend of Lord Auchinleck's, and Boswell is often torn between honoring and ridiculing him. When Monboddo gestures to his "poor old house" at greeting, the Lord gets in the first stroke: "'In such houses (said he,) our ancestors lived, who were better men than we.'—'No, no, my lord (said Dr. Johnson). We are as strong as they, and a great deal wiser'" (5:77). Clearly, both Monboddo and Johnson understand the parts assigned them in this event, and each welcomes his role. Boswell either fails to recognize this or recognizes that his role is to fail to recognize this: "I was afraid there would have been a violent altercation in the very close, before we got into the house" (5:77).

Boswell proceeds to record the details of their conversation, interspersing throughout the "points of similarity" he highlighted in a footnote when he first expressed a curiosity to see them together: "There were several points of similarity between them; learning, clearness of head, precision of speech, and a love of research on many subjects which people in general do not investigate. Foote paid Lord Monboddo the compliment of saying that he was 'an Elziver edition of Johnson.' It has been shrewdly observed [by Boswell?] that Foote must have meant a diminutive or pocket edition" (5:74 n.). In transcribing their conversation, Boswell notes, "Bravo! thought I; they agree like two brothers" (5:80); and later, "My lord was extremely hospitable, and I saw both Dr. Johnson and him liking each other better every hour" (5:81). Monboddo invites them to spend the night, but Boswell insists they must be in Aberdeen by night; on the road again, Johnson pronounces himself "much pleased" with Monboddo. Lord Monboddo had sent Gory, his black servant, to conduct them to the high road, and Boswell reflects "the circumstance of each of them having a black servant was another point of similarity between Johnson and Monboddo" (5:82).

After all the preparation, then, here at the very outset of Johnson's tour, the anticipated confrontation that threatens to break out "in the very close, before we got into the house," dissipates into a series of agreements and similarities. In the midst of these courteous exchanges, Boswell drops a one-line reference to what passed on "the familiar topick": "My lord and Dr. Johnson disputed a little, whether the Savage or the London Shopkeeper had the best existence; his lordship, as usual, preferring the Savage" (5:81). Here, one would expect the fireworks promised, "in the very close," and Boswell's biographer voices a disappointment that Boswell himself must have felt after bringing these two together:

> Soon came a touchier subject, the relative happiness of the savage (Monboddo, advocate) and the London shopkeeper (Johnson, advocate). We might wish some details of the discussion were preserved, since this reflected the central question (the respective merits of a semi-feudal and a commercial society) posed by the tour itself. But in this last oblique transposition of the quarrel between the Ancients and the Moderns the positions had become frozen, and Johnson was to admit he could have argued equally well on behalf of the savage. Perhaps this is why the argument remained amiable, and nothing was said, pro or con, about tails. (Brady 61)

Even, it would seem, when Johnson himself is prepared to spare Monboddo, Johnsonians and Boswellians rush forward, pointing to tails. While I agree strongly with Brady as to the centrality of this topic with respect to the tour itself, I differ from him as to the topic being frozen out of age and exhaustion. Moreover (as I hope to show) the debate, staged here at the outset of the journey, although it goes largely unrecorded, continues to echo throughout the tour. Certainly, Brady captures the artifice of the argument in assigning Monboddo and Johnson their respective roles as "advocates" for savages and shopkeepers. It is in the very nature of this "familiar topick" of philosophers that the subjects being compared are subordinated to the citizens of enlightenment who will adjudicate their claims to happiness in the rational discursive space of the bourgeois public sphere.

Johnson makes no mention of the debate in his *Journey;* Boswell quotes a single remark Johnson makes as they resume their trip: "He observed, that his lordship had talked no paradoxes today. 'And as to the savage and the London shopkeeper, (said he,) I don't know but I might have taken the side of the savage equally, had anybody else taken the side of the shopkeeper'" (5:83). Johnson's fullest account of the exchange occurs in his letter to Hester Thrale Piozzi, dated August 25, 1773:

> We . . . dined at Lord Monboddo's, the Scotch Judge who has lately written a
> strange book about the origin of Language, in which he traces Monkeys up to Men,
> and says that in some countries the human species have tails like other beasts. He
> enquired for these longtailed Men of Banks, and was not well pleased, that they
> had not been found in all his peregrination. He talked nothing of this to me, and I
> hope, we parted friends, for we agreed pretty well, only we differed in adjusting the
> claims of merit between a Shopkeeper of London, and a Savage of the American
> wilderness. Our opinions were, I think, maintained on both sides without full conviction; Monboddo declared boldly for the Savage and I perhaps for that reason
> sided with the Citizen. (*Letters,* no. 321, 1:344–45)

From the opening salvo, the entire tenor of this visit has been one where both advocates seem willing to stage their difference for Boswell's (and posterity's) benefit, more as public discursive exercise than as the articulation of deeply felt difference. Monboddo and Johnson are equally citizens of the Enlightenment, they agree about this as about so much else, and the rules of such citizenship require them to adopt adversarial positions, on "the familiar topick." When they part, whichever account we consult—Johnson's, Boswell's, or the letter to Hester Thrale—they part on friendly terms within the sanctioned space of rational dispute that defines humanity by enlightened citizenship.

The quarrel is unresolved, and its specter accompanies Johnson into the Highlands. Heretofore, Monboddo has represented the folly of the degenerative thesis through a comic personification in which he is collapsed into the figure of the wild man in the same way that the Scriblerians confused Tyson and

his pygmy. Monboddo's ability to play by the rules of civil debate without recourse to the paradoxical singularities that infuriated Johnson seem to have
won him Johnson's respect, if not agreement. The fundamental disagreement
continues to present itself, nonetheless, and it is not long before it arises again.
Less than a week later, Johnson and Boswell pay a visit in Cullen to William
Robertson, a former clerk of Monboddo's who had accompanied the lord to
France to interview the wild girl of Soigny.[9]

Johnson makes no mention of the meeting in either the *Journey* or his letters, but Boswell reports of their conversation that "Robertson said, he did not
believe so much as his lordship did; that it was plain to him, the girl confounded
what she imagined with what she remembered: that, besides, she perceived
Condamine and Lord Monboddo forming theories, and she adapted her story
to them" (5:110–11). One should, in fairness, wonder if Robertson, in the company of Boswell and Johnson, may not have been guilty of the same offence.
This conversation offers Boswell the opportunity to record some of Johnson's
remarks on Monboddo that would have seemed more out of place when the
lord was their host:

> "It is a pity to see Lord Monboddo publish such notions as he has done; a man
> of sense, and of so much elegant learning. There would be little in a fool doing it;
> we should only laugh; but when a wise man does it, we are sorry. Other people
> have strange notions; but they conceal them. If they have tails, they hide them;
> but Monboddo is as jealous of his tail as a squirrel." . . . He said he did not approve
> of a judge's calling himself *Farmer* Burnett and going about with a little round
> hat. (5:111)

Monboddo challenges Johnson's understanding of civil society as much as his
beliefs about natural philosophy. He does not approve of the lord's affectation
of rustication, and he is perplexed by his public singularity. To be wise and yet
voice such notions is as contradictory as any of Monboddo's vexing paradoxes.
Had Monboddo, perhaps, behaved with less courtesy or argued more eccentri-
cally (and, certainly, his writings show he was capable of eccentric argument),
he would have been less of a challenge to classify; but a wise and educated man
arguing for the kinship of all primates is as disturbing as *homo caudatus*—or
Farmer Burnett, Lord Monboddo.

Monboddo may have been troubling,, but he was also pleasing, and Johnson
seems genuinely to have grown fond of him. He takes to referring to him, as he
did to his closest friends, by a diminutive contraction of the first syllable of his

14. James Burnett, Lord Monboddo, in his affected dress of rustic simplicity (1773); his characteristic finger-pointing pose dramatizes his disputatious engagement in public sphere discourse.

name: just as Goldsmith became "Goldy" and Boswell "Bozzy," Monboddo becomes "Monny." At Dunvegan in Skye, Boswell finds Johnson on a Sunday morning with a singular (if not downright paradoxical) collection of reading material: Bacon's *Works, The Decay of Christian Piety,* Sterne's *Sermons,* and Monboddo's *Origin and Progress of Language.*[10]

The wild man operates as "other" to Johnson's "citizen" throughout his tour, and he does so in a variety of ways: inhabitant of wild nature, rather than civil society; rude and inarticulate, rather than polished and refined; solitary and independent, rather than loyal and social. These oppositions repeatedly define Johnson's encounters and perceptions, and frequently, as in the initial encounter with Monboddo, these oppositions collapse into one another. Johnson's long letter to Hester Thrale, written from September 15–21 and posted from Dunvegan in Skye, articulates this rhythm of collapsing oppositions, filtered through Johnson's own emotional rhythm of excitement and exhaustion:

Macleod has offered me an Island, if it were not too far off I should hardly refuse it; my Island would be pleasanter than Brighthelmston, if you and Master could come to it, but I cannot think it pleasant to live quite alone. . . . It has often happened that I have been often recognized in my journey where I did not expect it. . . . [MacQueen] had been *out* as they call it, in forty five, and still retained his old opinions. He was going to America, because his rent was raised beyond what he thought himself able to pay . . .

I sat down to take notes on a green bank, with a small stream running at my feet, in the midst of savage solitude, with Mountains before me, and on either hand covered with heath. I looked round me and wondered that I was not more affected, but the mind is not at all times equally ready to be put in motion. If my Mistress, and Master, and Queeny had been there we should have produced some reflections among us either poetical or philosophical, for though *Solitude* be *the nurse of woe,* conversation is often the parent of remarks and discoveries . . .

The Inhabitants, a very coarse tribe, ignorant of any language but Earse, gathered so fast about us, that if we had not had Highlanders with us, they might have caused more alarm than pleasure . . .

I cannot forbear to interrupt my Narrative. Boswell, with some of his troublesome kindness, has informed this family, and reminded me that the eighteenth of September is my birthday. The return of my Birthday, if I remember it, fills me with thoughts which it seems to be the general care of humanity to escape . . .

You are perhaps imagining that I am withdrawn from the gay and the busy world into regions of peace and pastoral felicity, and am enjoying the reliques of the golden age; that I am surveying Nature's magnificence from a mountain, or remarking her minuter beauties on the flowery bank of a winding rivulet, that I am invigorating myself in the sunshine, or delighting my imagination with being hidden from the invasion of human evils and human passions, in the darkness of a Thicket, that I am busy in gathering shells and pebbles on the Shore, or contemplative on a rock, from which I look upon the water and consider how many waves are rolling between me and Streatham.

The use of travelling is to regulate imagination by reality, and instead of thinking how things may be, to see them as they are. Here are mountains which I should once have climbed, but the climb steeps is now very laborious, and to descend them dangerous, and I am now content with knowing that by scrambling up a rock, I shall only see other rocks, and a wider circuit of barren desolation. Of streams we have here a sufficient number, but they murmur not upon pebbles, but upon rocks; of flowers, if Chloris herself were here, I could present her only with the bloom of Heath. Of Lawns and Thickets, he must read, that would know them, for here is little sun and no shade. On the sea I look from my window, but am not much tempted to the shore for since I came to this Island, almost every Breath of

15. The triumphant figure of
Dr. Johnson on tour in Scotland, wielding his immense
walking stick (1773); see also
the primates with walking
sticks in figures 1 and 2 (page
33).

air has been a storm, and what is worse, a storm with all its severity, but without its
magnificence, for the sea is here so broken into channels, that there is not a
sufficient volume of water either for lofty surges, or loud roar. . . .

The Wine circulates vigorously, and the tea and Chocolate and Coffee, however
they are got are always at hand.

I am Madam Your most obedient servant

Skie. Sep. 21. 1773   Sam: Johnson

We are this morning trying to get out of Skie. (353–61)

Johnson is well able to imagine the sublime delights of wild nature, but only in
the context of a realistic description of exhausting desolation. The melancholy
pleasures of solitude take a back seat to the social pleasure of the conversation
he must forego; and yet, what could be more vexing than to be feted on his
birthday when he wants nothing so much as to retreat in solitude to ponder the
approach of his own mortality? The weather is lousy, and it is not romantic—

it is just unpleasant; he is surrounded by savages who threaten to become threatening instead of remaining suitably picturesque. After reading this letter, I could not resist telling a colleague that I was "interested in accounts of large primates, capable of bipedal locomotion and of wielding a stick, but unable to comprehend the language of humans around them—for that is the condition of Dr. Johnson in Skye." [11]

Johnson in the Highlands would seem to reverse the experiment of the feral child. Instead of a natural man raised outside society reintroduced into society, Johnson presents himself as civilized man put into the wild, surrounded by tribes who speak only a barbaric tongue. Within the semiotic square, his ear might group Highlanders with Yahoos and orang-outangs, socially organized but without written language. Importantly, however, the Highlands provide a site for an alternative space of departure from the enlightened citizen—the space of the recluse, hermit, or exile. For the Highlands are identified with "the" solitary other to the citizen—the Pretender. On September 12, the party arrives at Skye: "To see Dr. Samuel Johnson, the great champion of the English Tories, salute Miss Flora MacDonald in the isle of Sky, was a striking sight; for though somewhat congenial in their notions, it was very improbable they should meet here" (5:184). That night, Johnson sleeps in the same bed where Charles Stuart slept, and the next day he hears from Flora MacDonald the romantic tale of her part in the prince's flight from Culloden.

Throughout the tour of the highlands, the romance of "the forty-five" animates the journey; often, as in the letter to Hester Thrale quoted above, allusions to that romance are associated with depopulation and emigration. Just as Johnson is repeatedly moved by the loyalty of the Highlanders to their prince in exile, so he is moved by their poverty forcing them into exile in the wilds of America. In each case, the poignancy of loss combines with the dissolving of social order. Rather than viewing Johnson's sympathy for the Highlanders as symptomatic of Jacobitism, I would prefer to read it as part of that ambivalent rhythm that prompted him to reflect that in the debate with Monboddo, the two could just as easily have reversed positions. [12]

Virtually the first stop on the journey after leaving Edinburgh had been at the home of Monboddo, who had attempted to help bring about a reconciliation between Boswell and his father, Lord Auchinleck, an old friend of Monboddo's. As the journey drew to a close, the last stop before Edinburgh was with Lord Auchinleck himself. If Boswell had hoped to stir controversy between Johnson and Monboddo, he positively hoped to prevent turmoil with his father, of whom Boswell writes: "He was as sanguine a Whig and Presbyterian, as Dr. Johnson was a Tory and church of England man . . . he used to call [Johnson] 'a Jacobite fellow.' . . . I was very anxious that all should be well; and begged of my friend to avoid three topicks, as to which they differed very widely; Whiggism, Presbyterianism, and—Sir John Pringle" (5:376).[13] The anticipated confrontation with Monboddo may have dissipated, but the visit to Auchinleck lasted six days, and before it was over, "Whiggism and Presbyterianism, Toryism and Episcopacy, were terribly buffeted" (5:384).

Brady represents the opening meeting with Monboddo as a disappointment because we do not hear the arguments pro and con on the relative happiness of savage and shopkeeper. The arguments themselves, however, must disappoint; they are static and frozen not of age, but out of its very artificial nature. Indeed, the dispute, at once caricaturing the postures of Johnson and Monboddo and showing their interchangeable nature, serves as an ideal introduction to the rhythm of the tour of the Highlands. In little ways, the events of that tour show that Johnson at least was aware of that rhythm in his responses to wild nature, emigration, Erse, Jacobite loyalty, and highland poverty. Shortly after Johnson's letter to Hester Thrale, the party encounters Donald MacLean, "Young Col."

Young Col is to be their guide for the longest part of the journey and plays a heroic role in the one genuinely life-threatening moment on the trip. Johnson had hoped to "escape" Skye on September 21, but the weather continued bad, and they were still bound to the island on October 3. Then, a break in the weather suggests they might make it to Icolmkill, but once they are underway the weather closes in again. Col undertakes to pilot the boat through the storm to the island of Col and—not without difficulty—pulls it off: "The master knew not well whither to go; and our difficulties might perhaps have filled a very pathetic page, had not Mr. Maclean of Col, who, with every other qualification which insular life requires, is a very active and skilful mariner, piloted us safe into his own harbor" (120). Both Johnson and Boswell lament the news that Col drowned in similar circumstances the following year. Col had been heir apparent to his father's role as feudal lord and had been preparing for that role by working on English farms in order to bring English principles of husbandry to the highlands. Both Johnson and Boswell comment favorably on this emulation of Russia's Peter the Great: "If the world has agreed to praise the travels and manual labours of the Czar of Muskovy, let Col have his share of the like applause, in the proportion of his dominions to the empire of Russia" (76).

Johnson is brief in enumerating Col's shortcomings ("I regret that he is not more intellectual"); Boswell at once clarifies and clouds the issue. Although he endorses Johnson's view, he notes that Col would speak forcefully and was not unwilling to disagree with Johnson. Boswell's greatest reservation was that Col did not yet command that respect and "dignity" that Boswell liked in his aristocrats; people liked Col but did not pay him the little gestures of respect that his position ought to command. When they take leave of Col for the last time on October 18, both Boswell and Johnson are effusive in their praise. "Dr. Johnson said, 'Col does every thing for us: we will erect a statue to Col'" (5:327). Boswell's narrative of the moment indicates that Dr. Johnson remains sensitive to the argument with Monboddo:

> Young Col told us he could run down a greyhound; "for, (said he,) the dog runs himself out of breath, by going too quick, and then I get up with him." I accounted for his advantage over the dog, by remarking that Col had the faculty of reason, and knew how to moderate his pace, which the dog had not sense enough to do. Dr. Johnson said, "He is a noble animal. He is as complete an islander as the mind can figure. He is a farmer, a sailor, a hunter, a fisher: he will run you down a dog: if any man has a *tail*, it is Col." (5:330)

The passage epitomizes the ambivalent rhythm of the shopkeeper/savage debate, as it manifests itself throughout the journey: Col possesses the physical superiority that Monboddo claimed on behalf of the savage life; Boswell counters that Col's victory demonstrates man's rational superiority to beast (though neither Boswell nor Johnson offer to demonstrate the technique themselves); Johnson classes Col as "a noble animal." Surely the reference to Monboddo's belief in the existence of *homo caudatus* is comic, but the comedy is unstable. If, on one hand, Johnson chooses to view this as one more occasion to smile at Monboddo's belief, he does so while granting the practical excellencies that Col possesses and that Monboddo has claimed as the virtues of savage life. It would be wrong to reduce Johnson's attitude to merely bestializing Col (and the highlanders), although he classes him as an animal; Johnson is, as the comparison to the "Czar of Muscovy" makes clear, a genuine admirer of Col's "noble" attributes. The shopkeeper/savage debate presumes clear distinctions; Col represents the liminal case that renders the debate inconclusive. If Monboddo challenged Johnson's expectations by behaving as a proper Citizen of Enlightenment, Col challenges those expectations by exemplifying the virtues Monboddo had claimed on behalf of the savage.

If when Johnson left Edinburgh he expected to meet the folly of one who believed in the kinship of primates and the knavery of one who professed to translate from a language that had no literature, we might ask how far those expectations were realized in the event. However much Johnson may develop sympathy for Monboddo's folly, he clearly hardens his position with respect to MacPherson's knavery. In his account of the "transit of Caledonia," Pat Rogers rightly links the intellectual roles played by Monboddo and MacPherson in the tour, in that they "illustrate the interconnections between such themes as Ossian and the state of primitive society" (8). Yet I believe his account understates the degree to which Johnson's stance with respect to Monboddo's claims for the natural condition of man exhibits far more flexibility than his stance with respect to MacPherson's claims on behalf of an Erse literature. Throughout the tour of the Hebrides, the nobility of the highlanders is indicated by their social impulses (loyalty, hospitality, industry, etc.); their savagery almost always is indicated by their barbarous language: "I have always difficulty to be patient when I hear authors gravely quoted, as giving accounts of savage nations, which accounts they had from the savages themselves. What can *McCraas* tell about themselves a thousand years ago? There is no tracing the connection of ancient nations, but by language; and therefore I am always sorry when any language is lost, because languages are the pedigree of nations" (5:224–25).

Over and over again, Johnson encounters Highlanders who support the claims of MacPherson, and every one he confronts with his skepticism. He leaves the Highlands more convinced than when he arrived of the impossibility of the claims to an Erse national epic. The dispute between Johnson and MacPherson is a literary dispute, and it is also a dispute as to national identity.[14] When, however, Johnson turns his attention fully to a sustained characterization of Erse, that characterization culminates in a rhetorical flourish that subordinates literary and national disputes to the border where natural history meets early anthropology: "But this is the age in which those who could not read have been supposed to write; in which the giants of antiquated romance have been exhibited as realities. If we know little of the ancient Highlanders, let us not fill the vacuity with Ossian. If we have not searched the Magellanic regions, let us however forbear to people them with Patagons" (119). Whatever flexibility Johnson has been willing to demonstrate in his engagement with Monboddo's claims for the natural condition of man disappears when the trope is brought forward to decide the dispute with MacPherson. For the lexicographer, the limits of language and literacy are as clear and distinct a border as the material body was for Tyson at the end of the previous century. Like Tyson, Johnson invokes the clear truth of natural history as the privileged alternative to "antiquated romance." And the consequence of such a border construction is to locate literate, cultured civilization squarely within the clearly defined realm of the human, while relegating oral cultures to the outlying Magellanic regions of quasi-human "Patagons" and "the giants of antiquated romance" on exhibition.

Johnson concludes his tour where he began, in Edinburgh. This is the final appearance of Monboddo in Boswell's narrative, for we are told that on one of Johnson's last evenings, the lord "disengaged himself on purpose to meet" him for supper. There is, however, another less direct appearance that Monboddo makes and that Johnson positions as his final comment in the *Journey*. He chooses to end his *Journey* with a description of Braidwood's academy—a description that again highlights the juxtaposition of nature/culture:

> There is one subject of philosophical curiosity to be found in Edinburgh, which no other city has to shew; a college of the deaf and dumb, who are taught to speak, to read, to write, and to practice arithmetick, by a gentleman, whose name is Braidwood. . . .
>
> I do not mean to mention the instruction of the deaf as new. Having been first practised upon the son of a Constable of Spain, it was afterwards cultivated with much emulation in England, by Wallis and Holder, and was lately professed by Mr. Baker, who once flattered me with hopes of seeing his method published. (162–63)

Henry Baker, to whom Johnson here alludes, was Defoe's son-in-law who instructed the deaf and was recommended by Defoe as a suitable tutor for Peter when he first arrived in England. Johnson proceeds to describe Braidwood's successes, focusing on a young lady who solves a problem in arithmetic that he sets for her. His conclusion, which stands as the conclusion of the *Journey*, generalizes from the condition of the deaf to the condition of the inhabitants of the wild Hebrides: "It was pleasing to see one of the most desperate of human calamities capable of so much help: whatever enlarges hope, will exalt courage; after having seen the deaf taught arithmetick, who would be afraid to cultivate the Hebrides?" (164)

Monboddo had repeatedly championed Braidwood's success in his accounts of attempts to teach language to Peter and enjoy the praises of extending humanity to those whom nature has set apart: "But if we could get an Ouran Outang, or a mute savage, such as he above mentioned, that was caught in the woods of Hanover, and would take the same pains to teach him to think that Mr. Braidwood takes to teach his scholars to speak, we should soon be convinced that the formal part of language was as difficult to be learned as the material" (*Origin* 186). The urbane debate regarding the savage and the shopkeeper with which this journey began is figured in Johnson's *Journey* as "the magnetism of . . . conversation," the very hallmark of civilization from which the deaf are by definition precluded.

Although we do not have the details of Johnson's opening debate with Monboddo, the narratives of the journey repeatedly evoke the ambivalent rhythms of that encounter. Once we are alerted to the figure of the wild man, we glimpse him again and again throughout the trip. "Monboddo's notion of Man," Barnard reminds us, "is explicitly not based on language, but depends rather on the ability and practice of making weapons and tools" (78). In this, he seems to stand in stark opposition to Johnson. As the journey continues, however, we can see Johnson (even in comic moments) returning to consider Monboddo's point. In the disputes over *Ossian,* Johnson insists on language as the trait that distinguishes savagery from civilization; but repeatedly his encounters with the Highlanders compromise that insistence. Certainly the final visit to Braidwood's academy is marked by none of the whimsical humor that marks his usual references to Monboddo, and the position he adopts is Monboddo's own. If there is a single moment of comic recognition of Monboddo's triumph, it may come when the reader recognizes that Johnson in the Highlands embodies not so much his own conception of man as Monboddo's: surrounded by barbarians with whom he shares no language, Johnson is reduced to the status of bipedal primate, wielding a large staff. There is good reason to believe that Johnson himself was aware of this comedy. On that initial visit to Monboddo, after their debate over the shopkeeper and the savage, as well as their agreement over the excellencies of that most bardic of poets, Homer, Johnson took leave of the lord with a telling allusion. Picking up his walking stick, an oak wattle taller than himself with part of the root still attached as a knob, he said, "My Lord, that's Homeric." The jest offers an olive branch (indeed, most of the tree) to Monboddo's passion for Homer, and it does so by casting the famous lexicographer in Monboddo's preferred role for the exemplary human: bipedal, weapon-wielding primate. That jest returns, in more pointed form, after Johnson's return to London when MacPherson contended in print with Johnson's strictures on language. When, after the publication of the *Journey* and its denunciation of *Ossian,* MacPherson sent Johnson an impudent and threatening letter, Johnson responded with a public allusion to that staff, printing his reply, which begins "I received your foolish and impudent letter. Any violence offered me I shall do my best to repel" (2:298). The preposterously large walking staff that yokes the image of Johnson astride the Scottish landscape (see figure 15) with the image of a pygmy chimpanzee astride the English landscape (see figure 1 and figure 2) recurs in startlingly opposite deployments in his encounters with Monboddo and MacPherson. Where the defining trope of the wild man is brought forward when he takes his leave of Monboddo, it serves to offer a bridge across their artificial debate to join hands in a negotiated settlement that at once privileges Homer and sociability. With MacPherson, however, Johnson wields his weapon in defiant animosity to the threatening pretensions of one who would claim civilization for those beyond the pale where literacy dissolves into oral tradition. To the extent that the figure of the wild man lurks on the periphery of human identity, defined by his relation to the normative along the axes of language and sociability, then Johnson's interactions with Monboddo and MacPherson throughout the tour of Scotland underline the shifting dynamics and affiliations surrounding the construction of a normative human identity. As Barnard reminds us, Monboddo's hypothesis of the wild man presumes that sociability and tool use characterize an essential humanity that provides the necessary precondition to language acquisition—orang-outangs constitute humans' "prior to" language; such a view, however much Johnson might oppose and ridicule it, proves ultimately unthreatening. MacPherson, however, is another case, and his claims on behalf of an oral culture as a rival to literary civilization are to be forcibly repudiated. The staff of the wild man with which Monboddo and Johnson consolidate their agreement to differ in sociable dispute becomes the weapon with which Johnson threatens to beat back MacPherson's challenge to literate civilization.

6

The End of Homo Ferus

*in which one feral child survives the
revolution in France and invents
special education, another feral
child returns to society (driving his
father into exile), an orangutan
establishes residency at Exeter
Change, and an Oran Haut-Ton
stands for parliament*

In some ways, perhaps this study should come to an end with Johnson's return from Scotland. Instead, I want to pursue the wild man one generation deeper into the modern world. Samuel Johnson was born in 1709 and died in 1784; Peter the wild boy was an almost exact contemporary, born circa 1712 and died in 1785.[1] Sometime in the next two or three years was born the most famous of eighteenth-century feral children, Victor of Aveyron. His story is as well documented and narrated as Peter's is obscure and forgotten; the different career paths of Peter and Victor (who died, in his forties, in 1828) offer some insight into the cultural transformations that took place within their lifetimes.[2]

First sighted in 1797 by peasants in south central France, the boy was seen gathering nuts and roots on several occasions, but he always fled into the forest. The following year he was captured and put on display in the village of Lacaune. For a few days he attracted attention, but when interest waned, he was soon able to escape. The following summer, hunters captured him again, and he was again taken to Lacaune and entrusted to the care of an old widow; after eight days, he again escaped. Instead of returning to the forest, he crossed the mountains into the department of Aveyron; that winter he was captured for a final time on January 8, 1800. Described in official reports in the months that followed, the boy enters civilization semiotically through letters, reports, and news accounts; soon, as a consequence of these reports, he is materially brought to Paris, where he is officially assigned to Dr. Jean-Marc Gaspard Itard. Itard takes charge of Victor's education and material care, but the doctor is also responsible for the youth's semiotic presentation and authors two reports (1801, 1807). After this last report, Victor's education is abandoned, and he is once again entrusted to the care of an old woman. Almost a decade later, in 1816, he is visited a final time by the naturalist Julien-Joseph Virey, who publishes an account. Twelve years later, he dies an obscure Parisian death. Virey's final notice of Victor, included in his contribution, titled "Hommes, Hommes des Bois, et Hommes Sauvages," to the *Nouveau dictionnaire* (1817) coincides with several literary representations of the wild man, particularly Thomas Love Peacock's little-known *Melincourt* (1817) and Mary Shelley's famous *Frankenstein* (1818).

The material-semiotic actor of the wild man found an advocate in Rousseau and a champion in Monboddo, but his eighteenth-century nemesis was certainly Johann Friedrich Blumenbach. For Monboddo—whose expansive notion of humanity included the orang-outang—Peter, as exemplary feral child, provided the strongest case for Linnaeus's category of *homo sapiens ferus*. Blumenbach set out to discredit this classification, and his principal target was Monboddo's assertion that "I consider his [Peter's] history as a brief chronicle or abstract of the history of the progress of human nature, from the mere animal to the first stage of civilized life" (*Antient Metaphysics* 3:57). Blumenbach's pointed opposition to Monboddo arises, in part, from his relation to the long-standing differences between Linnaen systematics and Buffon's natural history.

For the naturalist Buffon, the anatomical similarities between humans and apes were more than offset by the stark differences in their moral natures; nothing more dramatically signaled that natural difference than the possession of language. For Rousseau and for Monboddo, the evidence of language was, at best, inconclusive, and the wild man belonged in the human family. Linnaeus, maddeningly, left the matter unresolved. In an early edition of the *Systema,* humans and apes had been classed together as *Anthropomorpha* among the *Quadrupeds.* Linnaeus had been attacked on both points. *Anthropomorpha* meant "man-like," and although apes might be considered "man-like," men could hardly be classified as "like themselves." More urgent was the claim that bipedal man deserved to be elevated above the quadruped brutes. Privately,

Linnaeus maintained the position that bipedal locomotion was an acquired rather than a natural trait—infants must learn to walk; but, publicly, he revised his *Systema*. In the tenth edition, man was now listed first among a new order, *Primates*, at the head of the class of *Mammals* (who suckle their young). Within the order of primates, Linnaeus distinguishes between the orang-outangs (*simia*) and Man (*homo*); but he finesses the issue by including the wild man within the species *homo* as *homo sapiens ferus* and *homo troglodytes*. Blumenbach extends the logic of Linnaean systematics in order to effect Buffon's clear distinction between man and the wild man and jettison from Linnaeus's species classification Rousseau's and Monboddo's exemplary cases:

> Blumenbach's comparative anatomy of racial differences was judged altogether more reliable than the earlier speculative and even fabulous classifications of the varieties of man propounded by Linnaeus, and it soon came to be much preferred, as well, to the genetic and evolutionary perspective—on the racial deformations of a single human archetype—adopted by Buffon and his followers. Modern physical anthropology, in effect, may be said to have arisen in response to the hypothetical taxonomies and conjectural natural histories of the enlightenment. (Wokler 45)

Blumenbach's seminal work, *On the Natural Varieties of Mankind* (1775), opens the field of physical anthropology with an insistence on the unity of the human species. A proper classification of the species *homo* will mark an unbridgeable species distinction between those who constitute varieties descended from a common original and those who trace to another genesis. In this respect, his physical anthropology marks a culmination of the project Tyson had initiated with his comparative anatomy. Over the next two decades, Blumenbach sharpens his position in explicit contrast to Monboddo's consideration of the hypothesis that the orang-outang may be considered "an infantine member of the human species." Ultimately in 1811, Blumenbach focuses his attack on the Linnaean category of *Homo sapiens ferus;* in doing so, he seizes for rhetorical purposes on both Peter of Hameln and Lord Monboddo as his chosen combatants, and his success is largely responsible for consigning both figures to the obscurity of historical minutiae. The emergence of physical anthropology is, in no small part, the product of changing cultural forces, and one measure of the significance of those changes is to contrast briefly the careers of Peter of Hameln and Victor of Aveyron.

Like Peter before him, Victor entered civilization through the newspapers, through correspondence, and through public display. Just as descriptions of

Peter conflicted with one another over details while organizing themselves around the more or less stable categories of diet, locomotion, nakedness, passion, and speech, so too the initial discussions of Victor follow these same rubrics even as they contradict and qualify one another. Early accounts (most of which are reproduced by Harlan Lane) repeatedly note that he refuses bread and meat, eating only vegetables and showing a preference for nuts and potatoes (which, in some accounts, he at first ate only raw but soon began to eat cooked). He is generally described as quite fast, trotting when he walks, and sometimes moving rapidly on all fours. He is described as naked when found, though at least one of the early letters suggests some doubt on this point. He is in some accounts completely mute, in others he makes inarticulate cries; in some he is completely deaf, in others he betrays some sense of hearing. He is frequently described as insensitive to extremes of hot or cold, though some accounts describe his cries upon pulling a potato out of the fire; other accounts indicate he has a "pleasing laugh," that he is responsive to affection, and that he cries out in distress when one takes his food away. And, like Peter, he is a sensation and a spectacle—first in Lacaune, as Peter was in Hanover; subsequently in Paris, as Peter was in London. But beyond that surface similarity, the society Victor enters is not the society Peter entered, and from the beginning the two are constructed differently.

Peter's entry into society was into a court-centered society, and accounts of his arrival trade on that fact. His appearance in London is marked by his reception by the haut monde. Swift's earliest mention of Peter in correspondence remarks that he has been promised to the princess's court, but that his arrival has been delayed for two weeks, because he has proven such a popular attraction at the king's court. While the delineator may have hoped that his care and education would be entrusted to an educator who specialized in language acquisition (albeit that such a hope may have been prompted by mercenary motives), in fact he was turned over to the keeping of the Royal Physician. An early satiric pamphlet identified Peter's place in the royal household in part by his identification with the dwarf who served as Royal Page. The entrepreneurial pamphlet that sought Peter's virtual endorsement for a patent remedy for venereal disease identified royal patronage with Peter's upwardly mobile status. When Peter lost his cachet as a social attraction, he no longer held Arbuthnot's interest and was farmed out.[3]

Victor entered a very different society indeed. Eight years after the fall of the *ancien régime,* and six years after the end of the Reign of Terror, Victor entered the modern world of bureaucracy. The early correspondence initiated by his arrival in Lacaune spreads to include various local commissioners, orphanage and institute directors, the minister of the interior (Lucien Bonaparte), and the secretary of the recently founded Society of the Observers of Man. This last-named organization is officially charged with evaluating Victor, and after his arrival in Paris in August 1800, a select committee is assigned to report on him:

> The Society of Observers of Man appointed an impressive commission to study the boy and report its observations: [Philippe] Pinel, unequaled authority on mental disease; Sicard, linguist, educator, and director of the Institute for Deaf-Mutes; Jauffret, secretary of the society and a naturalist; De Gerando, philosopher and author of a prize-winning four-volume treatise on language and thought; Cuvier, the most celebrated anatomist of his time and secretary of the Academy of Sciences. (56)

By the end of the year Pinel's committee issues its report concluding that Victor is *pretendu sauvage,* a mere idiot. Nonetheless, he is entrusted to the care and keeping of Abbe Sicard's pupil, Itard, who two days later is appointed resident physician at the National Institute for Deaf-Mutes. Itard's first formal report is issued six months later, which concludes with reasonable caution that more definitive conclusions should await more detailed observation. For the next five years, Itard works with his student while Napoleonic France consolidates its gains under the now-imperial government. In June 1806 the minister of the interior writes the following letter to Itard: "I know, sir, that your care of the young Victor who was entrusted to you five years ago has been as generous as it has been diligent. It is essential for humanity and for science to know the results. I invite you therefore to send me a detailed account, which will allow me to compare his original condition with his current one, and to judge what hopes we may still entertain concerning this child and the type of vocation he should be assigned" (qtd. in Lane, *Wild Boy* 133).

These quite different cultural contexts construct the material/semiotic actor of the wild youth quite differently. However much the conclusion of Pinel's committee (that Victor is a *pretendu sauvage*) echoes Swift's earlier appraisal that he could not think Peter "wild, at least not in the sense they report him," the difference between private subjective appraisal and formal committee finding speaks to the markedly different cultural locations of these two feral children. Politically, Peter entered a public sphere that was still court-centered; Victor enters the realm of a bureaucratic, systematic Republic. Semiotically, Peter

was the subject of pamphlet literature of quacks and satirists; the former traf-
ficked in superstitious enthusiasm and pseudo-scientific optimism, the latter
checked this enthusiasm with the skepticism of satire. Victor, on the other hand,
is the subject of reports, both journalistic and medical, where romantic optimism of innate potential is checked by a cautious skepticism of scientific finding. Between the appearance of Peter and the appearance of Victor, the world
had seen the entire course of Peter's life, as well as the life of Marie-Angelique
Memmie Le Blanc, the wild girl of Soigny who had become a nun. The early efforts of individuals such as Henry Baker to tutor the deaf privately had become
institutionalized in settings such as Braidwood's academy in Scotland, and even
more so in France, where the schools of Sicard and Epee had formalized an alternative method of instruction. When Peter came to England, he seemed to be
(in the words of his delineator) "the experiment the learned world had long
wished for" to test Locke's notion of innate ideas, but no systematic apparatus
existed for conducting such an experiment. When Victor entered Paris, however, an institutionalized apparatus was readily available for testing the hypothesis of ideologues. Peter may have been entering a world of royal patronage
and pensions, but Victor was entering a world of systematic study in the service
of the state. Where Peter's innocent follies were at once humbling reminders
and the foil for satires on corruption and knavery, Victor—read through the
lens of the official reports of Bonaterre, Itard, and Virey—contains a spark of
romantic potential that flickers and gives way to sober disillusionment. Something of a similar tension may be discerned in the fictions of Mary Shelley's
Frankenstein (1818) and Thomas Love Peacock's *Melincourt* (1817) as they com-
pete for the attention of Romantic activist Percy Shelley.

    William Frankenstein has one of the briefest careers of any character in lit-
erary history: he speaks only twice before his violent death. For those of us who
remember the second grade, his brief life is true to the most obnoxious characteristics of a spoiled brat: prejudiced, mean-spirited, frightened, and belliger-
ent, he arrogantly swaggers in the confidence of an exaggerated sense of his
father's importance. In case you have forgotten, here is all that is recorded of
William's utterances: a shrill scream, followed by, "Let me go, monster! Ugly
wretch! You wish to eat me and tear me to pieces—you are an ogre—Let me
go, or I will tell my papa. . . . Hideous monster! let me go; My papa is a Syn-
dic—he is M. Frankenstein—he would punish you. You dare not keep me"
(96–97).

    In a narrative filled with lurid and sensational moments, this initial murder of an innocent is often lost amid the cascade of excesses that follow. Just as the moment opens up a variety of complications in the plot, so too I believe it opens up important avenues for considering the novel's historical location. The psychoanalytic and biographical questions concerning Mary Shelley's imaginative creation are familiar enough: she had, of course, recently given birth to a boy named William, who died of a fever shortly after the novel's publication. In the complex biographical nexus of psychological determinants, her child and his murdered namesake in the novel both bear the name of the father who had encouraged Mary to hold herself responsible for the death of her own mother in childbirth. Moreover, the episode engages both Miltonic and Lacanian frames of reference. William's fate is sealed by his second utterance, which at a stroke identifies the name of the father ("M. Frankenstein"), the order of the law ("a Syndic"), and the punitive superego ("he would punish you") with a direct challenge ("you dare not"). Such an overdetermined symbolic articulation of the ego's rebellion may also be read in the Miltonic paradigm, where willful disobedience is defined against "the Son" whose triumph consists in his entire self-denial in relation to the Father ("not my will, but thine"). The crime scene of this narrative, in a nutshell, casts the monstrous disobedient offspring of a distant father into the role of exacting his revenge by the murder of an innocent child who subordinates all claim to independent volition to the activity of a powerful father.

In a profound psychological sense, the events that flow from this crime repeat this incident's obsessive concern with ambivalent binaries, but I want here to make use of a third frame—one less often noted, and one that is suggested by the creature's utterance articulated between William's only two speeches. When William first threatens to tell his father, but significantly, before he names that father, the creature replies: "Boy, you will never see your father again; you must come with me." That ominous-sounding formula reproduces the opening dynamic of initiation rituals: "Everywhere the mystery begins with the separation of the neophyte from his family, and a 'retreat' into the forest. In this there is already a symbolisation of death" (Eliade 197). The creature's reflections indicate that at this time, his urge is to remove the child from a society that will teach him to hate, and to educate him outside society. Only at the name "Frankenstein" does that plan give way to murderous revenge, the symbolic death of initiation replaced by the actual death of retaliation. The verbal exchange, then, between William and the creature identifies the creature with a liminal initiatory figure of the wild man, only to immediately subvert that identification with another of the murderous monster.[4] Pursuing that identification opens up a larger consideration of how Mary Shelley's novel engages contemporary anxieties over the limits of the human.

The most immediate connection between Shelley's novel and the eighteenth-century discussion of wild men that precedes and informs it has been established by Marilyn Butler in discussing the novel's debt to William Lawrence's radical science.[5] Lawrence's materialist attacks on John Abernethy's vitalist position brought down on himself the wrath of the *Quarterly Review,* which successfully sought to censor and silence his *Lectures:*

> Something more is necessary for the satisfaction of the public and the credit of the institution. It appears to us imperative on those who have the superintendence of the Royal College of Surgeons, to make it an indispensable condition of the continuance of Mr. Lawrence in the office of lecturer, not only that he should strictly abstain from propagating any similar opinions in future, but that he should expunge from his lectures already published all those obnoxious passages which have given such deserved offence, and which are now circulating under the sanction of the College. (Editorial 34)

The *Review* succeeded in curbing Lawrence's public airing of his dangerous science, but only at the end of an eight-year debate, during which materialist and vitalist arguments on the principle of life had become accepted as an appropriate subject for discussion in the bourgeois public sphere. The silencing of Lawrence's radical views is required for the "satisfaction of the public and . . . the institution." The vitalist debate of the early nineteenth century itself emerges from a rational public discussion among enlightenment philosophers on "the speculative general issue, whether the wild man is a sub-species, and if so how he relates both to advanced man and to the primates" (Butler, Introduction xxxvii–xxxviii). That discussion—involving Rousseau, Condillac, Condorcet, Buffon, Linnaeus, Monboddo, Itard, Blumenbach, and eventually Lawrence— ironically consists on the one hand of an exemplary instance of the Habermasian public sphere (a rational discussion, appealing to argument rather than authority, on the nature of man) and at the same time focused repeatedly on those problematic figures who were marked by their exclusion from that discussion—orang-outangs and feral children. Repeatedly, the rational discussion of European philosophers on the relation of these three beings revolved around the terms of language use and sociability that the public sphere required. More-over, whenever that discussion stooped from abstract formulations to eviden-tiary matters of fact and empirical observation, the discourse of natural phi-losophy is marked by a traffic with the vulgar discourses of advertisement, legendary accounts, and sensationalized travel narrative.

Lawrence Lipking is at times remarkably humorous at the expense of his Ro-manticist colleagues who, in the past quarter century, have elevated *Franken-stein* to canonical status while at the same time achieving a remarkable critical consensus on certain issues.[6] One of his wittily malicious paragraphs is organ-ized around the necessary blindness of a "kinder, gentler" political correctness that dominates contemporary literary criticism of the novel: "To be contempo-rary, evidently, is to link arms against wrong-headed or *uncontemporary* read-ings. Late-twentieth-century critics, when they look at Frankenstein's creation, no longer see a Monster, as earlier generations did; they now see a Creature" (317). Lipking, here, is exactly right—in the way that half-truths often are. The (I believe, significant) strength of Lipking's essay is his insistence that central to *Frankenstein*'s appeal is the novel's dramatizing of ambivalence—"The novel firmly answers Yes and No" (330)—on profound intellectual questions. But while Lipking identifies the labeling of Frankenstein's creation a "creature" rather than a "monster" with contemporary criticism, that particular ambiva-lence is as old as the novel itself. Not only are both labels applied within the nar-rative, but the reading Lipking marks as "contemporary" was shared by Shel-ley's contemporaries as well. The anonymous reviewer in *Knight's Quarterly* in 1824 is clearly enrolled in the "creaturist" camp:

> For my own part, I confess that *my* interest in the book is entirely on the side of the
> monster. His eloquence and persuasion, of which Frankenstein complains, are so
> because they are truth. The justice is indisputably on his side, and his sufferings are,
> to me, touching to the last degree. . . . The poor monster always, for these reasons,
> touched me to the heart. Frankenstein ought to have reflected on the means of giv-
> ing happiness to the being of his creation, before he *did* create him.[7]

Don't be misled by that initial "monster"; this is a "poor monster" of the crea-ture school of interpretation, and this first-generation *Frankenstein* critic is every bit as dogmatic and one-sided as any representative "late-twentieth-cen-tury" variety Lipking can dig up; there is nothing new about this reading of the novel. To Lipking's credit, however, his argument with this reading is not that it is incorrect, only that it is incomplete: "for the relatively cut-and-dried didactic formulas of *Frankenstein* do not do justice to the double-mindedness it induces in a reader" (325). Well, yes, maybe. But, as the example from *Knight's Quarterly* suggests, the remarkably single-minded readings Lipking laments have been just as readily (perhaps more readily) induced in some readers. For better or worse, whether it is a sign of aesthetic complexity or of intellectual indecision, this novel offers equally fertile ground to those readers who like their meanings ambiguous and indeterminate and to those who prefer to discern a deeply important doctrine.

Lipking's own reading belongs to the ambiguous and indeterminate variety: "Indeed, the capacity for arguing both sides of a question, or for providing material to undermine its own first premises, accounts for much of the fascination—as well as the terror—of *Frankenstein*" (330). Moreover, Lipking's reading identifies this capacity with Romanticism generally and with Jean-Jacques Rousseau in particular: "in this respect also Romanticism follows the track of Rousseau" (330). Indeed, however much Lipking may argue against viewing "Frankenstein's Monster" as "Victor's Creature," his argument tends strongly to the view that it makes sense to think of "Mary Shelley's *Frankenstein*" as a creature of Jean-Jacques Rousseau's.[8] I think he is right—and, of course, also wrong.

Or, more accurately, I think Mary Shelley's departures from Rousseau are as significant as her borrowings. There are two fundamental ways that Lipking sees Rousseau—and especially, *Émile*—lurking behind *Frankenstein*. The first, at the level of content, sees the novel as conducting a thought experiment on the relation of society and human nature suggested by Rousseau's writings. The second, at the level that may be thought of as a habit of mind, is the characteristic Romantic preoccupation with the haunting question "what has gone wrong?" On both of these points, but especially the second, I find myself agreeing. Just two weeks before the "ghost story contest" that gave birth to *Frankenstein*, Mary Shelley wrote to her half-sister Fanny, from their new cottage on Lake Geneva, describing the surroundings:

> To the south of the town is the promenade of the Genevese, a grassy plain planted with a few trees, and called Plainpalais. Here a small obelisk is erected to the glory of Rousseau, and here (such is the mutability of human life) the magistrates, the successors of those who exiled him from his native country, were shot by the populace during that revolution, which his writings mainly contributed to mature, and which, notwithstanding the temporary bloodshed and injustice with which it was

polluted, has produced enduring benefits to mankind, which all of the chicanery of statesmen, nor even the great conspiracy of kings, can render vain. From respect to the memory of their predecessors, none of the present magistrates ever walk in Plainpalais. (174)

When Mary Shelley set about writing *Frankenstein,* she was certainly under the influence of "the glory of Rousseau" and also preoccupied with the question of "what had gone wrong" with the French Revolution; to anyone who shared Rousseau's habit of mind, of course, that latter question—as Mary's letter suggests—was virtually identical with "what had gone wrong with the glory of Rousseau?" I want to consider one way that this version of Rousseau's quintessential Romantic question troubles Mary Shelley's novel and is at least partly responsible for its double-mindedness.

That is the element of *Frankenstein* recently discussed by Marilyn Butler as "Radical Science." Butler has laid the groundwork for a consideration of the novel's relation to the vitalist debates of the second decade of the nineteenth century as something more than the stitching together (as it were) of various allusions to contemporary science: "some ideas from Erasmus Darwin and Humphrey Davy also figure here and there in the novel. But the coincidences between Lawrence's best book and Mary Shelley's are so different in scale that they need following through as, in effect, a single intermeshing story" (305). I think Butler is right in focusing on William Lawrence (who was Percy Shelley's physician during the years of the vitalist debates, 1814–19, when *Frankenstein* was created). Without rehearsing all the evidence that Butler puts forward about the Lawrence-Abernethy (organicist-vitalist) debates, or how the substance of those debates came to be represented in Mary Shelley's novel, I would like to extend that discussion a bit further to consider how those debates enabled Mary Shelley to reassess the position of Rousseau on human nature.

When Lawrence replies to Abernethy's charges "that there is a party of modern sceptics, cooperating in the diffusion of these noxious opinions with a no less terrible band of French physiologists, for the purpose of demoralizing mankind" (4), he wastes little time in pointing out the chauvinist political agenda underwriting this particular "science war": "the French . . . seem to be considered our natural enemies in science, as well as in politics" (5). Now Lawrence may very well be guilty of a bit of disingenuousness himself here, but nonetheless Abernethy seems to have been motivated by a conservative fear of the dangerously radical position of the materialists that he identified with the dangers of the French Revolution. Indeed, Coleridge's receptivity to Abernethy's vitalist position may well be ascribed to their sharing at this moment a desire to turn away from the dangerous radicalism associated with materialism. Lawrence's reply enables him to claim almost all the high ground: British liberty, a defense of the public sphere, the disinterestedness of objective science all combine in the service of Lawrence's defense:

> here I take the opportunity of protesting, in the strongest terms,—in behalf of the interests of science, and of that free discussion—which is essential to its successful cultivation,—against the attempt to stifle inquiry by an outcry of pernicious tendency; . . . Science, the partisan of no country, but the beneficent patroness of all, has liberally opened a temple where all may meet. . . .
>
> Science requires an expanded mind, a view that embraces the universe. Instead of shutting himself up in an island, and abusing all the rest of mankind, the philosopher should make the world his country, and should trample beneath his feet those prejudices, which the vulgar so fondly hug to their bosoms. (13, 15)

By the end (there is quite a bit of rhetoric here), Lawrence has neatly folded Abernethy into the joint character of a pompous Houyhnhnm and a conservative Briton.

At precisely the moment when the vitalist debate was kindling in England, in 1816, Julien-Joseph Virey paid a final visit to Victor of Aveyron; his final description was included in the lengthy entry "L'Homme" published the following year in the *Dictionnaire de l'histoire naturelle . . . Deterville*. Virey was an ideologue and a student of Rousseau's who continued to maintain the Rousseauian position on natural man and the pernicious influence of society. His was the sort of position that provoked Abernethy: "We are denaturalized by education, law, etc.," Virey wrote; "men are only what they are made. . . We are born, when all is said, apes; it is education which renders us human" (qtd. in Blanckaert 135). Virey's reputation is primarily that of a popularizer, but that is all the better for illustrating the Rousseauian position on the border identities of quasi-humans at the time of *Frankenstein*. And it is worth noting that on precisely this issue—the potential kinship of humans and apes—Lawrence dissociates himself from the position of Rousseau and Monboddo; his means of accomplishing that dissociation is not via an appeal to some spiritual addition, but via the anatomical studies of Blumenbach and other continental zoologists and physiologists. In a word, Lawrence's lectures allowed the radical Romantics in the Shelley circle to retain an internationalist materialism, while maintaining a uniquely privileged position for human potential that was at risk in Rousseau's doctrine that society should be modeled more closely on natural demands.

Lawrence takes as his task a scientific study of man in relation to his animal nature: "I design, on the present occasion, to consider man as an object of zoology,—to describe him as a subject of the animal kingdom" (103). This is, of course, precisely the design that had been so controversial when Linnaeus gestured in that direction a generation earlier when he first proposed including humans as "subject" to that "kingdom" that Christianity insisted was properly their "dominion." And Lawrence is well aware that he is treading on dangerous ground; almost his first step is to distance himself dramatically from the most dangerous tendencies of his most radical predecessors—Rousseau and Monboddo:

> That the greatest ignorance has prevailed on this subject, even in modern times, and among men of distinguished learning and acuteness, is shewn by the strange notion very strenuously asserted by Monboddo and Rousseau, and firmly believed by many, that man and the monkey, or at least the oran-outang, belong to the same species, and are no otherwise distinguished from each other than by circumstances which can be accounted for by the different physical and moral agencies to which they have been exposed. The former of these writers even supposes that the human race once possessed tails; and he says, "the orang-outangs are proved to be of our species, by marks of humanity that I think are incontestable." A poor compliment to our species; as any one will think, who may take the trouble of paying a morning visit to the orang-utang at Exeter Change. (106)

One of those who took the trouble (at least twice, according to her journal) was Mary Shelley, who records two visits to "a most curious monkey" at Exeter Change in the spring of 1815. Understandably, critics have for some time attended to the literary influences on the composition of *Frankenstein;* after all, Mary Shelley's journal bears a striking resemblance to the reading log of an ambitious graduate student. When not being mined for literary influences, the journal has been (with equal success) consulted for what it tells us about the psychological dimension of a remarkably creative young woman. In this respect, many have acknowledged the poignant appositeness of the entry of March 19, 1815, in which she records a particularly disturbing dream that registers the distressing death of her first child a month earlier: "Dream that my little baby came to life again. That it had only been cold, and that we rubbed it before the fire and it lived. Awake and find no baby. I think about the little thing all day.

16. An infant orangutan placed on display in London's Exeter Change in the early nineteenth century. Mary Shelley visited this "curious monkey" in the week in which she began *Frankenstein.* Assessing this animal's claim to humanity, William Lawrence observed (with chilling detachment): "[he] certainly never laughs: his keeper informs me that he has seen him weep a few times."

Not in good spirits" (41). The following day's entry begins "dream again about my baby," and as Moers has noted, she wrote to Leigh Hunt in 1817, saying that such dreams recurred throughout the composition of the novel. Two days after recording these dreams in her journal, she pays her first visit to Exeter Change and returns the following day to view the infant orangutan that she calls "a most curious monkey" (42).

Beyond the observation that Mary Shelley's journal entry indicates that she concurred with Lawrence (and almost all of Europe) in rejecting the idea of kinship between humans and apes proposed by Monboddo and Buffon, I want to emphasize the important contribution Lawrence makes in offering a materialist argument for species distinction. For Lawrence, any claim of a species distinction that rested on an untestable a priori assertion of the existence of a soul begged the question under discussion; instead, Lawrence found a basis for such distinction in the recent zoological and physiological research being carried on in Europe, especially by Johann Blumenbach.[9]

Blumenbach provided Lawrence with a mechanism for distancing his own radical biology from the heterodox positions of Rousseau and Monboddo. Of particular importance—both to Lawrence's argument and to its intellectual relation to *Frankenstein*—is Blumenbach's attack on the category of *homo ferus* and particularly on the credibility of accounts of Peter. Lawrence reproduces in the second chapter of his *Natural History of Man* most of Blumenbach's discrediting of Peter's wild status. The terms in which Lawrence introduces Blumenbach's discussion make clear that for Lawrence, the importance of this attack has directly to do with its discrediting of "natural man," either as a term for a biological entity (as suggested by Linnaeus) or as a philosophic ideal (as represented in the writings of Rousseau and Monboddo):

> The chief support of this notion concerning the human subject being naturally quadruped, has been derived from the examples of *wild men;* that is, children lost in the woods, and growing up in a solitary state. Even Linnaeus has kindly taken them under his protection, and has provided a respectable situation for them in his *Systema Naturae,* under the head of "homo sapiens *ferus,*" to whom he assigns the epithets *tetrapus, mutus, hirsutus.*
>
> What is this "homo ferus" of Linnaeus? How are we to consider these wild men? In different countries of Europe, a few individuals—and very few indeed are authentically recorded—have been met with in a solitary state;—young persons, wandering alone in the woods, or mountainous regions. To unsophisticated common sense, they appear poor, half-witted, stupid beings, incapable of speech, with faculties very imperfectly developed, and therefore probably escaping from or abandoned by their parents or friends. But their case has been eagerly taken up and warmly defended by some philosophers, who employ them to exemplify *natural* man—the original uncorrupted creature—in opposition to those who have become vitiated and degenerate by civilization. (117)

The suspect "philosophers" of Lawrence's last sentence include, of course, Rousseau and Monboddo. Lawrence claims for his position the populist rhetoric of "unsophisticated common sense," but one contemporary source reveals that both positions were well represented in folk idiom: Grimm's *Fairy Tales.* Their 1815 collection included one tale, "The Wild Man," in which a hairy wild man captured in the forest becomes a "magical helper" and powerful initiator for a little prince who liberates him from the captivity of his parents. In subsequent editions, this variant was replaced by the very similar variant commonly known today as "Iron Hans"; in that variant, the wild man speaks the same shamanistic formula as Frankenstein's creature when he first abducts William

("You will never see your mother and father again"). If Iron Hans can be seen as one folk tradition of the powerful liberatory potential of the wild man that Lawrence assigns to "some philosophers," then there is a pleasant irony in the diminution of that figure put forward on behalf of commonsense science by Blumenbach and Lawrence. For Blumenbach's retelling of what he considers the more probable version of Peter's "wild" origins leaves Peter sounding less like "Iron Hans" and more like "little Hansel" of "Hansel and Gretel": "it was ascertained that a widower at Luchtringen had had a dumb child; who, having been lost in the woods in 1723, returned home again; but, on his father's second marriage, was driven out again by his stepmother" (119). As so often happens when scientists quarrel, a lay audience is left to choose their preferred fairy tale.

If Lawrence is interested in discrediting and disavowing Rousseau's idealization of the noble potential of natural man, his challenge—"how are we to consider these wild men?"—propounds the thought experiment that Mary Shelley enacts in *Frankenstein*. Whether or not one can discount the story of Peter or any of the other cases instanced by Rousseau and Monboddo, her novel imagines one in the position described by Lawrence: a young person, wandering alone in woods or mountainous regions, in a purely solitary state, who appears to unsophisticated folk to be poor, stupid, speechless, with imperfectly developed faculties, abandoned by his parents; is this the original uncorrupted creature? I think Shelley's novel is as responsible as modern commentators for answering this question with "why not?" For *Frankenstein* neither embraces nor disavows the Rousseauian notion that man is innately good and is corrupted by civilization. The famous opening line of *Émile* ("Everything is good as it leaves the hands of the Author of things; everything degenerates in the hands of men") is not the moral of *Frankenstein* as much as it is the radical proposition that is to be tested by the narrative itself.

There are some difficulties presented by the reading Lipking assigns to the current critical consensus: "Item: Frankenstein's abandonment of his Creature is an act of unforgivable irresponsibility; Not Worth Mentioning: the Creature murders a small child and frames an innocent woman for the crime" (317). In Lipking's cautionary tale, the chief villain is Anne Mellor's articulation of what Lipking terms "coercive" pedagogy: "'Only by reading the sublime, the unknowable, as lovable can we prevent the creation of monsters, monsters both psychological and technological, monsters capable of destroying all human civilization.' Love thy Creature *or else.* I wonder how many students disagree at this point; or if they do, how many dare to speak up" (318). The criticism of

pedagogy here I find excellent, for Mellor's statement is extremist in two directions: human civilization is in imminent peril, and only one solution will work.
I doubt both of these formulations, and almost every fiction I have encountered
that depends upon them. Just as important as those reservations, however, is a
deeper reservation about what the novel itself has to say about the reading that
both Lipking and I associate with Rousseau's grand opening gesture: "everything is good as it leaves the hand of the Author of things." However much
Mary Shelley may have identified with the abandoned condition of Frankenstein's creature (and his condition certainly seems to draw upon some of her
own experiences), she creates a very different experience for Victor Frankenstein: "no creature," we are told, "could have had more tender parents than myself" (19). If this novel purports to teach us that, as Mellor advises, we must love
even the monstrous to avoid annihilation, or to warn us that, as Percy Shelley
moralized the tale, "treat a person ill, and he will become wicked" (186); then
we must also acknowledge that it teaches something far more sobering about
the limits of both pedagogy and parenting as well. One can, according to this
novel, provide the most loving and idyllic household, complete with the most
enlightened and liberal education, and one careless off-the-cuff dismissal of the
folly of Cornelius Agrippa can prompt your child to pursue a chain of night-
marish activities that will destroy the lives of those nearest and dearest to you
and unleash monsters that could terrorize the planet. Neither of these readings
seems to me inherently more—or less—accurate than the other. If Blumenbach was right—and his conjecture certainly strikes me as a good deal more
plausible than the fanciful notion that Peter was raised from infancy by a bear
with an overactive maternal instinct—then a heartless stepmother coercing her
husband to abandon his autistic offspring in the wilds of a forest does not create a murderous monster, but a rather genial and inoffensive simpleton who
lives a long, quiet, and simple life, interrupted only occasionally by visits of the
learned and a whirlwind four-month visit at court.

If Mellor and others follow (perhaps too closely) the teachings of Rousseau
and the moralizing of Percy Shelley in judging that "Frankenstein's abandonment of his Creature is an act of unforgivable irresponsibility," then Lipking
is right to ask us to consider the extent of that creature's responsibility for
the murder of William and the events that follow from it. As central as this
crime is to the plot of the novel, it is dramatically overshadowed by numerous
other confrontations between Frankenstein and his creature. But I believe that
crime—and its setting—point us toward the novel's fundamentally ambivalent

attitude toward Rousseau's doctrine of the natural condition of man. The crime itself occurs offstage, and we learn of it twice: the first time, along with Victor, when he receives a letter from home; the second time, from the creature, as he tells his story in his meeting with Victor on the *mer de glace*.

The creature's narrative of the crime is the one I quoted from above, and it is calculated to arouse our sympathies not on behalf of the victim (whom we barely know) but on behalf of the perpetrator. Indeed, the murder itself is told as a crime of passion, the almost unthinking culmination of a string of outrages and injuries suffered by the innately good and innocent creature. After the detailed and pathetic tale of the creature's self-education in the hovel adjoining the DeLacey's cottage, he speaks of his banishment in terms drawn directly from the close of *Paradise Lost*—one of five texts in his small but select library. His first impulse is to seek not revenge, but justice, from the hands of his creator. On the way, he interrupts an idyllic pastoral scene, reminiscent of that first Paradise, and unlike those quasi-human brutes that Lawrence reported were unable to laugh with joy or weep from grief, this sensitive creature weeps Romantic tears: "Half surprised by the novelty of these sensations [gentleness and pleasure], I allowed myself to be borne away by them; and, forgetting my solitude and deformity, dared to be happy. Soft tears again bedewed my cheeks, and I even raised my humid eyes with thankfulness towards the blessed sun which bestowed such joy upon me" (95).[10] This lyric interlude is interrupted by a pastoral couple vaguely reminiscent of those innocents of Eden; this rural Eve approaches, "laughing as if she ran from some one in sport" (95), only to slip and fall into the river below. In such a calamity, our pure natural creature performs the role of hero admirably, first saving the girl and then attempting primitive CPR, only, of course, to have his actions misconstrued by her swain, who compounds insult with injury by firing at—and wounding—the creature.[11]

By this point in the narrative, one need not be Rousseau to feel sympathy for the creature. Nor, pace Lipking, must one belong to a culture characterized by a "collective identification with victims." Even at this point, however, this creature is not a monster, but an ideal Rousseauian pedagogue—or, if one prefers the version collected by the Brothers Grimm, an Iron Hans seeking a civilized pupil in need of some (super)natural education:

> At this time a slight sleep relieved me from the pain of reflection, which was disturbed by the approach of a beautiful child, who came running into the recess I had chosen with all the sportiveness of infancy. Suddenly, as I gazed on him, an idea

seized me, that this little creature was unprejudiced, and had lived too short a time
to have imbibed a horror of deformity. If, therefore, I could seize him, and educate him as my companion and friend, I should not be so desolate in this peopled
earth. (96)

The original motive may well be benign—to provide a better, more natural
education. Perhaps it is only when the child utters his triply threatening name
that the generous first impulses of the creature turn monstrous. But monstrous
they do turn, and the dream of educating innocence outside the corrupting
influence of civilization is immediately succeeded by the terrifying reality of a
brutal "exultation and hellish triumph" over the corpse of the very innocent
whose improvement had been intended.

My last sentence, of course, describes not only the scene in *Frankenstein* but
also the cautionary tale of the French Revolution, and in doing so (like Mary's
letter to her sister, haunted by the question of "what had gone wrong" with "the
Glory of Rousseau") it prompts us to return to an earlier moment in the narrative when Victor receives a letter informing him of William's murder. The letter tells him that William's body has been discovered where it was last seen, in
the grassy plain called Plainpalais just south of Geneva. Victor immediately
returns home from Ingolstadt and arrives in Geneva after the city's gates have
already closed. Unable to sleep, "I resolved to visit the spot where my poor
William had been murdered. As I could not pass through the town, I was
obliged to cross the lake in a boat to arrive at Plainpalais" (47). The scene, then,
where the creature confronts, attempts to seize, and winds up murdering William is the promenade that Mary Shelley described to her sister Fanny, with the
obelisk to "the glory of Rousseau" and the troubling aftermath of "that revolution, which his writings mainly contributed to mature," that it conjured up for
her. When Victor arrives at this scene of the crime, amid a sublime thunder-
storm, a flash of lightning suddenly illuminates the creature, who Victor immediately recognizes as his brother's killer. The tortured reflections that ensue
on this occasion follow something like the tortured syntax of Mary Shelley's
letter, wrestling with her ambivalent reaction to Rousseau's implication in the
events following the French Revolution:

> I revolved in my mind the events which I had until now sought to forget: the whole
> train of my progress towards the creation; the appearance of the work of my own
> hands alive at my bed side, its departure. Two years had now elapsed since the
> night on which he first received life; and was this his first crime? Alas! I had turned

loose into the world a depraved wretch, whose delight was in carnage and misery; had he not murdered my brother? (48–49)

If the creature's account of the murder offers us a self-justifying narrative, one in which the murderous outcome of well-intended idealism results at least as much from society's indifferent cruelty as from the actions of a malevolent agent, then Victor's account carries something of the agonized self-indictment of one whose best intentions have perhaps turned loose on the world an unimaginable horror. Percy Shelley perhaps remained unwaveringly loyal to Rousseau's idealism, and he may moralize the tale precisely as the creature himself would; he would not be alone in doing so even today. But Mary Shelley had more doubts, and the doubled narrative of creator and creature allows her to unfold a doubled response to Rousseau's doctrine on natural man. Both the rebellious mob and its most obvious recent manifestation—the French Revolution—exist, but only obliquely, in Shelley's novel. The political anxiety at the heart of the novel is not narrated directly but instead is projected onto its monstrous representative: "even though the demonic personification [of the Jacobins] remains intact, and though the story is nominally set in the 1790s, the French Revolution has simply disappeared" (Sterrenburg 157).

If we may glimpse from time to time the specter of Rousseau in the shadows of *Frankenstein*, then it is much easier to find Monboddo in the pages of *Melincourt*, where lengthy quotations from that author provide a veritable forest of footnotes sufficient to make the novel's most extraordinary character, Sir Oran Haut-ton, feel completely at home. The two novels were composed during the same summer and fall of 1816, though Peacock's appeared the year before *Frankenstein*. Peacock had been part of the "Shelley circle" since 1812 (the year of Percy's first brief meeting with Mary), and although Carl Dawson says Mary "never liked Peacock" (xiv), he was frequently a fixture in the Shelley household during their stays in England at this time. After Percy Shelley's death in 1822, Peacock served as executor of his estate in England on Mary's behalf. As Marilyn Butler has noted, "the best and most responsive reader *Melincourt* has ever had was [Percy] Shelley" (Peacock 99). While *Frankenstein* has become ever more central to discussions of Romantic fiction, *Melincourt* has become (if such a thing is possible) ever more obscure, but if Mary Shelley can be seen to struggle with her doubled response to Rousseau (and Monboddo) in a tragic vein, Peacock's novel presents in the vein of comic satire a similar struggle with respect to Monboddo (and Rousseau). Instead of a difficult confrontation with the consequences of Rousseau's ideal, Peacock presents a satire in which the un-deniably eccentric and comic Monboddo functions simultaneously as a comic foil and an implicit norm against which Peacock can lash the corruptions of a complacent political status quo. Perhaps one explanation for the great disparity in the reception of these two novels is the very great degree to which Peacock's novel looks back to models of eighteenth-century satire and romance, whereas Shelley's novel looks forward to those still popular modes of gothic and science fiction. Ending our consideration of the wild man in the public sphere with a consideration of *Melincourt* may allow us to reflect on what has come before.

To speak of *Melincourt* as a novel is something of a mistake, albeit a neces-sary one. Northrop Frye is surely right to locate Peacock's fiction in the tradi-tion of Menippean satire that includes Rabelais, Swift, and Voltaire; that is especially apt for the case of *Melincourt*. Alternately, his fictions have been identified with the "novel of talk," and certainly the "talkiness" of this narrative form presents itself as the literary representative of an idealized salon public sphere. It is in some respects impossible to identify a more quintessentially Habermasian bourgeois public sphere than the one described in *Melincourt*, where virtually nothing happens without the rational articulations of represen-tatives of a literary- inflected bourgeoisie.

The plot of *Melincourt* is slight. Anthelia Melincourt is a wealthy and beau-tiful young heiress of remarkably good sense, in possession of £10,000 a year and a castle in the Lake District; consequently, it is determined by all except the lady herself that she must be in want of a husband. In the vicinity (though the two are unknown to each other) is Sylvan Forester, who is well matched to An-thelia in all requisite points: age, appearance, property, and, most importantly, of course, intellect and principle. That these two will wind up united is obvious. Most of the talk and much of the merriment that intervenes arises from the cast of suitors and matchmakers (male and female) that descend on Westmoreland with other designs. The evil designs necessary to complicating the plot of such a romance are unspectacularly provided by the foppish Lord Anophel Achthar and his tutor, Rev. Grovelgrub, who kidnap the fair Anthelia not once, but twice (the first abduction being thwarted without their identities being revealed).

This, in summary, is the main action of the romance; what is most material to the fiction that this summary leaves out includes satirical portraits of those first-generation Romantic poets who are perceived to have betrayed their early professions of liberty in exchange for comfortable livings; much pointed po-litical satire on issues on the opposition agenda, notably slavery in the West

Indies, the devastating effects of paper currency on the agricultural economy, and the desperate need for political reform in parliamentary elections; and the fact that Sylvan Forester's loyal friend and protégé is an Angolan ape, Sir Oran Haut-ton, Bart., for whom Forester has procured a knighthood and purchased a seat in Parliament. His election to Parliament as one of two representatives of the borough of Onevote is literally, as well as figuratively, central to the satire of the novel.

"It is hard to do justice to Sir Oran Haut-ton, who is probably the most memorable and amiable of Peacock's characters," states Butler (*Peacock* 77). One is tempted to suggest that this is because he is mute in a "novel of talk," but certainly Butler is right in her assessment. Oran is a comic figure, and his election to Parliament is first and foremost a political joke at the expense of the corrupt practice of "rotten boroughs" and "virtual representation." But, beyond that, Peacock seems genuinely to share a number of Monboddo's beliefs and attitudes, and Sir Oran's physical vigor and virtuous actions repeatedly give Monboddo the chance to speak at length in the footnotes while Oran remains mute in the text. If Mary Shelley's doubled attitude toward Rousseau spans the Romantic emotional compass from idealized natural potential to the torment of blasted hopes and tragic ruin, then Peacock's correspondingly doubled attitude toward Monboddo alternates between the satirists' poles of bemused disbelief and cynical approbation.

Although Sir Oran is himself mute, he is triply ventriloquized: first, through the footnotes that quote Monboddo at length; again, at frequent intervals in the text when the protagonist, Sylvan Forester, who embodies many of Monboddo's real (and theoretical) virtues speaks on his behalf; and a third time, when his brother candidate for Parliament, Sir Simon Sarcastic, speaks on the hustings at the election at Onevote. In *Frankenstein*, the political threat of the mob was famously displaced onto the solitary figure of Victor's monstrous creation.[12] In *Melincourt*, that political threat is dramatized—albeit in a comic vein—when the "swinish multitude" of the city of Novote, plied with alcohol for the election speeches, break out in unfocused rioting. Ironically, Sir Oran Haut-Ton becomes not the embodiment of such revolution but the heroic chivalric rescuer of the endangered heroine, as he vigorously swings his staff in order to clear a path through the rabble. Throughout *Melincourt*, and increasingly through the final third of the narrative, Peacock makes caustic and deeply ironic allusions to the ministry's dismissal of the "swinish multitude"; the novel's explicit engagement with this radical and unruly dimension of the public sphere stands in pointed contrast to Mary Shelley's muting of the voice of rebellion in *Frankenstein.* One cannot help but suspect that Peacock needed to introduce the third voice of Sir Simon Sarcastic in order to preserve the integrity and sincerity of Forester, who could not have delivered the necessarily bitter parody of electioneering self-interest without damaging his credentials as a hero of Romance. Each of these voices has something to recommend it, and each in turn undercuts itself; Sir Oran, advocated by each, but himself innocent of every excess, comes off rather well.

Peacock's technique of having Monboddo speak through footnotes to the mute Sir Oran Haut-ton constitutes a particularly vivid illustration of our "material-semiotic actor." That is, Sir Oran Haut-ton is a manifestly imaginary and fictional character—a strictly semiotic actor (as Gulliver, for instance, or Victor Frankenstein). But he also gestures more than those characters, though perhaps not quite so completely as Robinson Crusoe does, to a real material actor. Just as considering the material-semiotic actor Robinson Crusoe requires us to think of both Defoe's imaginary character and the real-life Alexander Selkirk, Sir Oran is both Peacock's creation and a representative (pun intended) of real "nonhuman primates." The footnotes from Monboddo articulate the doubly significant identity of this particular genus of material-semiotic actor: what Monboddo asserts as the "material" significance of orangs is, of course, a construction that depends on their mobilization as semiotic actors within a particular construct. What orangs are scientifically will be ultimately determined by the outcome of a semiotic competition, a contest that may be thought of as the one between Lawrence's rendering of orang identity and Monboddo's. That competition is, of course, not simply rhetorical—but neither is it simply "matter of fact." Lawrence's physical anthropology is in many cases (though not all) better than Monboddo's, and his descriptions of orangs are to that extent "better." But he also constructs what evidence will and will not be admitted—as the examples from grief and laughter cited above attest. Peacock's strategy of glossing the mute orang with the commentary of Monboddo in effect grants a public airing to Monboddo's view; Sir Oran signifies semiotically not just as any literary character does, but also as a marker of the contested arena of human/quasi-human identity where he represents the most radical position in that rhetorical debate.

To the considerable extent that *Melincourt* is a self-conscious parody of Romance, Sir Oran is quite recognizably the ultimate parody of "the strong, silent type"—a reclusive Heathcliff with hair. I do not want to appear oblivious to this important comic element in his character. But with that not insignificant caveat, Sir Oran escapes the eccentricity of Monboddo, the cynicism of Simon Sarcastic, and (for lack of a better phrase) the tedious sincerity of Forester. It is hard to escape the impression that each of these characters embodies both virtues that Peacock approved of and deficits he sought to guard against.

Perhaps some of Monboddo's beliefs were "dotty"—certainly they seemed so to Peacock's contemporaries, but many of them were principled and admirable, and Peacock was willing to admire them. Among these were a profound respect for classical literature, for the virtues those works were willing to praise, and for the dignity of labor, especially agricultural labor. Monboddo prided himself, as Forester does in this novel, on maintaining reasonable rents and manageable farms on his estate, with the result, in both cases, that the number of families living above poverty is greater than on any comparable estates in the vicinity. That is, Forester looks back and emulates the practice of Monboddo, who already fifty years earlier was anachronistic in priding himself on the successful management of an essentially feudal agricultural economy. Without question, this is an attitude endorsed by Peacock in *Melincourt,* and it is perhaps one reason why A. E. Dyson imagined Forester as an "exponent of that brand of optimistic Toryism which can afford to be good-humoured and genial" (188). Marilyn Butler has made the case, and made it well, that Peacock's politics in 1816 are closer to the radical agrarianism of Cobbett, and that these are the views championed by Forester. Before following that affiliation into its implications for the satire on campaign reform, political poetry, and the public sphere, we might first look at one of Forester's positions that was shared with Peacock, though too radical for Cobbett—a principled, pragmatic opposition to slavery in the West Indies. Forester practices—as did Peacock—a boycott of sugar, refusing to participate in his personal life in supporting the economy that depended on slavery:

> If I wish seriously to exterminate an evil, I begin by examining how far I am myself, in any way whatever, an accomplice in the extension of its baleful influence. My reform commences at home. . . .
>
>   If every individual in this kingdom, who is truly and conscientiously an enemy to the slave-trade, would subject himself to so very trivial a privation as abstinence from colonial produce, I consider that a mortal blow would be immediately struck at the roots of the iniquitous system. (Peacock, *Works* 42, 43)

There is a rather wonderful irony here, in that Peacock's fiction is often slighted (justifiably) on the grounds that it is too narrowly topical (and *Melincourt* is generally perceived as his most pointed and narrowly topical satire). Yet there are some remarkable affinities between issues dear to Peacock and those that we generally think of as current: social justice (particularly with respect to anti-colonialism) and a commitment to ecological protection that warns against both industrial development and exploitative tourism. Intensifying that irony is Peacock's commitment to a notion of grass-roots political activism in which "the personal is political." It is, of course, naive to imagine that an individual boycotting colonial produce can alter significantly the politics of colonialism, but it is a commonplace of late-twentieth-century social movements that such a boycott—originating in the domestic realm—can by virtue of entering the public sphere bring about such social change. Indeed, this is the centerpiece of public sphere opposition to state authority. Arguably, that is precisely what Peacock seeks to accomplish in *Melincourt*. Moving beyond his own personal boycott, Peacock has his virtuous protagonist articulate the basis for such an action; Forester develops in conversation with Sir Telegraph Paxarett the justification for a boycott in chapter 5, "Sugar." The promise of that chapter is fulfilled in chapter 27, "The Anti-Saccharine Fete." Here, a social entertainment is provided, sugar-free, at which Forester lobbies his guests on behalf of the "Anti-Saccharine Society" (an unfortunate acronym, but that may not have been so relevant in a society that had not yet developed the marketing refinements of T-shirts and bumper stickers). This chapter not only enables Peacock to enlarge on the position laid out in the beginning of the novel but actually models for a public readership a mechanism for spreading and extending political action beyond the domestic realm into the social arena.

We are only now catching up with Peacock in this regard. Postcolonial criticism has rightly begun to direct serious attention to what Keith Sandiford aptly labels "the Cultural Politics of Sugar." In his rich and provocative discussion of "Creolization" and *"negotium"* in narratives of colonialism in the West Indies, Sandiford locates Matthew "Monk" Lewis's *Journal of a West Indian Proprietor* (1834) within the framework of "multiple public spheres," overlapping and mutually constituting one another (156–63). Sandiford's focus, however, is clearly on the West Indies rather than on the discussion taking place in England; and frequently, when postcolonial criticism turns its gaze back from margin to metropolis, it follows the line of vision described by Edward Said in *Culture and Imperialism*. There, in an important discussion of Jane Austen's *Mansfield Park*, Said observes that Austen's novel is silent about, while dependent upon, the West Indian slave economy of sugar production; the force of Said's observation is in the claim that Austen's novel here reproduces the central dynamic of

British imperialism, where the economy of slavery is met with "dead silence."[13]
Often, even when Said's arguments about Austen are contested, the underlying
premise of cultural "dead silence" is tacitly granted:

> I will grant that Said's depiction of Austen as unthinking in her references to An-
> tigua fits logically with his overall contention that nineteenth-century European
> culture, and especially the English novel, unwittingly but systematically helped to
> gain consent for imperialist policies (see *Culture* 75). . . . [The novel] was, Said as-
> serts, one of the primary discourses contributing to a "consolidated vision," virtu-
> ally uncontested, of England's righteous imperial prerogative (*Culture* 75). (qtd.
> in Fraiman 805)

Said's own method of "contrapuntal" reading should encourage us to be careful about too quickly universalizing this "'consolidated vision,' virtually un-
contested"; instead, we would do well to attend to ways in which novelists such
as Peacock sought (however unsuccessfully) to resist and contest that vision of
empire. Instead, the tendency has begun to tilt in the other direction, constructing a myth of "dead silence" more pervasive than in fact it was. In what is generally a fine and supple articulation of the cultural politics of sugar, James
Walvin, for instance, notes that it would be a mistake (albeit one commonly
made) to "take the universal taste for sweetness for granted." Instead, he rightly
makes the case that whatever the physiological factors involved, there is a cultural history behind constructing that taste; but he then goes on to presume
something like the universalizing of Said's "dead silence": "Put simply, cheap
accessible cane sugar was a function of British economic and colonial power.
But who thought this, who thought about the slaves—the instruments of sugar
cultivation—when adding sugar to their tea or coffee in 18th century Britain?"
(22). Walvin intends his question rhetorically, but in fact it has an answer, and
not the one he is thinking of. If Austen's *Mansfield Park* may be considered to
exemplify hegemonic British imperial culture, with a model polity built on a
colonial edifice about which it wishes to remain silent, then *Melincourt* may be
thought of as exemplifying those troubling voices within the public sphere,
who insist on articulating models of resistance to that hegemony. If, in Austen's
novel, neither slaves nor sugar are mentioned, in Peacock's novel, precisely the
opposite is true: the link between sugar and slavery is explicitly named, it is
identified as a site for direct political action, and that action is, in turn, modeled
as a constituent element of the novel's plot.

Ultimately, this seems to me the most interesting feature of *Melincourt.*

Much of the critical disenchantment with this text arises from the degree to which political speeches substitute for novelistic dialogue, and from the fact that the action of the novel dramatizes political positions more than domestic relationships; but these are (as others have pointed out) criticisms of genre—the text fails our novelistic expectations. As satiric intervention in current politics, however, *Melincourt* may be seen as remarkable in the degree to which it actively seeks to participate directly in political events of the time. Setting himself in pointed opposition not only to the Tory ministry but also to those Romantic poets whom he considered to have sold themselves to this ministry (Southey, Coleridge, and Wordsworth), Peacock turns his pen to taking a message of political resistance and opposition directly to the people. That his effort and his cause both failed does not make the attempt any the less interesting. Peacock is seldom read today beyond "The Four Ages of Poetry," which is generally read as the specific provocation of his friend Shelley's "Defense of Poetry," where Shelley famously identifies poets as "the unacknowledged legislators of the world." It makes sense to read *Melincourt* as Peacock's testing of that hypothesis (and therefore, "The Four Ages of Poetry" as his disillusioned rendering of the test results). If, however, poets are "the unacknowledged legislators of the world," then unread poets must be "the unacknowledged minority legislators of the world"—and this is Peacock's fate with *Melincourt.*

One sign that Peacock's political sympathies lay close to Cobbett's radical agrarianism can be seen in his correspondence with Shelley following the publication of *Melincourt* and *Frankenstein.* Throughout that summer, Peacock kept Shelley informed about Cobbett's latest attacks on the government and mailed copies of Cobbett's *Political Register* to Shelley in Italy. This paper had been for some time the leading voice for radical reform, but the government effectively rendered it beyond the means of working men and women by imposing a tax via the Paper Stamp that effectively raised the cost by 50 percent. In 1816, Cobbett responded to the Paper Stamp by publishing separately—as a broadsheet—the lead essay from each issue of the *Political Register.* Evading the tax on newspapers, this broadsheet was sold for tuppence and quickly became known as "Cobbett's Twopenny Trash." George Spater identifies this development as "representing three significant steps in the making of the English working class: it gave them a feeling of their worth, it was a manifesto of their political rights, and it was a means of educating them in the exercise of such rights" (348).

Cobbett's grass-roots populism put him in direct opposition with the one-time voices of radicalism, William Wordsworth and Robert Southey. The sinecure position Wordsworth had accepted from the administration in 1813 was stamp distributor of Westmoreland, which put him in the position of imposing the stamp designed to silence Cobbett, and which the Twopenny Trash effectively circumvented. Southey, that former radical turned poet laureate, authored an anonymous essay in the *Quarterly Review* in the fall of 1816 that responded to the Twopenny Trash by calling for government censorship (Butler, "Frankenstein" 91–94). Peacock's response, in *Melincourt,* is to parody Southey in the character of Mr. Feathernest and Wordsworth in the character of Mr. Peter Paypaul Paperstamp. The culmination of these parodic characterizations comes near the novel's conclusion, in a chapter entitled "Mainchance Villa," the residence of Mr. Paperstamp. Peacock has been faulted for his attack on Southey and Wordsworth, but as Butler has observed, the satire amounts to little more than putting into the mouths of Feathernest and Paperstamp the published words of Southey and Wordsworth. Indeed, one instance of such quotation neatly anticipates this line of criticism, when Feathernest (echoing Southey's printed comments in *Quarterly Review 31*) solemnly intones: "Poets, Sir, are not amenable to censure, however frequently their political opinions may exhibit marks of inconsistency" (415).

For Peacock, as for Shelley, the irony at the heart of the events of 1816 was the peculiar situation in which poets famed for radical sensibilities deploy their rhetorical skills on behalf of silencing growing dissent within the public sphere. When Southey declaimed against the dangerous tendencies of Cobbett's liberty of the press, Peacock's Mr. Forester replied, "I cannot now remember what names of true greatness and unshaken devotion to general liberty, are associated with these heathy rocks and cloud-capped mountains of Cumberland. We have seen a little horde of poets, who brought hither from the vales of the south, the harps which they had consecrated to Truth and Liberty, to acquire new energy in the mountain-winds: and now those harps are attuned to the praise of luxurious power, to the strains of courtly sycophancy, and to the hymns of exploded superstition" (386).

Cobbett's radical agrarian movement, and both his Twopenny Trash and Peacock's avowedly political satire, speak to a radical transformation within the bourgeois public sphere, as the unruly voice of agrarian populism raises a clamor within the discursive realm, advocating more thoroughgoing political reform than any call issued in the previous century. Moreover, the explicitly agrarian inflection of that clamor underlines an economic irony of history. When Defoe wrote *Robinson Crusoe,* the practice of enclosure was a technology of cultivation that domesticated the wild and materially benefited the small landowner and yeoman farmer. Just as the hedges on Juan Fernández islands, however, soon ran wild and overran the island, so the economic effects of enclosure soon overran the rural economy of England. What had, in the early eighteenth century, promised benefit to the small farmer became by the early nineteenth century the mechanism of his ruin, and the resulting dissent fueled the political upheaval of Cobbett's radical agrarian movement. In an irony that Peacock fully appreciated, enclosure was—in England, as well as on Juan Fernández—"sportive wood run wild" with a vengeance that Wordsworth no longer intended.

If *Melincourt*, however, was intended to enter the public sphere alongside Cobbett's Twopenny Trash in opposition to the pens of Wordsworth and Southey, then Peacock was definitely a loser in this particular unacknowledged legislative battle; one might say his bill never made it out of committee. *Melincourt* appeared in March 1817; on the first of that month, Parliament passed the first peacetime suspension of habeas corpus in more than a century. A series of treason acts followed, and by May Cobbett was on a ship to America. From there, he continued writing essays back to England, and although his popular readership declined, and the essays were necessarily less current than when he was in England, Peacock continued to forward them to Shelley in Italy:

> Cobbett is indefatigable. He gives us a full close-printed sheet every week, which is something surprising, if we only consider the quantity, more especially if we take into account the number of his other avocations. America has not yet dimmed his powers, and it is impossible that his clear exposures of all the forms of political fraud should fail of producing a most powerful effect.
>
> The *Courier* calls fiercely for a Censorship of the Weekly Press. (May 30, 1818; 192–93)

Peacock was more optimistic about the effects of Cobbett's "clear exposures" than he should have been. His letters to Shelley of June and July carry another shipment of Cobbett's broadsheets and notices of the reviews of *Frankenstein*. The July 5 letter concludes with a discussion of Wordsworth's political interventions:

> Brougham is contesting Westmoreland against the Lowthers. Wordsworth has published an *Address to the Freeholders,* in which he says they ought not to choose so poor a man as Brougham, riches being the only guarantees of political integrity. He goes farther than this, and actually asserts that the Commons ought to be chosen

by the Peers. Now there is a pretty rascal for you. Southey and the whole gang are supporting the Lowthers, *per fas et nefas,* and seem inclined to hold out a yet more flagrant degradation to which self-sellers can fall under the dominion of seat-sellers. . . . Of course, during the election, Wordsworth dines every day at Lord Lonsdale's.[14] (199)

Two weeks later, Peacock's letter completes the predictable tale: "No number of 'Cobbett' has been published for three weeks . . . Brougham has lost the Westmoreland election by a small difference of number. The Cumberland Poets, by their own conduct on this occasion, have put the finishing stroke to their own disgrace. I am persuaded there is nothing in the way of dirty work that these men are not abject enough to do, if the blessed Lord [Lonsdale] commanded it, or any other blessed member of the holy and almighty seat-selling aristocracy to which they have sold themselves, body and soul" (Peacock, *Letters* 201). The outcome of the election confirms the characterization in *Melincourt* the previous winter of Cumberland poets tuning their harps in praise of luxurious power. As pointedly topical as the political satire of that novel is, its bitterest irony is reserved for the world of letters. If Feathernest and Paperstamp are transparent caricatures of Southey and Wordsworth, whose speeches quote the published writings of these most public poets, then it is worth contemplating that their venal corruption in the novel is countered by the virtues of one who is mute.

However much the election of 1818 disappointed Peacock's reformist hopes, the novel of 1817 does not end with the cynical glee at Mainchance Villa.[15] Indeed, Forester and Mr. Fax immediately take their leave of the genial venal glee and in the ensuing chapter, "The Hopes of the World," unfold in conversation the novel's positive moral doctrine. That conversation begins with an exchange glossed with quotations from Samuel Johnson and Lord Monboddo, respectively: Mr. Fax citing Johnson in his indictment of "the abject servility and venality by which [literary character] is so commonly debased" (420); and Forester, concurring with him, citing Monboddo that "it is lamentable to reflect that there is most indigence in the richest countries" (423). If Johnson and Monboddo here, once again, "agree like brothers" as to the sorry degenerate state into which contemporary letters have fallen, where then do the hopes of the world reside? Peacock's answer is clear, if somewhat surprising: Canada.

Linnaeus may have listed the Canadians among his *homo monstrosus,* but in the spring of 1815, while writing *Melincourt,* Peacock began reading Weld's

Travels in Canada; and here, he seems clearly to have found a Romantic ideal that would answer the betrayal and venal corruption he saw in England. Indeed, he was so moved by the prospect—and no doubt by his own indebtedness— that he began planning to move there. Mary Shelley records in her journal for April 17: "Peacock comes; tells us of his plan of going to Canada, and taking Marianne; talk of it after dinner" (44). The plan, of course, came to nothing (neither did the relationship with Marianne), but it seems clear that what mo- tivated Peacock's interest was an idealized depiction of socialist primitivism. *Melincourt* is a talky novel of speeches and footnotes, but Weld's *Travels in Can- ada* is cited only once, and then as a gloss on Forester's speech that serves as the culmination of the novel's most explicit statement of doctrine[16]:

> We talk of public feeling and national sympathy. Our dictionaries may define those words, and our lips may echo them: but we must look for the realities among the less enlightened nations. The Canadian savages cannot imagine the possibility of any individual in a community having a full meal, while another has but half an one:* still less could they imagine that one should have too much, while another had nothing. Theirs is that bond of brotherhood which nature weaves and civiliza- tion breaks, and from which, the older nations grow, the farther they recede.

The footnote reads:

> * "It is notorious, that towards one another the Indians are liberal in the extreme, and for ever ready to supply the deficiencies of their neighbours with any super- fluities of their own. They have no idea of amassing wealth for themselves individu- ally; and they wonder that persons can be found in any society so destitute of every generous sentiment, as to enrich themselves at the expense of others, and to live in ease and affluence regardless of the misery and wretchedness of members of the same community to which they themselves belong." (Weld, letter 35)

Throughout this book, I have been arguing that for the eighteenth century what doubly defined the "wild man" in opposition to his cousin, the citizen, was language use and sociability. Although the novels of both Peacock and Shelley revolve around problematic human identities, Shelley's novel translates that figure into a modern internalized literature of the psyche that ultimately enables her to turn away from political engagement with immediate events of the day. Peacock's novel, on the other hand, even while voicing a Romantic primitiv- ism about natural brotherhood and the bonds of civilization, embraces fully a construction of literature's engagement in the public sphere from which

Frankenstein retreats. In this respect, *Melincourt* occupies a curious relationship to its predecessor in the writings of Swift. Swift worked diligently within the public sphere in opposition to both the state authority and the presumption of the emergent public sphere within which he labored. Peacock worked diligently (and with despair reminiscent of Swift's attitude to the Irish) on behalf of a public that prefers to remain quietist. The attack on Coleridge, Wordsworth, and Southey arises from their willingness to encourage such torpor. The pointed satire of Sir Oran Haut-ton's election to Parliament at the center of the novel enables an attack on the current practice of "virtual representation" where ministry and opposition agreed not to oppose one another in a corrupt administration of mutual back-scratching. With the regular organs of the public sphere (popular press) compromised, one answer was Cobbett's Twopenny Trash; another was Peacock's practice in the third volume of turning his novel into direct participation in political discussion and debate. Peacock's novel, positioned in a Romantic era but looking backward to Augustan models of satire and literary involvement in the public sphere, brings both sociability and language use center stage in seeking to redefine the role of the responsible citizen. Tellingly, in this talky novel, Forester's speech articulating the "hopes of the world" begins by calling attention to how we define our relation to sociability through speech; and he does so particularly by calling attention to the public sphere and emergent constructions of national identity. But by the end of his brief speech, it is sociability—and its economic correlative, socialism—that is naturalized, and thus, in his final image, "nations . . . recede" from that condition of sociability like a feral child fleeing society and returning to a state of barren isolation.

Notes

INTRODUCTION

1. My project may in this respect be seen as complementing that of Helen Deutsch and Felicity Nussbaum in *Defects: Engendering the Modern Body:* "Our brand of literary and cultural criticism hopes to worry the tenuous link between literature and science, between 'subjective' and 'objective' forms of knowledge. . . . In the process we hope to begin to restore to 'natural history' what it would not write, the beginnings of a genealogy of human nature" (19).

2. See, for instance, Christopher Fox, Roy Porter, and Robert Wokler's *Inventing Human Science.* See also Douthwaite, *The Wild Girl.*

3. Cf. Deutsch and Nussbaum, *Defects,* 23. Marianna Torgovnick's *Gone Primitive: Savage Intellects, Modern Lives* pursues a not dissimilar set of concerns. Her study of gender and the history of anthropology does much to trouble the simple binary of self and other underwriting Western constructions of primitive cultures, while at the same time emphasizing the continuities between modern and postmodern formulations. Although this study differs from hers in numerous ways, it returns to view through a nonmodern lens a moment in the prehistory of that construction.

4. "The pair human-nonhuman is not a way to 'overcome' the subject-object distinction but a way to bypass it entirely" (Latour, *Pandora's* 308); "I think analyses of what gets called 'nature' and analyses of what gets called 'culture' call on the same kinds of thinking since what I'm interested in most of all are 'naturecultures'—as one word—implosions of the discursive realms of nature and culture" (Haraway, *How* 105).

5. The public sphere model presented by Habermas may be characterized as offering an optimistic view of modern social organization, and most of the very fine criticism of the Habermasian model has focused on the degrees to which that optimism is often purchased at the expense of those who are excluded from participation within the public sphere. In particular, one might cite Erin Mackie, John Bender, Beth Kowaleski-Wallace, Seyla Benhabib, Katherine Wilson, Nancy Fraser, and Michael Warner among those who have significantly contributed to an active, vigorous, and expanding field of revising Habermas. The touchstone of this critique, as Benjamin Lee among others has noted, is a commitment to a "postmodern theory . . . [that arises] from the embattled fields of American identity politics, whose basic premises were formed by the civil rights movement of the sixties and still shape the debates over the canon, feminism, and multiculturalism" (Calhoun 405). Although not without significant validity, this postmodern critique of the liberal optimism detected in Habermas returns us to something not unlike what constituted, as Craig Calhoun has noted, the original

precondition for Habermas's thesis: "[*The Structural Transformation*] is part of Habermas's lifelong effort to reground the Frankfurt School project of critical theory in order to get out of the pessimistic cul de sac in which Horkheimer and Adorno found themselves in the postwar era" (5).

6. Here, and throughout this book, I am aware of the appropriately doubled sense of the word "figure." The term refers at once to material embodiment, as when Crusoe offers us "a sketch of [his] figure" (108); but, of course, it is also a rhetorical term of art for metaphor (i.e., figurative language). The "figure of the wild man" is both a real material being and a richly evocative metaphor.

7. As I was completing this book, David Zaret published *Origins of Democratic Culture: Printing, Petitions, and the Public Sphere in Early Modern England*. In many respects, I am very sympathetic to his account and am pleased to see what I take to be affinities between our projects. Zaret's strongest challenge to Habermas's original formulation is the contention that one can trace the democratic culture of the public sphere back to the print history of petitions in the 1640s. It is, I believe, an important observation, but one that I am inclined to view as establishing what might be thought of as a "prehistory" to the public sphere. To begin with, Habermas himself was clear from the beginning that the structural transformation that he assigns to eighteenth-century Europe occurred on a slightly more accelerated timeline in England, one that dates back to the last third of the seventeenth century, or even (in its earliest forms) to "around the middle of the seventeenth century" (32; cf. 22). Arguably, Habermas is at such moments speaking only of the material conditions for public sphere discourse, not the actual articulation of that discourse that Zaret documents. But there does exist, as well, the objection to aligning the discursive formations that Zaret describes with what Habermas labels "a category of bourgeois society." As Calhoun (rightly, I believe) glosses this phrase, Habermas is interested in the "public sphere," not as in itself bourgeois, but as a constituent category of a social structure in which the bourgeoisie is hegemonic. Although such a description can be used quite effectively to describe English society since the reign of William and Mary in the late Restoration, it is considerably more problematic to extend such a notion back to the 1640s. What one may think of as the radical eruption of a revolutionary public sphere in the 1640s is promptly silenced by the Restoration of monarchy in the 1660s, only to arise again in a more modulated and successful form under the bourgeois accommodation that accompanied the accession of William and Mary. In one sense, some of the voices I am most interested in attending to in this book belong to those participants in the bourgeois public sphere who trace their own heritage back to the unruly ancestors of Zaret's model.

1. A PYGMY IN LONDON

1. Critical examination of the process whereby "matters of fact" came to be established during the scientific revolution has become a major feature of science studies since the publication of Steven Shapin and Simon Schaffer's *Leviathan and the Air-Pump:* "we stress . . . that producing matters of fact through scientific machines imposed a special sort of discipline on this public. . . . we shall describe the nature of the discursive and social practices that Boyle recommended for the generation of the matter of fact" (39–40). Lorraine Daston writes of scientific fact: "those nuggets of experience purified of all inference and interpretation which we recognize as cousins if not twins of our modern facts are the creations of seventeenth-century natural philosophy" (42).

2. Broberg, 156–94; Thomas, 130; Sloan, 117–21.

3. Cf. Wiseman, 215–38.

4. And, indeed, it is a confusion that I must to some degree compound. Tyson never used the word "chimpanzee" because that word did not arrive in England until 1738. For over two hundred years thereafter, the scholarly literature referring to Tyson has often referred (somewhat anachronistically) to "Tyson's chimpanzee." In 1967, noted primatologist Vernon Reynolds concluded that the animal Tyson anatomized was in all likelihood not a chimpanzee but the more recently discovered bonobo (see Reynolds 80–87). This new identification is only slowly entering the secondary literature on Tyson.

5. This is a context to which we now seem to be returning. From the time bonobos were described by Schwarz in 1934, there has been considerable discussion as to whether the bonobo was a subspecies of chimpanzee or a distinct species. Recent studies in cladistics and molecular genetics contend that not only should the bonobo be considered a subspecies of chimpanzee, but that, in fact, we are overdue for a reclassification of the primate order: "We propose that the gorilla, chimpanzee, and orang-utan be included in the family *Hominidae* together with the human; and that the chimpanzee and gorilla be included in the genus *Homo*, thereby assuming the names *Homo niger* and *Homo gorilla*, respectively (Watson, Easteal, and Penny 307–18).

6. See Shapin and Schaffer on "the modesty of experimental narrative," 65–69.

7. "The doctrine was so well established by the early eighteenth century, in fact, that it had overshadowed all other explanations of the causes of monstrous birth, and it was turned to almost automatically to account for a wide variety of anomalies and malformations" (Todd 47).

8. In an interesting discussion, medievalist Joyce Salisbury locates this taboo's origin in Europe with the arrival of the Christian narrative: "early Christian thinkers inherited two main traditions that had something to say about bestiality, the Germanic myths and the classical Greco-Roman literature. In the mythology of both, humans and animals had intercourse" (85). By the eighteenth century, of course, the taboo against bestiality was firmly in place, and interspecies sexuality was understood to be sterile. Robert J. C. Young discusses the perceived relation between species identity and reproductive sex: "the generally accepted test for distinct species, formulated by the Comte de Buffon in France and John Hunter in Britain, was that the product of sexual intercourse between them was infertile" (7).

I would note the particular "semiotic relationship" between species identity and sexual reproduction, in which each term was available to serve as a sign for the other. Thus, species identity could be signaled by sexual reproduction, and species difference could be signaled by the failure of such union. At the same time, barrenness (or even a purported diminishing of reproductive potential over time) could signal species difference. Young discusses how this semiotic relationship was read differently by monogenesists and polygenesists in construction of racial identities. The logic of this relationship is powerfully self-defeating: only successful reproduction can signal species identity, but the presumption of species difference prohibits the sexual interaction that would test that identity.

9. "This circumstance shows the elephant to be endowed with sentiments superior to the nature of common brutes. To feel the most ardent passion, and at the same time to deny the gratification of it, to experience all the fury of love, and not to transgress the laws of modesty, are perhaps the highest efforts of human virtue; and yet in these majestic animals they are only common and uniform exertions" (Buffon 1:534; see also 531, 537, 540, 543, 548–50).

10. European mythological tradition typically represented the figure of the "wild man"

wielding a stick, a staff, or in some instances a small tree; cf. Bernheimer, *Wild Men in the Middle Ages*.

11. Maynard Mack's influential essay "The Muse of Satire"

12. Swift, *Correspondence*, 1:82. As Alan Bewell writes, "It is ironic that empirical philosophy was preeminently a discourse about marginal people. . . . In describing these 'remarkable cases,' in transforming marginal peoples into living laboratories where theories about the origin of mankind could be tested and corroborated, medical, philosophical, and literary writing found a domain of shared concerns, a place where fact and fiction, theory and observation, the fantastic and the everyday could intermingle" (25–26). Nor is twenty-first-century London very far removed from the questions raised by Helena and Judith. In the fall of 2000, deliberating on the legal and ethical dilemma posed by the question of whether or not to separate conjoined twins, Lord Justice Henry Brooke asked of the more physically advanced half of the pair, "What is this creature in the eyes of the law?" That was, of course, precisely the question posed in the *Memoirs*.

13. Felicity Nussbaum observes the satire's parody of Clarke's "fawning flattery" that dwelt heavily (and heavy-handedly) on Caroline's role as an exemplary mother (*Torrid Zones* 59–60). It is difficult not to see that flattery as the gendered complement to the bourgeois fantasy that praised Tyson, at his death, for having "devoted himself to celibacy."

14. G. S. Rousseau offers a helpful discussion of the parallels between *Madame Chimpanzee* and Clarke's panegyric on the late queen, as well as bringing together relevant contemporary accounts of Madame Chimpanzee's brief stay in London, in "Madame Chimpanzee," *Enlightenment Crossings*.

2. THE FERAL CHILD AT COURT

1. See Novak's "The Wild Man Comes to Tea." Recently, Julia Douthwaite's very interesting "*Homo Ferus*: Between Monster and Model" discusses Peter and other feral children in relation to Enlightenment arguments about "perfectibility." I have benefited also from her "Rewriting the Savage: The Extraordinary Fictions of the 'Wild Girl of Champagne.'" As I was completing this manuscript, I encountered Michael Newton's "Bodies without Souls: The Case of Peter the Wild Boy."

2. *Mere Nature Delineated* was attributed to Defoe by John Robert Moore. The recent bibliographic research of P. N. Furbank and W. R. Owens has called into question large parts of the impossibly huge canon attributed to Defoe, without deciding one way or another about *Mere Nature Delineated*. Defoe's most recent biographer, Paula Backscheider, has written: "My own use of the received canon is conservative . . . I have reexamined and reevaluated every work attributed to Defoe, used for significant arguments only those about which I am certain, scrupulously noted my reservations about others, and avoided the use of those I consider not Defoe's, or probably not Defoe's" (xiv). Nowhere does she mention *Mere Nature Delineated*.

3. In discussing Wordsworth's "The Idiot Boy," Alan Bewell writes: "In its fervor to show that nature and isolation were the causes of idiocy, the Enlightenment rejected the obvious possibility that the wild child found in the woods might simply be a 'lost idiot.' By insisting upon this alternative, Wordsworth allows us to see the wild child for what he is: an exotic invention of empiricist philosophy" (65). Wordsworth's position has much in common with

that put forward by Blumenbach, and as the ensuing discussion should make clear, many of Peter's contemporaries had already recognized "the obvious possibility."

4. That, at least, is the image in the copy in the Clark Library reproduced in Maximilian Novak's "The Wild Man Comes to Tea." The three copies I examined in the British Library differ slightly. In the centerpiece, Peter is stouter with bushier hair, his face is more detailed, and one cannot see his right arm. Each of these illustrations is clearly derived from sketches for William Kent's portrait of Peter on the King's Staircase at Kensington Palace, discussed in chapter 4.

5. "Certain categories of traditional 'news' items from the repertoire of the broadsheets were also perpetuated—the miracle cures and thunderstorms, the murders, pestilences, and burnings" (Habermas 21).

6. In all likelihood, this author was Francis Tanner, who was certainly the author of the shorthand method and was variously referred to as "Dr. Anodyne Necklace Tanner," "Dr. Anodyne," and "Anodyne Tanner." Francis Doherty surveys evidence linking Tanner to both the Anodyne Necklace and *The Practical Scheme,* but he generally emphasizes the loose and corporate nature of the patent remedy concern, documenting the active involvement, in addition to Tanner, of both George and Henry Parker, Robert Bradshaw, Mrs. Garway, and many others over time.

7. Paulson's note on this engraving suggests that the Anodyne Necklace may have been used for treating venereal disease as well as teething, but I think he may be misreading both the contemporary advertising and the engraving. He cites an advertisement in the *Craftsman* that "claims curative power 'for Children's Teeth, Fits, Fevers, Convulsions, &c and the great Specifick Remedy for the Secret Disease.'" There is no reason to believe that this does not advertise two remedies—the necklace indicated by those symptoms ending with "&c" and a second for venereal disease—available at the sign of the Anodyne Necklace. This would have been consistent with other advertisements in the early decades of the eighteenth century. Moreover, since "The Practical Scheme" was given away with each purchase of "The Specific Remedy," and since it always advertised the remedy as available at "the Sign of the Anodyne Necklace," it would seem likely that the broken dish and substance on the floor with the pamphlet is the Specific Remedy itself.

8. Daniel Defoe, in *Mere Nature Delineated* (published in August 1726), and James Burnett, Lord Monboddo and Johann Blumenbach, writing about Peter later in the century, all accept without comment the attribution to Swift.

9. See Leland Peterson's discussion of the difficulties involved here.

10. Under "irresponsible attributions," Lester Beattie includes this discussion of *The Most Wonderful Wonder:*

The text of *The Most Wonderful Wonder,* telling of an old bear which had been brought to London because it was the foster-mother of the wild boy, and ending with a Gulliverian dialogue between the two, has been reprinted by Aitken among the doubtful works; but the insinuation that Swift was the author, and allusion in the text to a "Scotchman by birth" who was to civilize the bear's cubs, do not inspire confidence. It is clear also that the phrase "the Copper-farthing Dean," the notion of the bear, and the "full and true account of a most horrid and bloody Battle between Madam Faustina and Madam Cuzzoni," which forms one of the episodes of *The Devil to Pay at St. James,* all go back to that part of the title of *It Cannot Rain* which was deferred "to some following papers"—that is, which was never worked up at all by the original author. A more transparent trick for connecting these three papers with Arbuthnot could hardly be imagined. (310)

It should be noted that, despite his reference to "three papers" in the final sentence, Beattie's arguments apply only to *The Most Wonderful Wonder* and *The Devil to Pay at St. James;* the third paper alluded to *The Manifesto of Lord Peter* is not connected to the allusions of the title page and, I argue below, was at least partly the production of Arbuthnot. We should also note that Beattie's reasons for resisting attributing *Most Wonderful Wonder* and *Devil to Pay* to Arbuthnot apply just as strongly against attributing them to Swift. If anything, the "transparent" commercial trick applies with much more force to the suggestion that Swift may be the author, and Swift is hardly more likely than Arbuthnot himself to allude to the doctor as a "Scotchman by birth."

11. Beattie here distorts the original text slightly, which originally read "though he is ignorant both of ancient and modern languages" (6). As I discuss later in the chapter, the satirist's treatment of Peter's facility with language is one of the unique aspects of this satire and points to Swift's authorship.

12. Welcher and Bush review the bibliographical problem without offering an opinion, and they omit *The Manifesto of Lord Peter* from their collection. As becomes clear from the ensuing discussion, I consider the pamphlets to be part of a collective Scriblerian project, however one divides authorial responsibility.

13. Johnson kept detailed Minute-Books of the meetings of the Spalding Gentlemen's Society, and a facsimile reproduction of his manuscript, selected and introduced by Dorothy M. Owen, has been published by the Lincoln Record Society.

14. The Stationers' Register records *It Cannot Rain but it Pours, Or London Strow'd* as entered by James Roberts on April 21, 1726.

15. Shortly after Swift returned to Ireland in 1726, he received a "cheddar letter," jointly authored by Gay, Pope, Bolingbroke, Mrs. Howard, and William Pulteney. It included a verse recipe for stewing veal, which (though in Gay's handwriting) is commonly assigned to Pope, who was unable to write because of an injury to his hand. The poem contains a couplet—and a gloss on the couplet—that identifies Swift as "the Copper farthing Dean": " 'Put this pot of Wood's mettle* / In a hot boiling kettle.' The note reads: *Of this composition see the Works of the Copper farthing Dean" (Swift, *Correspondence* 3:168).

16. Until there was a "George II," "George I" would simply be identified as "King George."

17. "I have past six weeks in quest of health, and found it not" is the opening of a letter from Pope to Swift, dated "Bath, 12 Oct. 1728" (Swift, *Correspondence* 3:302).

18. Cf. Thorne: "This observation alone should do much to complicate Habermas's suggestive but perhaps somewhat too blithe notions of a Tory fourth estate. For the consistent effect of Tory satire is, in fact, to expose England's early modern political culture as a dictatorship of the public, as a catastrophic attempt to predicate power on public opinion rather than on virtue" (533).

19. Although I recognize that current scholarship alternates between assigning this pamphlet to Arbuthnot and leaving its authorship undetermined, for the reasons given earlier and for some others that are discussed later in a subsequent chapter, I find it useful to return to the attribution to Swift that was prevalent at the time.

20. At the time that Walpole married his son to the fourteen-year-old Margaret Rolle, he had himself just begun his relationship with Maria Skerrett, who was his mistress until his wife died and then became his second wife. Maria Skerrett was from the Rolle family, and the

lodge that Walpole had built at Richmond Park as a wedding gift to his son in fact served as a trysting spot for his own liaisons with Maria Skerrett.

21. Margaret Rolle was, indeed, "aged fourteen and some months" when she was married to Robert, Baron Walpole, in 1724. Accordingly, early editions of Lady Mary's letters dated this letter in that year. On the basis of other events mentioned in the letter, however, Robert Halsband has assigned this letter to early in June of 1726—at the very time when Peter was present at court, and Swift was writing his satire. See M. W. Montagu, 2:67.

22. The quote is from the pamphlet *It cannot Rain but it Pours: or, London strow'd with Rarities* (5–6), which is not to be confused with its companion piece, *It cannot Rain but it Pours: Or, The First Part of London strow'd with Rarities.*

23. Certainly, this would seem to be indicated by those pamphlets whose authorship has become confused with the Scriblerian pamphlets. Especially remarkable in this regard is *The Devil to Pay at St. James.*

24. Cf. Thorne, 540.

3. THE TRAVELS OF A WILD YOUTH

1. Samuel Johnson made this observation with respect to his own failure to comprehend Erse in the Highlands: "After supper, the ladies sung Erse songs, to which I listened as an English audience to an Italian opera, delighted with the sound of words which I did not understand" (51).

2. See also Nicholas Mirzoeff, *Silent Poetry: Deafness, Sign and Visual Culture in Modern France.*

3. One notable exception, discussed later in the chapter, is Richard Grove, *Green Imperialism.*

4. This account, incidentally, is also the source for Friday's gesture of political submission in placing Crusoe's foot on his head.

5. Robert Allen's *Enclosure and the Yeoman* makes a similar point, if anything more starkly: "There were two agricultural revolutions in English history—the yeomen's and the landlords'. . . . The conclusion is unavoidable—most English men and women would have been better off had the landlords' revolution never occurred" (21).

6. Although I focus in this chapter on the relationship between Robinson Crusoe and Alexander Selkirk, Defoe was also familiar with the case of Peter Serrano, a Spaniard who was shipwrecked alone on a Caribbean island, and who was widely reported to have degenerated, losing speech, acquiring hair, and becoming remarkably adept at rapid quadrupedal locomotion. Glyndwr Williams discusses other castaway narratives that may have contributed to Defoe's novel (180ff.).

7. Anson, 119. See also Lamb 232ff.

8. There are, of course, cannibals; but strictly speaking they are foreigners—nonnative natives, as it were—who only venture to Crusoe's island when dining out. In terms of daily threats of predation, Crusoe's island is as void of natural predators as was Defoe's.

9. The figure of the "man in skins" is at least as old as Gilgamesh and can be seen in the twelfth-century Georgian poem "The Knight in the Panther Skin." For Defoe's contemporaries, he was most familiar in the figure of Orson from "Valentine and Orson," but he soon becomes better known in the Timon-like character of The Man on the Hill from *Tom Jones*: "This person was of the tallest size, with a long beard as white as snow. His body was clothed

with the skin of an ass, made something into the form of a coat. He wore likewise boots on his legs, and a cap on his head, both composed of the skin of some other animals" (Fielding 8.10.376).

10. Jonathan Lamb discusses the plight of this sailor in terms of his failure to reconcile his sense of self with his own self-accusations (180–82). Lamb's discussion centers on a pamphlet, *The Just Vengeance of Heaven* (1730), that seems to be fashioned from an account of this castaway published two years earlier ("An Authentic Relation"). Though I place greater reliance on the authenticity of the earlier account, like Lamb, I accept the account as probably genuine. I am grateful to Evan Davis for showing me an unpublished essay discussing the bibliographic questions surrounding these accounts and their claims to factual validity.

4. UNIMAGINABLE COMMUNITIES

1. The literary opposition was alluded to by Habermas; see the brief discussion in chapter 2, above.

2. Periodically, wire service reports inform us of similar Gulliverian dilemmas. In 1981, "an orangutan grabbed and kissed a naked woman who was about to take a bath in a river in Borneo"; in 1993, "an orangutan ambushed a French tourist as he was strolling in a Malaysian park on Borneo and stripped him naked." Laura Brown's perceptive reading of this moment in Gulliver's narrative details how the episode simultaneously invites conflicting readings on the vexed question of the relation of race and species (Ends 196–97).

3. In the opening paragraph of *Gulliver's Travels*, Gulliver describes his family, education, and apprenticeship to a surgeon named James Bates. He runs through most of the permutations for alluding to this apprenticeship before his final reference, which triggers his desire to leave his family and go to sea: "But my good Master Bates dying . . . "

4. Ward's description is fulsome: "At last out comes an Epitome of a Careful Nurse, drest up in a Country Jacket, and under her Arm a Kitten for a Nurslin, and in her contrary Hand a piece of Cheese; down sits the little Matron, with a very Motherly Countenance, and when her Youngster mew'd, she Dandled him, and Rock'd him in her Arms, with as great Signs of Affection as a Loving Mother could well show to a disorder'd Infant; then bites a piece of Cheese, and after she had mumbled it about in her Mouth, then thrust it in with her Tongue into the Kittens, just as I have seen Nasty Old Sluts feed their own Grand children."

5. This seems—for us, as well as for Gulliver—the more important context in which to frame the critique of imperialism observed by Laura Brown. For Brown's configuration of race, gender, and colonialism ultimately produces a supple and powerful reading, fully confident of its own political legitimacy: "Swift's satire registers the complex interdependency of categories of the oppressed in this period of English imperialism, and the interchangeability figured in part 4 enables us to move beyond misogyny in itself or racism in itself to a dialectical critique that provides equal priority to both gender and race" (Ends 198). As far as it goes, Brown's reading effectively foregrounds the complexity of Swift's satire of the colonialist fantasy underwriting English imperialism, but that reading presumes as settled the solid ground of species identity, when in fact the terms of Swift's satire consistently remind us that this was an identity very much still in play. The "interchangeability" and fluid border crossing of identity politics are not here restricted to gender and race but involve the more vexing term of species itself. With the comforting cushion of nineteenth- and twentieth-century science intervening, we are quite comfortable choosing between discrete and separable readings

of the Yahoos in book 4: either they are nonhuman brutes (i.e., apes), or they are non-European savages; for Swift and his contemporaries, however, these were not necessarily discrete options, and the recognition that "human" identity comprised considerably more than European identity left very much in play the precise limit point at which primate identity became "nonhuman." From an anatomical perspective, apes and Yahoos equally verge on the human; from the perspective of the naturalist, what counts as "human" nature becomes—as the satire of Houyhnhnm and Yahoo reminds us most pointedly—a point on which we are all too prone to delude ourselves.

6. The *Edinburgh Caledonian Mercury* of Tuesday, December 21, 1725, quoted the following from the *St. James Evening Post,* December 14, 1725, soon after Peter's capture in Hanover: "[Peter is] supposed to be about fifteen years of age, who was found some time ago in a wood near Hamelin, about twenty-eight miles off this city, walking upon his hands and feet, climbing up trees like a squirrel, and feeding upon grass, and moss of trees." After he was brought to England, the following description appeared in the *Edinburgh Evening Courant,* August 8, 1726, reprinted from the *Country Gentleman,* no. 10, April 11, 1726: "He was found naked in the woods of Hamelin in Germany, running upon all four, and sometimes climbing up the trees, like a squirrel." Both descriptions are cited in Monboddo (Burnett), *Antient Metaphysics* 3:58, 60. In her essay on the wild girl of Soigny, Julia Douthwaite cites a similar description of that wild child by Monboddo: "she climbed trees like a squirrel, and leapt from one branch to another, upon all-four, with wonderful agility" (qtd. in "Rewriting" 183).

7. One potentially dramatic rendering of opposition hopes in comic verse appeared in the *British Journal,* June 3, 1727, just one week before the death of King George. Ostensibly, the poem is an elegy on the death of Peter, but it is hard not to believe that the rumors that summer of Peter's death were a screen for the anticipated death of the king:

> Epitaph on PETER, the Wild Youth;
> Occasioned by the Report of his Death.
> > Ye Yahoos mourn; for in this Place
> > Lies dead the Glory of your Race;
> > One, who from Adam had Descent,
> > Yet ne'er did what he might repent;
> > But liv'd unblemish'd, to Fifteen,
> > And yet (O Strange) a Court had seen!
> > Was solely rul'd by Nature's Laws,
> > And dy'd a Martyr in her Cause!
> > Now reign, ye Houyhnhnms; for Mankind
> > Have no such Peter left behind;
> > None, like the dear departed Youth,
> > Renown'd for Purity and Truth.
> > He was your Rival, and our Boast,
> > For Ever, Ever, Ever lost!

If one reads ironically Peter as an innocent alternative to George, then Yahoos and Houyhnhnms are once again mobilized on behalf of opposition and court, respectively, although the fictional premise of the poem reverses the poles of who is in and who is out by imagining the positions reversed on the occasion of this important death.

8. This signature, of course, plainly alludes to the list of comic code words that Gulliver

encounters at the academy at Lagado, where "a Seive" denominates "A Court Lady." My suggestion, here, is that within opposition circles that winter, the signature "Seive Yahoo" would be understood as "A Court Lady of the Opposition Party."

9. I am indebted to Evan Davis for first pointing this out to me.

10. In one instance, Jorry is said to have attacked a maid of the Countess of Portland and then a footman who tried to defend her. George had his page tried by the Board of Green Cloth, and when he was found guilty, the king placed him in solitary confinement on bread and water for fifteen days.

11. Ulrich's nickname of "Young Turk" may glance at his affiliation with Mehemet and Mustapha in George's court.

5. WALK SCOTLAND AND CARRY A BIG STICK

1. The threat of rustication was a staple of Restoration comedy. *The Country Wife*, of course, plays on moral associations of city and country living, and the ambiguous ending of Etherege's *The Man of Mode* turns on the question of Dorimant's promise to pursue Harriet, even into the deserts of rustic Hampshire.

2. Cf. "Origin of the Sciences," discussed in chapter 1.

3. In many respects, the argument of this chapter travels through territories recently visited by Pat Rogers in *Johnson and Boswell: The Transit of Caledonia*, especially chapter 4 and the appendix. Like Rogers, I consider the writings of James Burnett, Lord Monboddo and the tour of Scotland as related contributions to an Enlightenment discourse on the nature of man. Like Rogers, I find considerations of human nature deeply connected with the issue of Ossian's poetry in Johnson's journey. If, at times, we differ over the significance of particular events and exchanges, there is a fundamental agreement in our evaluation of Monboddo's importance to the tour.

4. Cf. Wokler.

5. One might see in "the Lady who had seen him in England" in Monboddo's account an echo of the various court ladies satirized for their unruly desires in the pamphlets accompanying Peter's original stay at court.

6. "At Nairn," Johnson tells us, "we may fix the verge of the Highlands; for here I first saw peat fires, and first heard the Erse language" (25).

7. The enmity between Johnson and Monboddo resumed after the tour of Scotland, although most accounts represent Monboddo as "hateful" and Johnson as condescending. Dr. James Beattie wrote in 1785: "Lord Monboddo's hatred of Johnson was singular. . . I never heard Johnson say anything severe of him; though when he mentioned his name, he generally 'grinned horribly a ghastly smile.'"

Boswell records in his journal (January 12, 1786) a cold meeting with Monboddo, which he takes as license for his representation in the *Life:* "I understood afterwards that he was violent against me. I did not care. I considered that it would make him *fair game* in Dr. Johnson's *Life*."

8. This opening evaluation foreshadows a recurrent (often jocular) observation of Johnson's, as he indulges the fantasy of owning an island.

9. See Julia Douthwaite's discussion of this case in "Rewriting."

10. In the Pottle and Bennett edition of Boswell's *Tour,* it is this very day according to Boswell that Johnson denominates Monboddo his friend: "He came the length this day of

contracting Monboddo and calling him 'Mony.' This was a piece of kindness, for he does so to all his friends" (189). The Hill and Powell edition of Boswell's *Life* omits these two sentences. I suspect the change is Boswell's. He had flattered himself that he had made friends of Johnson and Monboddo, but by the 1780s Monboddo was clearly hostile to Johnson, and Boswell seems to have played some role in that as well. Certainly, he at some point related to Monboddo the story of Johnson (before the meeting in Scotland) laughing at the lord as one "who does not know he is being foolish."

11. Cf. Pat Rogers: "A large paradox underlies Johnson's journey into the unknown. The cosmopolitan goes to see a primitive society in action. He aims to test the theories of Rousseau and others on natural man—but finds he has *become* natural man" (106).

12. I share Pat Rogers's reservations about the usefulness of the term "emotional Jacobitism." Labels used to identify political allegiances—particularly extremist ones—become less helpful the more they require modification. It makes sense to describe those who sought to return the Stuarts to the throne as Jacobites—extending the term to those who did not share that objective creates more problems than it solves.

13. In introducing his father into the narrative, Boswell reminds us of Monboddo by citing his characterization: "he was remarkable for 'humour, *incolumi gravitate*,' as Lord Monboddo used to characterise it" (v. 375). Johnson's response to Boswell's anxiety reminds us that he well knew what was expected of him in these situations, both in terms of hospitality and Boswell's designs; his words might well be applied to the meeting with Monboddo: "'I shall certainly not talk on subjects which I am told are disagreeable to a gentleman under whose roof I am; especially I shall not do so to *your father*'" (Boswell 5:376).

14. On this point, see Katie Trumpener, *Bardic Nationalism,* especially 67–96, and Leith Davis, *Acts of Union.* Where Trumpener identifies one dimension of the Johnson-MacPherson dispute as that between "imperial ethnography" (68) and "nationalist mythmaker" (77), Davis argues for the interesting proposition that MacPherson represents not so much a nationalist resistance to British imperialism, but rather an alternative British imperialism that challenges Johnson's ideas. Where Johnson valorizes a British identity premised on heterogeneity not unlike Defoe's "True-Born Englishman," MacPherson offers a homogeneous—and Caledonian—myth of British origin. Though her discussion makes no mention of Monboddo, primitivism, orang-outangs, or evolution, the relevant chapter bears the happy title "Origin of the Specious."

6. THE END OF *HOMO FERUS*

1. The "end of *Homo Ferus*" coincides with the French Revolution. In 1789, while the Bastille was being stormed, the thirteenth edition of Linnaeus's *Systema natura* appeared, with the categories of *homo ferus* and *homo troglodytes* omitted. This chapter suggests that one may find significance in that coincidence.

2. Victor has been the subject of numerous historical studies, as well as one outstanding biography, Harlan Lane's *The Wild Boy of Aveyron* (as much about Victor's teacher, Jean-Marc Gaspard Itard, and the history of education, as about Victor) and one extraordinary feature film, Francois Truffaut's *The Wild Child.*

3. Indeed, aside from a brief flurry of Royalist excitement when he is suspected of being a Jacobite incendiary, if not the Pretender himself, Peter's life is one of sedate British rural retirement.

4. I might add that if William's naming of the father seals his doom, he still accomplishes an appropriate revenge on his killer; for in the cultural imaginary that killer is identified not as "Victor's creature," but as "Frankenstein's monster."

5. Butler's analysis identifies each of the novel's three volumes with a relevant aspect of Lawrence's views. The first volume, in which the creature is brought to life, imagines the "what if" proposition of the vitalists, whom Lawrence ridiculed; the second volume, in which the creature narrates his own education, applies a similar "what if" imagining to the educational program Itard proposed for Victor of Aveyron, and which Lawrence followed Blumenbach in dismissing; the third volume "repeatedly illustrates, but ironically, Lawrence's scholarly observations about parenting" (xliv) and his interest in the effects of heredity and environment on variation in the human species (Butler, Introduction xl–xlv). Although my principal interest in this presentation is with the material that informs the second volume, the interrelatedness of these three themes should be underlined.

6. "Is *Frankenstein* a story of homophobic paranoia? The repression of the proletariat? An abandoned woman? Collectively, the response of modern criticism has been, Why not?" (Lipking 314). Or, "Which of us, in Frankenstein's position, would not invite the Creature home, give him a good hot meal, plug him into Sesame Street, enter him in the Special Olympics, fix him up with a mate, and tell him how much we love him?" (319). Rhetorical questions are often more funny than fair, and these are no exception. In the body of my text, I give some reasons why I think Lipking's charges are ultimately unfair, but here in the notes, I concede that some of my laughter is nervous; like Lipking, I also worry that the proliferating critical discussion of *Frankenstein* may be too heavily inflected by differences that are not disagreements, too thoroughly dominated by certain unchallengeable critical preconceptions.

7. The anonymous review in the 1824 *Knight's Quarterly Review* is reprinted in Mary Shelley's *Frankenstein*, edited by J. Paul Hunter (197–200).

8. Himself a practitioner of the doubled readings he admires in the writings of Romantic (and other) authors, Lipking both disclaims and repeats such a formulation: "My evidence for this proposition will consist of a look at a single source for Mary Shelley's novel. . . . If ever a work was overdetermined—psychologically and historically bombarded with multiple influences—that work is *Frankenstein*. Nevertheless, one source stands out, for its impact on Mary Shelley's sense of the age in which she lived as well as on her writing" (321). I am, myself, of two minds about what Lipking says here. The kinder, gentler version of myself (call him Creature) says that Lipking here demonstrates an admirable evenhandedness, balancing a legitimate insistence on Rousseau's impact on Shelley with an awareness that such claims can easily slide into reductivism. The harsher judgmental version (call him Monster) rolls his eyes and snorts that Lipking is trying to have it both ways once again.

9. "It is only of late years, and principally through the labours, the lectures, and the excellent writings of Blumenbach, that the natural history of man has begun to receive its due share of attention" (Lawrence 109). Others cited by Lawrence as contributing to this important development include Zimmermann, Meiners, Soemmering, Ludwig, Hunter, Kaimes, Smith, and Prichard.

10. Lawrence's doubt is expressed in one of the more unintentionally chilling passages of animal observation since Descartes: "That many animals besides man secrete tears is well known; but whether they weep from grief is doubtful. . . . Whether any animals express mirth or satisfaction by laughter is more doubtful, to say nothing of the other causes of smiling or laughter in our species. The fact has been asserted, for instance, by Le Cat, who says that he saw the chimpanzee both laugh and weep. The orang-utang brought from Batavia by Mr. Abel

certainly never laughs: his keeper informs me that he has seen him weep a few times" (205). One hardly needs to add to that final sentence the observation that orang-outang in Exeter Change had more reason to display grief than glee.

11. In my summary, I have deliberately likened this pastoral interlude to Adam and Eve, but a more likely conjecture as to literary influence would be that the passage is an ironic retelling of the Sir Satyrane episode of Spenser's *Faerie Queene.* In that episode, a virtuous maiden in a similar plight is saved by the wild man, Sir Satyrane, and her guardian knight is nursed back to health by him. Mary Shelley read Spenser the year before writing *Frankenstein,* and Percy Shelley was reading the *Faerie Queene* aloud as Mary prepared the final copy of the novel and Percy then "corrected" it. Perhaps the manuscript in the Bodleian indicating Percy's corrections might shed some light on whether this episode was interpolated into the narrative at this point.

12. Sterrenburg's discussion of this displacement underlines the degree to which serves the larger interest of shifting the ground of such discussions from the Enlightenment field of political theory to the internal Romantic terrain of the individual psyche: "we shift our attention from the social object to the perceiving subject" (159). In one respect, I hope to counter a trend in *Frankenstein* criticism during the quarter-century since Sterrenburg's essay appeared by insisting that we recognize how deeply engaged Mary Shelley's novel is with Enlightenment concerns, and how fully it participates in those concerns within an Enlightenment framework. At the same time, however, as the subsequent discussion of Peacock's *Melincourt* should clarify, Mary Shelley's novel does look forward to a dramatically more modern aesthetic—one that can be identified with this shift from the political to the personal.

13. "Did not you hear me ask him about the slave-trade last night? . . .—but there was such a dead silence!" (Austen 215).

14. For a review of Wordsworth's relationship to the Lowther family, see Johnston, *The Hidden Wordsworth,* esp. 19–31. Like Wordsworth himself, Johnston sees a significant difference between James Lowther ("Tyrant Lonsdale") and the cousin, William, who succeeded him; Peacock, like most historians of political reform, sees little more difference than Pope observed between the first two Georges ("Still Dunce the Second reigns like Dunce the First"; Pope, *Dunciad* 1:6).

15. The chapter concludes with a quintet—Mr. Feathernest, Mr. Paperstamp, Mr. Anyside Antijack (i.e., Canning), Mr. Vamp (i.e., Gifford, editor of the *Quarterly Review*), and Mr. Killthedead (i.e., John Wilson Croker)—singing "We'll all have a finger in the Christmas Pie." To balance that song, two chapters later, immediately before Anthelia is rescued, she recites a poem, the last of several poems interspersed throughout the narrative, and one clearly intended by Peacock as a true Romantic lyric ode to freedom. The final stanza of that poem seems explicitly to assert the political responsibility of poetry:

> And, Freedom! thy meridian blaze
> Should chase the clouds that lower,
> Wherever mental twilight dim
> Obscures Truth's vestal flame,
> Wherever Fraud and Slavery raise
> The throne of blood-stained Power,
> Wherever Fear and Ignorance hymn
> Some fabled daemon's name!

The bard, where torrents thunder down
Beside thy burning altar,
Should kindle, as in days of old,
The mind's ethereal fire;
Ere yet beneath a tyrant's frown
The Muse's voice could falter,
Or Flattery strung with chords of gold
The minstrel's venal lyre.

16. In speaking of the novel's "doctrine," I am here returning to Irvin Ehrenpreis's notion of the term as he defines it in *Literary Meaning and Augustan Values*. One measure of the anachronism of Peacock's novel is the degree to which Ehrenpreis's formulation applies to it. Earlier, I put forward the proposition that, for better or for worse, Shelley's *Frankenstein* "offers equally fertile ground to those readers who like their meanings ambiguous and indeterminate, and to those who prefer to discern a deeply important doctrine." Perhaps this is the sharpest contrast between Shelley's Romantic novel and Peacock's Menippean satire, looking back to what Ehrenpreis characterizes as more typical of literature "before the Romantic movement . . . [and its attendant] flight from explicit meaning" (33).

Works Cited

Aitken, George A. *Life and Works of John Arbuthnot.* Oxford: Clarendon Press, 1892.

Allen, Robert. *Enclosure and the Yeoman.* Oxford: Clarendon Press, 1992.

"An Authentick Relation of the many Hardships and Sufferings of a Dutch Sailor." *The Harleian Miscellany.* Vol. 11. London, 1810. 197–208.

Anderson, Benedict. *Imagined Communities: Reflections on the Origin and Spread of Nationalism.* New York: Verso, 1991.

Anonymous. "Review of Frankenstein." *Knight's Quarterly* (Aug.–Nov. 1824). Rpt. in *Frankenstein: Contexts, Nineteenth-Century Responses, Criticism.* Ed. J. Paul Hunter. New York: Norton, 1995. 197–200.

Anson, George Lord. *A voyage round the world: In the years MDCCXL, I, II, III, IV.* Compiled by Richard Walter. London: Printed for John and Paul Knapton, 1748.

Austen, Jane. *Mansfield Park.* 1814. Ed. Tony Tanner. London: Penguin Books, 1966.

Backscheider, Paula. *Daniel Defoe: His Life.* Baltimore: Johns Hopkins UP, 1989.

Barnard, Alan. "Monboddo's Orang Outang and the Definition of Man." *Ape, Man, Apeman: Changing Views since 1600.* Ed. Raymond Corbey and Bert Theunissen. Leiden, Netherlands: Leiden University, 1995. 71–86.

Beattie, J. M. *The English Court in the Reign of George I.* London: Cambridge UP, 1967.

Beattie, Lester. *John Arbuthnot.* New York: Russell & Russell, 1967.

Beeckman, Daniel. *A Voyage to and from the Island of Borneo, in the East Indies.* London, 1718. Rpt. in *A General Collection of the Best and Most Interesting Voyages and Travels in All Parts of the World.* Ed. John Pinkerton. Vol. 11. London: Longman, Hurst, Rees, Orme & Brown, 1812. 96–158.

Benedict, Barbara. *Curiosity: A Cultural History of Early Modern Inquiry.* U of Chicago P, 2001.

Bernheimer, Richard. *Wild Men in the Middle Ages: A Study in Art, Sentiment, and Demonology.* New York: Octagon Books, 1970.

Bewell, Alan. *Wordsworth and the Enlightenment: Nature, Man, and Society in the Experimental Poetry.* New Haven: Yale UP, 1989.

Blanckaert, Claude. "J.-J. Virey, observateur de l'homme (1800–1825)." *Julien-joseph Virey, naturaliste et anthropologue.* Ed. Claude Bénichou and Claude Blanckaert. Paris: J. Vrin, 1988.

Blumenbach, Johann Friedrich. *On the Natural Varieties of Mankind: De generis humani varietate nativa.* Trans. and ed. Thomas Bendyshe. New York: Bergman, 1969.

Blunt, Wilfrid. *Black Sunrise.* London: Methuen, 1951.

Boswell, James. *Boswell's Life of Johnson, Including Boswell's Journal of a Tour to the Hebrides and Johnson's Diary of a Journey into North Wales.* Ed. George Birkbeck Hill. Oxford: Clarendon Press, 1887.

Bourne, W. R. P., M. de L. Brooke, G. S. Clark, and T. Stone. "Wildlife Conservation Problems in the Juan Fernandez Archipelago, Chile." *Oryx: The Journal of the Fauna and Flora Society* 26.1 (1992): 43.

Brady, Frank. *James Boswell: The Later Years, 1769–1795.* New York: McGraw-Hill, 1984.

Braithwaite, John. *The History of the Revolutions in the Empire of Morocco.* London, 1729. Miami: Mnemosyne, 1969.

Broberg, Gunnar. "Homo Sapiens: Linnaeus's Classification of Man." *Linnaeus: The Man and His Work.* Ed. T. Frangsmyr. Berkeley: U of California P, 1983. 156–94.

Brown, Laura. *Ends of Empire: Women and Ideology in Early Eighteenth-Century English Literature.* Ithaca: Cornell UP, 1993.

———. *Fables of Modernity: Literature and Culture in the English Eighteenth Century.* Ithaca: Cornell UP, 2001.

Buffon, Georges Louis Le Clerc, comte de. *A Natural History, General and Particular, Containing the History and Theory of the Earth, a General History of Man, the Brute Creation, Vegetables, Minerals, &C, &C.; Translated from the French by William Smellie.* London: Printed for T. Kelly, 1862.

Burnett, James, Lord Monboddo. *Antient Metaphysics.* New York: Garland, 1977.

———. *Of the Origin and Progress of Language.* New York, Garland, 1970.

Butler, Marilyn. "Frankenstein and Radical Science." *Frankenstein: The 1818 Text, Contexts, Nineteenth-Century Responses, Modern Criticism.* Ed. J. Paul Hunter. New York: Norton, 1996. 302–13.

———. Introduction. *Frankenstein, or the Modern Prometheus: The 1818 Text.* By Mary Shelley. New York: Oxford UP, 1993.

———. *Peacock Displayed: A Satirist in His Context.* Boston: Routledge & Kegan Paul, 1979.

Calhoun, Craig. *Habermas and the Public Sphere.* Cambridge: MIT Press, 1992.

Castle, Terry. "Why the Houyhnhnms Don't Write: Swift, Satire, and the Fear of the Text." *Jonathan Swift's Gulliver's Travels: Complete, Authoritative Text with Biographical and Historical Contexts, Critical History, and Essays from Five Contemporary Critical Perspectives.* Ed. Christopher Fox and C. Ross-Murfin. Boston: Bedford, 1995. 379–95.

Chambers, Douglas. *The Reinvention of the World: English Writing, 1650–1750.* New York: Arnold, 1996.

A Compleat History of Europe: Or, a View of the Affairs thereof, Civil and Military, for the Year 1708. London: Henry Rhodes, 1709.

Cussins, Charis. "Confessions of a Bioterrorist: Subject Position and Reproductive Technologies." *Playing Dolly: Technocultural Formations, Fantasies, and Fictions of Assisted Reproduction.* Ed. E. Ann Kaplan and Susan Squier. New Brunswick, N.J.: Rutgers UP, 1999. 189–219.

Dampier, William. *A New Voyage round the World.* London: Argonaut Press, 1927.

Damrosch, Leopold. *God's Plot and Man's Stories: Studies in the Fictional Imagination from Milton to Fielding.* Chicago: U of Chicago P, 1985.

Daston, Lorraine. "Strange Facts, Plain Facts, and the Texture of Scientific Experience in the Enlightenment." *Proof and Persuasion: Essays on Authority, Objectivity, and Evidence.* Ed. Suzanne Marchand and Elizabeth Lunbeck. Turnhout, Belgium: Brepols, 1996. 42–59.

Davis, Leith. *Acts of Union.* Stanford: Stanford UP, 1998.

Dawson, Carl. *His Fine Wit: A Study of Thomas Love Peacock.* London: Routledge & Kegan Paul, 1970.

[Defoe, Daniel]. *Mere Nature Delineated.* London, 1726.

———. *Robinson Crusoe: An Authoritative Text, Contexts, Criticism.* Ed. Michael Shinagel. New York: Norton, 1994.

Deutsch, Helen, and Felicity Nussbaum. *Defects: Engendering the Modern Body.* Ann Arbor: U of Michigan P, 2000.

The Devil to Pay at St. James. London: A. Moore, 1727.

Dougherty, Frank. "Missing Link, Chain of Being, Ape and Man in the Enlightenment: The Argument of the Naturalists." *Ape, Man, Apeman: Changing Views since 1600.* Ed. Raymond Corbey and Bert Theunissen. Leiden, Netherlands: Leiden University, 1995. 63–70.

Douthwaite, Julia. "*Homo Ferus:* Between Monster and Model." *Eighteenth-Century Life* ns 21.2 (1997): 176–202.

———. "Rewriting the Savage: The Extraordinary Fictions of the 'Wild Girl of Champagne.'" *Eighteenth Century Studies* 28.2 (1994–95): 163–92.

———. *The Wild Girl, Natural Man, and the Monster: Dangerous Experiments in the Age of Enlightenment.* Chicago: U of Chicago P, 2002.

Dyson, A. E. *The Crazy Fabric: Essays in Irony.* London: Macmillan, 1965.

Edgeworth, Maria, and Richard L. Edgeworth. *Practical Education.* London, 1798.

Ehrenpreis, Irvin. *Literary Meaning and Augustan Values.* Charlottesville: UP of Virginia, 1974.

Eliade, Mircea. *Rites and Symbols of Initiation: The Mysteries of Birth and Rebirth.* New York: Harper & Row, 1965.

An Enquiry How the Wild Youth, Lately taken in the Woods near Hanover, (and now brought over to England) could be there left, and by what Creature he could be suckled, nursed, and brought up. London: Henry Parker, 1726.

An Essay towards the Character of the late Chimpanzee Who died Feb. 23, 1738–39. London: Gilliver & Clarke, 1738.

Fielding, Henry. *The History of Tom Jones, a Foundling; with an introduction and commentary by Martin C. Battestin.* Ed. Fredson Bowers. Middletown, Conn.: Wesleyan UP, 1975.

Fox, Christopher, Roy Porter, and Robert Wokler. *Inventing Human Science: Eighteenth-Century Domains.* Berkeley: U of California P, 1995.

Fraiman, Susan. "Gender, Culture and Imperialism." *Critical Inquiry* 21.4 (1995): 805–21.

Gildon, Charles. *Robinson Crusoe Examin'd and Criticis'd; Or, a New Edition of Charles Gildon's Famous Pamphlet Now Published with an Introduction and Explanatory Notes, Together with an Essay on Gildon's Life, by Paul Dottin.* London: J. M. Dent & Sons, 1923.

Greimas, A. J. *Structural Semantics: An Attempt at a Method.* Trans. Daniele McDowell, Ronald Schleifer, and Alan Velie. Lincoln: U of Nebraska P, 1983.

Grove, Richard. *Green Imperialism: Colonial Expansion, Tropical Island Edens and the Orgins of Environmentalism, 1600–1860.* New York: Cambridge UP, 1995.

Habermas, Jürgen. *The Structural Transformation of the Public Sphere: An Inquiry into a Category of Bourgeois Society.* Trans. Thomas Burger with Frederick Lawrence. Cambridge: MIT Press, 1989.

Hanafi, Zakiya. *The Monster in the Machine: Magic, Medicine, and the Marvelous in the Time of the Scientific Revolution.* Durham: Duke UP, 2000.

Haraway, Donna. *How Like a Leaf: An Interview with Thyrza Nichols Goodeve*. New York: Routledge, 2000.

———. *Primate Visions: Gender, Race, and Nature in the World of Modern Science*. New York: Routledge, 1989.

———. *Modest Witness@Second Millennium.FemaleMan©Meets OncoMouse™: Feminism and Technoscience*. New York: Routledge, 1997.

———. "The Promises of Monsters." *Cultural Studies*. Ed. Lawrence Grossberg, Cary Nelson, and Paula A. Treichler. New York: Routledge, 1992. 295–337.

Homer. *The Iliad of Homer*. Trans. Alexander Pope. Ed. Maynard Mack. 2 vols. New Haven: Yale UP, 1967.

Houghton, John. *A Collection for the Improvement of Husbandry and Trade. Consisting of Many Valuable Materials Relating to Corn, Cattle, Coals, Hops, Wool, &C: with a Compleat Catalogue with Several Sorts of Earths . . . ; Full and Exact Histories of Trades . . . ; an Account of the Rivers of England, &C. . . . 3* vols. London, 1727.

It cannot Rain but it Pours: Or, The First Part of London strow'd with Rarities. London: J. Roberts, 1726.

Jameson, Frederic. *The Prison-House of Language*. Princeton: Princeton UP, 1972.

Jefferson, Thomas. *Notes on the State of Virginia*. Ed. William Peden. Chapel Hill: U of North Carolina P, 1955. Published for the Institute of Early American History and Culture, Williamsburg, Va.

Johnson, Samuel. *A Journey to the Western Isles of Scotland*. Ed. Mary Lascelles. New Haven: Yale UP, 1971.

———. *The Letters of Samuel Johnson*. Ed. R. W. Chapman. Oxford: Clarendon Press, 1963.

Johnston, Kenneth R. *The Hidden Wordsworth: Poet, Lover, Rebel, Spy*. New York: Norton, 1998.

Jordan, Winthrop D. *White over Black: American Attitudes toward the Negro, 1550–1812*. New York: Norton, 1977.

Krakaeur, Jon. *Into the Wild*. New York: Anchor Books, 1997.

Lamb, Jonathan. *Preserving the Self in the South Seas, 1680–1840*. Chicago: U of Chicago P, 2001.

Lane, Harlan. *When the Mind Hears: A History of the Deaf*. New York: Vintage Books, 1989.

———. *The Wild Boy of Aveyron*. Cambridge: Harvard UP, 1976.

Latour, Bruno. *Pandora's Hope: Essays on the Reality of Science Studies*. Cambridge: Harvard UP, 1999.

———. *We Have Never Been Modern*. Trans. Catherine Porter. Cambridge: Harvard UP, 1993.

Lawrence, William. *Lectures on Physiology, Zoology, and the Natural History of Man*. London: Callow, 1819.

Levine, Joseph M. *Dr. Woodward's Shield: History, Science, and Satire in Augustan England*. Berkeley: U of California P, 1977.

Linné [Linnaeus], Carl von. *A General System of Nature: Through the Three Grand Kingdoms of Animals, Vegetables, and Minerals: Systematically Divided into Their Several Classes, Orders, Genera, Species, and Varieties, with Their Habitations, Manners, Economy, Structure, and Peculiarities*. London: Printed for Lackington, Allen, and Co., Temple of the Muses, Finsbury-Square, 1806.

Lipking, Lawrence. "*Frankenstein*, the True Story; or, Rousseau Judges Jean-Jacques."

Frankenstein: Contexts, Nineteenth-Century Responses, Criticism. Ed. J. Paul Hunter. New York: Norton, 1995. 313–31.

Lock, F. P. *The Politics of Gulliver's Travels*. New York: Oxford UP, 1980.

Mack, Maynard. "The Muse of Satire." *Yale Review* 41 (1951): 80–92.

Mackie, Erin. *Market à la Mode: Fashion, Commodity, and Gender in* The Tatler *and* The Spectator. Baltimore: Johns Hopkins UP, 1997.

Matar, Nabil. *Turks, Moors and Englishmen in the Age of Discovery*. New York: Columbia UP, 1999.

Memoirs of Martinus Scriblerus. Ed. Charles Kerby-Miller. New Haven: Yale UP, 1950.

Merchant, Carolyn. *The Death of Nature*. New York: Harper & Row, 1980.

Mirzoeff, Nicholas. *Silent Poetry: Deafness, Sign and Visual Culture in Modern France*. Princeton: Princeton UP, 1995.

Montagu, Ashley. *Edward Tyson, M.D., F.R.S., 1650–1708, and the Rise of Human and Comparative Anatomy in England: A Study in the History of Science*. Philadelphia: American Philosophical Society, 1943.

Montagu, Lady Mary Wortley. *The Complete Letters of Lady Mary Wortley Monatagu*. Ed. Robert Halsband. 2 vols. Oxford: Clarendon Press, 1966.

The Most Wonderful Wonder, that ever appeared to the Wonder of the British Nation . . . Written by the Copper-Farthing Dean. London, 1726.

Natural History Museum of Los Angeles County. "Documented Changes in the Flora." Robinson Crusoe Islands. http://www.lam.mus.ca.us/lacmnh/departments/research/botany/robcru/changes.html (1998; not currently accessible).

Newton, Michael. "Bodies without Souls: The Case of Peter the Wild Boy." *At the Borders of the Human: Beasts, Bodies, and Natural Philosophy in the Early Modern Period*. Ed. Erica Fudge, Ruth Gilbert, and S. J. Wiseman. New York: St. Martin's Press, 1999. 196–214.

Novak, Maximilian. "The Wild Man Comes to Tea." *The Wild Man Within: An Image in Western Thought from the Renaissance to Romanticism*. Ed. Edward Dudley and Maximilian Novak. Pittsburgh: U of Pittsburgh P, 1972. 183–221.

Nussbaum, Felicity. *Torrid Zones: Maternity, Sexuality, and Empire in Eighteenth-Century English Narratives*. Baltimore: Johns Hopkins UP, 1995.

Owen, Dorothy M. *The Minute-Books of the Spalding Gentlemen's Society, 1712–1755*. Selected and introduced by Dorothy M. Owen with S. W. Woodward. Lincoln Record Society 73. Lincoln, England: Lincoln Record Society, 1981.

Peacock, Thomas Love. *The Letters of Thomas Love Peacock*. Ed. Nicholas A. Joukovsky. 2 vols. New York: Oxford UP, 2001.

———. *The Works of Thomas Love Peacock*. Ed. H. F. B. Brett-Smith and C. E. Jones. London: Constable; New York: G. Wells, 1924.

Peterson, Leland. "Jonathan Swift and a Prose 'Day of Judgement.'" *Modern Philology* 81 (1984): 401–6.

Pope, Alexander. "Mary Gulliver to Capt. Lemuel Gulliver." *The Poems of Alexander Pope*. Ed. John Butt. New Haven: Yale UP, 1963. 486–88.

Poyntz, John. *The Present Prospect of the Famous and Fertile Island of Tobago*. London, 1683.

"Providence Display'd: Or, a very surprising account of one Mr. Alexander Selkirk." *Harleian Miscellany* 11. London, 1810. 40–45.

Quarterly Review 22 (1820): 1–34. [Review of Lawrence et al.]

Ray, John. *Synopsis methodica animalium quadrapedum et serpentini generis.* London: S. Smith & B. Walford, 1693.

Reynolds, V. "On the Identity of the Ape Described by Tulp in 1641." *Folia Primatologica* 5 (1967): 80–87.

Richetti, John. *"Robinson Crusoe:* The Self as Master." *Robinson Crusoe: An Authoritative Text, Contexts, Criticism.* Ed. Michael Shinagel. New York: Norton, 1994. 357–73.

Rogers, Pat. *Johnson and Boswell: The Transit of Caledonia.* Oxford: Clarendon Press, 1995.

Rogers, Woodes. *A Cruising Voyage round the World.* London, 1726. New York: Dover, 1970.

Rooy, Piet de. "In Search of Perfection: The Creation of a Missing Link." In *Ape, Man, Apeman: Changing Views since 1600.* Ed. Raymond Corbey and Bert Theunissen. Leiden, Netherlands: Leiden University, 1995. 195–207.

Rousseau, G. S. *Enlightenment Crossings: Pre- and Post-modern Discourses: Anthropological.* New York: Manchester UP, 1991.

Said, Edward. *Culture and Imperialism.* New York: Knopf, 1993.

Salisbury, Joyce. *The Beast Within: Animals in the Middle Ages.* New York: Routledge, 1994.

Sandiford, Keith A. *The Cultural Politics of Sugar: Caribbean Slavery and Narratives of Colonialism.* New York: Cambridge UP, 2000.

Schiebinger, Londa. *Nature's Body: Gender in the Making of Modern Science.* Boston: Beacon Press, 1993.

Schonhorn, Manuel. *Defoe's Politics: Parliament, Power, Kingship, and Robinson Crusoe.* New York: Cambridge UP, 1991.

Shapin, Steven, and Simon Schaffer. *Leviathan and the Air-Pump: Hobbes, Boyle, and the Experimental Life.* Princeton: Princeton UP, 1985.

Shelley, Mary. *Frankenstein: Contexts, Nineteenth-Century Responses, Criticism.* Ed. J. Paul Hunter. New York: Norton, 1995.

———. *Mary Shelley's Journal.* Ed. by Frederick L. Jones. Norman: U of Oklahoma P, 1947.

A short Philosophical Essay Upon Actions on Distant Subjects. Wherein are clearly explicated according to the Principles of the new Philosophy, and Sir Isaac Newton's Laws of Motion, all those Actions commonly attributed to Sympathy and Antipathy: As, the Celebrated Supplemental Nose of Taliacotius, mentioned in Hudibras: How it happened to fall off from the Gentleman's Face at Brussels, at the very instant of time when the Porter that own'd it died 500 miles off at Bologna? London, 1715.

Singh, J. A. L., and Robert M. Zingg. *Wolf-Children and Feral Man.* Hamden, Conn.: Archon Books, 1966.

Sloan, Philip. "The Gaze of Natural History." *Inventing Human Science: Eighteenth-Century Domains.* Ed. Christopher Fox, Roy Porter, and Robert Wokler. Berkeley: U of California P, 1995. 112–51.

Slocum, Joshua. *Sailing Alone around the World.* Annapolis, Md.: Naval Institute Press, 1985.

Spater, George. *William Cobbett, the Poor Man's Friend.* New York: Cambridge UP, 1982.

Spence, Joseph. *Observations, Anecdotes, and Characters, of Books and Men.* London: John Murray, 1820.

Stallybrass, Peter, and Allon White. *The Politics and Poetics of Transgression.* Ithaca, N.Y.: Cornell UP, 1986.

Sterrenburg, Lee. "Mary Shelley's Monster: Politics and Psyche in Frankenstein." *The Endurance of Frankenstein: Essays on Mary Shelley's Novel.* Ed. George Levine, U. C. Knoepflmacher, and Peter Dale Scott. Berkeley: U of California P, 1979. 143–71.

Swift, Jonathan. *Correspondence.* Ed. Harold Williams. Oxford: Clarendon Press, 1963–65.

————. *Prose Works of Jonathan Swift.* Ed. Herbert Davis et al. 14 vols. Oxford: B. Blackwell, 1939–68.

[Swift, Jonathan]. *It Cannot Rain but it Pours; or London strow'd with Rarities.* London: J. Roberts, 1726.

Thomas, Keith. *Man and the Natural World: Changing Attitudes in England, 1500–1800.* New York: Oxford UP, 1996.

Thorne, Christian. "Thumbing Our Nose at the Public Sphere: Satire, the Market, and the Invention of Literature." *PMLA* 116.3 (May 2001): 531–44.

Todd, Dennis. *Imagining Monsters: Miscreations of the Self in Eighteenth-Century England.* Chicago: U of Chicago P, 1995.

Torgovnick, Marianna. *Gone Primitive: Savage Intellects, Modern Lives.* Chicago: U of Chicago P, 1990.

Trumpener, Katie. *Bardic Nationalism: The Romantic Novel and the British Empire.* Princeton: Princeton UP, 1997.

Tulp, Nicolas. *Observationes Medicae.* Amsterdam, 1641.

Turner, Victor. "Betwixt and Between: The Liminal Period in Rites of Passage." *Betwixt and Between: Patterns of Masculine and Feminine Initiation.* Ed. Louise Carus Mahdi, Steven Foster, and Meredith Little. LaSalle, Ill.: Open Court Press, 1987.

Tyson, Edward. *Orang-Outang, sive Homo Sylvestris: or, The Anatomy of a Pygmie Compared with that of a Monkey, an Ape, and a Man. To which is added, A Philological Essay Concerning the Pygmies, the Cynocephali, the Satyrs, and Sphinges of the Ancients: Wherein it Will Appear That They Are All Either Apes or Monkeys, and Not Men, as Formerly Pretended.* London: Printed for T. Bennett and D. Brown, 1699.

Wain, John. *Samuel Johnson.* New York: Viking Press, 1975.

Wallis, John. "Method of Teaching the Deaf and Dumb to Read." *The History of the Life and Surprising Adventures of Mr. Duncan Campbell.* Vol. 4. *The Works of Daniel Defoe.* Ed. G. H. Maynadier. New York: George D. Sproul, 1903.

Walvin, James. "Sugar and the Shaping of Western Culture." *White and Deadly: Sugar and Colonialism.* Ed. Pal Ahluwalia, Bill Ashcroft, and Roger Knight. Commack, N.Y.: Nova Science, 1999. 21–31.

Ward, Edward. *The London Spy.* Ed. Paul Hyland. East Lansing, Mich.: Colleagues Press, 1993.

Watson, Elizabeth E., Simon Easteal, and David Penny. "*Homo* Genus: A Review of the Classification of Humans and the Great Apes." *Humanity from African Naissance to Coming Millennia.* Ed. Phillip V. Tobias, Michael A. Rath, Jacopo Moggi-Cecchi, and Gerald A. Doyle. Firenze, Italy: Firenze UP, 2000. 307–18.

Welcher, Jeanne K., and George E. Bush Jr. *Gulliveriana V: Shorter Imitations of Gulliver's Travels.* 8 vols. Gainesville, Fla.: Scholars Facsimiles and Reprints, 1970–99.

Weld, Isaac. *Travels through the states of North America and the provinces of Upper and Lower Canada, during the years 1795, 1796, and 1797.* London: J. Stockdale, 1799.

Wester, L. "Invasions and Extinctions on Masatierra (Juan Fernández Islands): A Review of Early Historical Evidence." *Journal of Historical Geography* 17(1991): 18–34.

White, Hayden. *Tropics of Discourse: Essays in Cultural Criticism.* Baltimore: Johns Hopkins UP, 1978.

Williams, Glyndwr. *The Great South Sea: English Voyages and Encounters, 1570–1750.* New Haven: Yale UP, 1997.

Wiseman, Susan. "Monstrous Perfectibility: Ape-Human Transformations in Hobbes,

Bulwer, Tyson." *At the Borders of the Human: Beasts, Bodies, and Natural Philosophy in the Early Modern Period.* Ed. Erica Fudge, Ruth Gilbert, and S. J. Wiseman. New York: St. Martin's Press, 1999. 215–38.

Wokler, Robert. "Anthropology and Conjectural History in the Enlightenment." *Inventing Human Science: Eighteenth-Century Domains.* Ed. Christopher Fox, Roy Porter, and Robert Wokler. Berkeley: U of California P, 1995. 31–52.

Yerkes, Robert M., and Ada W. Yerkes. *The Great Apes: A Study of Anthropoid Life.* New Haven: Yale UP, 1929.

Young, Robert J. C. *Colonial Desire: Hybridity in Theory, Culture, and Race.* New York: Routledge, 1995.

Zaret, David. *Origins of Democratic Culture: Printing, Petitions, and the Public Sphere in Early Modern England.* Princeton, N.J.: Princeton UP, 2000.

Index

Italicized page numbers refer to illustrations

Winners of the
*W*alker Cowen Memorial Prize

Elizabeth Wanning Harries
The Unfinished Manner:
Essays on the Fragment in the Later Eighteenth Century

Catherine Cusset
No Tomorrow:
The Ethics of Pleasure in the French Enlightenment

Lisa Jane Graham
If the King Only Knew:
Seditious Speech in the Reign of Louis XV

Suvir Kaul
Poems of Nation, Anthems of Empire:
English Verse in the Long Eighteenth Century

Richard Nash
Wild Enlightenment:
The Borders of Human Identity in the Eighteenth Century